# 100 HUT WALKS IN THE ALPS

*Col de Reidmatten between Arolla and Cabane de Dix*

# 100 HUT WALKS IN THE ALPS

by
Kev Reynolds

**CICERONE PRESS**
MILNTHORPE, CUMBRIA, ENGLAND
www.cicerone.co.uk

ISBN 1 85284 297 0
A catalogue record for this book is available from the British Library

## ACKNOWLEDGEMENTS

Thanks to walking and climbing friends who, over the past thirty-odd years, have shared some great days in the Alps, and visited with me a number of huts described in this book – especially Alan Payne, Roland Hiss, Nigel Fry and, of course, my wife. Thanks too, to the guardians and members of various mountain clubs who keep the huts maintained, often in very difficult circumstances. I am indebted to both Marion Telsnig at the Austrian National Tourist Office, and Heidi Reisz at the Swiss National Tourist Office, who have both provided generous assistance on many occasions. As ever I am grateful to my publishers for adding this book to their rapidly-growing list of Alpine guides, and for their encouragement during the two decades of our association. It's been a fruitful and highly enjoyable partnership.

*Kev Reynolds*

**Cicerone guidebooks by the same author :**
Walking in the Alps
Walks in the Engadine – Switzerland
The Valais
The Bernese Alps
Ticino – Switzerland
Central Switzerland
The Jura (with R. Brian Evans)
The Alpine Pass Route
Chamonix to Zermatt: The Walker's Haute Route
Tour of the Vanoise
Walks and Climbs in the Pyrenees
Annapurna: A Trekker's Guide
Everest: A Trekker's Guide
Langtang, Helambu and Gosainkund: A Trekker's Guide
Kangchenjunga: A Trekker's Guide
Manaslu: A Trekker's Guide
Walking in Kent Vols I & II
Walking in Sussex
The South Downs Way and The Downs Link
The Wealdway and The Vanguard Way
The Cotswold Way
*Front Cover: The Tasch Hut*

# CONTENTS

## ITALY

*Glacier scenery in the heart of the Ötztal Alps (Tirol)*

## Advice to Readers

Readers are advised that whilst every effort is taken by the author to ensure the accuracy of this guidebook, changes can occur which may affect the contents. It is advisable to check locally on transport, accomodation, shops etc but even rights–of–way can be altered.

The publisher would welcome notes of any such changes.

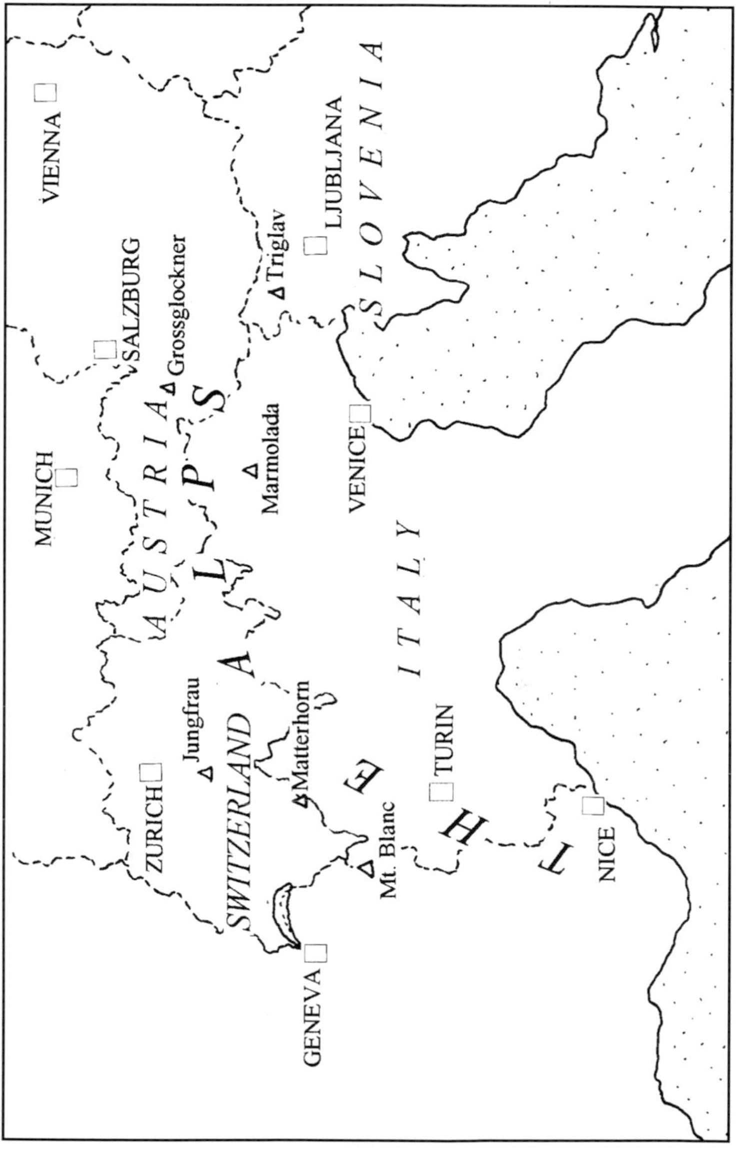

VIENNA

SALZBURG
Grossglockner

Triglav
LJUBLJANA

*S L O V E N I A*

MUNICH

*A U S T R I A*

*A L P S*

Marmolada

VENICE

*I T A L Y*

ZURICH

Jungfrau

*SWITZERLAND*

Matterhorn

Mt. Blanc

TURIN

NICE

GENEVA

# INTRODUCTION

Extending in a huge arc of more than 1000km (620 miles) from the Mediterranean coast near Nice to the low, wooded foothills outside Vienna, the Alps display the full gamut of mountain landscape features. With such a varied panoply of dramatic and spectacular scenery, there's nothing remotely comparable anywhere else in Europe – maybe in the World – and for two centuries and more walkers, mountaineers and general tourists have been flocking there in increasing numbers, and coming away enriched.

Walking is unquestionably the best method of exploring, and it is the mountain walker for whom journeys in the Alps reveal some of the finest views, the greatest contrasts. This book then is a guide to just 100 walks out of the many thousands possible, with a geographical span that ranges from the Maritime Alps of southern France to the Julians of Slovenia, from Italy's Gran Paradiso to the little-known Türnitzer Alps of eastern Austria, from the ice-bound giants of the Bernese Oberland to the green rolling Kitzbüheler Alps and the bizarre towers of the Dolomites of South Tirol, the routes having been especially selected in an attempt to show the amazing diversity of this wonderful mountain chain.

There are walks to suit every taste: gentle and undemanding, long and tough, and everything in between. Most of the routes avoid climbing of a technical nature, beyond the odd scramble aided by a fixed rope. Glacier crossings where crevasses lurk for the unwary have also been avoided in the main, although just a small handful of walks stray onto ice in order to reach a distant hut. And it is, of course, the huts which give this collection a unique flavour.

Mountain huts are found right across the Alpine chain and provide a focus for these walks. On some of the outings a hut will be reached in time to have lunch in the dining room, or outside on the terrace with a view, and then return to your valley base. But some are located too far from the valley to make a round-trip in a single day, so one would need to spend a night there. On a few occasions I've suggested making a short hut to hut tour, as an introduction to one of the most satisfying methods of spending an active mountain holiday. Some of the huts visited will be familiar to regular Alpine walkers and climbers, but I've also included a number that are likely to be unheard of. Each has its particular merit, its own character, and will be worth seeking out.

## MOUNTAIN HUTS

The Alpine hut system is a tremendous boon to both walkers and climbers. Initially built as simple overnight bases in order to reduce the time mountaineers might need to tackle a chosen peak, a comprehensive series of huts (cabane, capanna, refuge, or rifugio) gradually developed that were of use to mountain walkers too. It is now virtually possible to traverse the Alps from one end to the other using huts throughout. Most have been built by mountaineering clubs, but there are many – especially in Austria – that are privately-owned but open to all. Accommodation is not cheap, so if it is your intention to stay in a number of them during your holiday, consider joining the British Mountaineering Council (BMC) or an Alpine club to benefit from a discount on each overnight, although meals are not subject to reductions. Note that in Italian huts members should be of the same nationality as the club they belong to in order to benefit from discounts. Addresses are given in Appendix A, but it is worth noting that it is cheaper to join the Austrian Alpine Club, which has a UK branch, whose membership card is accepted for reduced rates in all huts other than those that are privately owned. (Another benefit of AAC membership is that of automatic insurance for mountain rescue, medical treatment and repatriation worldwide.)

Strategically placed, most huts visited in this book are looked after in the summer season by a guardian, or warden, who provides hot meals, snacks and drinks or, in a number of Swiss huts, will cook food carried in by the visitor. French huts often have a separate room for self-catering where you can prepare food on your own stove. Meals provided by the guardian are usually served at set times. They may not be haute cuisine, other than by definition of the hut's altitude, but they are often good and fairly substantial as to quantity – apart from breakfast, that is. In huts owned by the Austrian Alpine Club there's usually a choice of menu, the cheapest item being the Bergsteigeressen (literally the mountaineer's meal) which must contain at least 500 calories. It is often possible to buy a jug of boiled water to make your own hot drinks, so it's worth taking your own tea bags or coffee. A bag of muesli, pre-mixed with milk powder (simply add water), could also be carried to enhance a breakfast that would otherwise be limited to a few meagre slices of bread and jam or cheese.

Sleeping arrangements in huts vary little from one end of the Alps to the other. Dormitory accommodation is the norm. Not in individual youth hostel-type bunks, but on a large communal 'shelf' of mattresses with a space allocated by the guardian. Blankets and pillows are provided, but not bed linen, so it is advisable to carry a sheet sleeping bag (obligatory in AAC huts). There is no segregation of the sexes, and in the more popular buildings in the height of the season these dormitories can become overcrowded and airless. If it's a climbing hut, expect disturbance in the early pre-dawn darkness as climbers get up to begin their route; at the same time you should be aware of the need for quiet during the evening while others try to get a few hours of sleep before making their 1:00 or 2:00am start. Some huts operate a 'silent time' from 10:00pm until 6:00am, while in the larger huts, and this is especially true in Austria, it's possible for a couple or a family to have a two- or four-bedded room as opposed to sleeping in a communal dormitory – at a higher cost, naturally, but often well worth the price.

Nearly all huts have a supply of slippers, or 'hut shoes', stored on racks in the boot room at the entrance. On arrival you should exchange your boots for a pair of these slippers, and leave trekking poles, ice axe and/or crampons on a rack too. It's unacceptable to take these into the hut's communal rooms, whether you plan to stay overnight or just call in for a bowl of soup in the middle of the day. In some huts rucksacks are banned beyond the boot room, and in such cases a basket is usually supplied in which you place your essentials to carry into the hut proper.

The ambience of a hut often depends as much on the sociability of the guardian as on other users. The best are hospitable and friendly, who tend their hut with care, and have a deep love of the surrounding mountains. Most are knowledgable with regard to the condition of onward routes, and their advice can be usefully sought. Some are known to produce a guitar or accordian and at the drop of a hat will fill the evenings with music. The service they provide is to be appreciated.

Except in the more remote and little-known regions (some of which are included in this book) it will be rare indeed to have a hut to yourself. In the height of the summer season, or at weekends, a number of huts will be fully booked, and it is advisable to make a phone call in

*Monte Rosa, from the terrace of the Hörnli Hut on the Matterhorn*

*The Lauterbrunnen Breithorn, viewed from above Mürren*

advance should it be your intention to stay. Telephone numbers are given with the walk descriptions.

## WALKING IN THE ALPS

The key to a successful walking holiday in the Alps lies in preparation. To gain the most from such a holiday it is important to get fit before leaving home, then you'll enjoy each day's exercise, from first to last. Alpine walking can be demanding, so don't be over ambitious as soon as you arrive, but instead gradually increase distance and height-gain as the holiday progresses. Acclimatisation to altitude varies from one person to another. Unless you attempt to climb one of the 4000m peaks during the first few days of your holiday, it's unlikely that you'll notice much change, although some may be a little breathless above 1800m or so even when walking on the flat. Headaches and loss of appetite may be experienced, but these should disappear as you acclimatise. First-time visitors to the Alps sometimes find the sheer scale of the mountains intimidating, but this will soon pass as you become accustomed to wandering amongst them.

Choosing the right footwear to take is of prime importance. Good walking boots will be needed on practically every hut approach described in these pages. Anything less and you're bound to regret it. If you've never walked among mountains abroad you may be surprised to find that trekking poles are almost universally used. I recommend their use too, for they certainly ease the strain on knees and thighs especially when tackling steep descents. On multi-day routes they are almost indispensable.

When planning your day's walk read the route description beforehand and study the map so you can follow the route upon it and thereby gain an idea of what to expect. Although an estimated time is given at the head of each walk described, be aware that this is walking time only and you should therefore allow extra for rests, photography and delays. Plan your walk so as to reach your destination (be it the hut or return to the valley) with daylight to spare.

Check the weather forecast before setting out. The larger resorts usually have a guides bureau which displays a forecast, as do some of the tourist offices. Otherwise enquire at your hotel, hostel or campsite. If staying at a hut, the guardian will be able to give you an official forecast. Once you've set off keep alert for changes in the weather; in the mountains such changes can occur rapidly, so be prepared by taking appropriate clothing with you – see Appendix B for recommendations. Remember that a gentle valley breeze may be a piercing wind just 300m (1000ft) up the hillside, and as you wander higher so the weather intensifies, and when the sun goes behind a cloud the temperature can drop alarmingly. As a general guide, the temperature drops about 6°C for every 1000m of ascent. Should the weather deteriorate, or the route become hazardous, don't be too proud to turn back. Carry some food and a litre of liquid per person, also a map and compass – and know how to use them. A first-aid kit, whistle and torch should be included in the rucksack.

Leave details of your planned route and expected time of return with a responsible person. When staying in a mountain hut always make a point of writing your name and route details in the book provided. This information enables the authorities to plot your movements in the event of an accident. Be insured, for mountain rescue in the Alps, whilst highly organised, is very expensive.

Most walks described in this book follow established routes along marked trails, but on occasion wild terrain is encountered when extra caution should be adopted. Some routes are on trails safeguarded in places with fixed ropes, chains or cables. Although you may feel confident on these sections, the safeguards have been provided for very good reasons, so take care. Be vigilant when crossing mountain streams, exposed rocks or snow, and don't stray onto glaciers unless you have first learned the special techniques necessary for safe travel, or are in company with others experienced in glacier travel and with equipment to deal with crevasse rescue. Avoid icefalls and hanging glaciers, and be careful not to knock stones onto anyone who happens to be below.

## PATHS AND WAYMARKS

Mountains have always been seen as obstacles to communication, and throughout the Alpine chain for centuries the only way for most people to journey from one valley to the next was to walk, often over difficult or dangerous terrain. Routes taken by generations of farmers, hunters and traders going about their daily business steadily developed into a network of trails that have been adopted by today's recreational walker and climber. This network now forms a basic grid from which many more paths have sprung. Some have been created by official footpath organisations, like the Swiss Footpath Protection Association (Schweizerische Arbeitsgemeinschaft für Wanderwege), others by members of a mountaineering club in order to reach a hut, or the base of a popular climb.

With increased popularity in mountain walking, local communes in many Alpine regions have taken it upon themselves to improve and expand these footpaths further, to waymark and place signposts at strategic junctions, while other groups have added fixed rope safeguards in areas of potential danger. Some of these 'improvements' do little to enhance the mountain environment, but fortunately there is still a lot of wild country left, where activists need to use judgment and mountain sense.

Since many of the huts visited in this book are situated in fairly remote locations, walkers ought to be familiar with basic navigational procedures before tackling some of the longer routes described. Most waymarks in the Alpine ranges consist of paint flashes (usually red and white bands) on rocks, trees, posts or buildings. In the French Alps a number is sometimes added, which refers to a GR (Grande Randonnée) route. Signposts, where they appear, usually convey basic information, while in Switzerland yellow metal signposts appear at many trail junctions. These bear a central white plate which records the name of that junction and the altitude, while the finger pointers give the name or names of landmarks or villages and an estimate of the time it will take to walk there. In the Gran Paradiso National Park in Italy waymarks are often yellow; in Austria there are also yellow and black bands, as well as red and white. Numbers are frequently painted on Austrian waymarks, but these do not always agree with route numbers marked on some of the maps, so confusion can arise. In Slovenia waymarks are in the form of a red circle with a white centre.

## SAFETY IN THE MOUNTAINS

It may be that one day, despite having received a positive forecast, the weather turns nasty when you're still far from your destination. A storm breaks, and lightning begins to flash. In such instances, stay clear of metallic fixtures and dispose of any metal objects you have with you (ice axe, trekking pole etc) which can be retrieved later when the storm abates. Keep away from ridges and prominent features that stand above open ground. Do not shelter beneath over-hanging rocks or trees, and should you be caught in high open country, squat or curl up on your rucksack (assuming it does not have a metal frame) so as not to attract the lightning.

In the unfortunate event of an accident, stay calm. If your party is large enough to send for help while someone remains with the patient, make a careful written note of the precise location where the victim can be found. Should there be a mountain hut or farm nearby, seek assistance there. If valley habitation is nearer, find a telephone and call for help. Emergency numbers are usually prominently displayed. In the Chamonix region of France this is 0450 531689. In Switzerland dial 1414. In Italy dial 118 (or in Valle d'Aosta, 0165 238222). In Austria dial 140 for mountain rescue.

Should you be unable to leave the victim, give the recognised distress signal:-

---

### International Distress Signal
**Six blasts on a whistle (or flashes with a torch after dark)
spaced evenly for one minute, followed by a minute's pause.
Repeat until an answer is received. The response is
three signals per minute followed by a minute's pause.**

---

**The following signals are used to communicate with a helicopter:**

---

**Help needed:**
raise both arms
above head to
form a 'V'

**Help not required:**
raise one arm above
head, extend other arm
downward.

---

### THE ALPINE ENVIRONMENT
Concern for the mountain environment through which you walk ought to be second nature, but a few pointers are worth noting.
* Alpine flowers are to be appreciated, but not picked. Many are protected by law, but even those that are not specifically listed should be left for others to enjoy.
* Wildlife should not be disturbed.
* Leave no litter, but take your rubbish back to the valley for proper disposal.

* Take care not to foul water supplies.
* Make no unnecessary noise.
* Light no fires.
* Don't take shortcuts on mountain paths, for this can damage the soil and add to problems of erosion.

## RECOMMENDED MAPS AND GUIDES

### Maps

At the head of each walk description a note is given in regard to the map or maps recommended for that particular route. These are mostly at a scale of either 1:25,000 or 1:50,000, with a few at 1:30,000 or 1:40,000, depending on the publisher responsible. Not all are entirely accurate, although I found each one adequate for the walker's needs.

The Didier Richard sheets recommended for walks in the French Alps are based on maps of the official French survey, l'Institut Geographique National (IGN), with paths, huts, National Park boundaries etc overprinted upon them.

Those suggested for use in the Swiss Alps and marked with the initials LS are by the Swiss National Survey, Landeskarte der Schweiz. A few Wanderkarte are also noted; some of these are produced by local tourist authorities under licence, others published by Kümmerley and Frey with easy-to-read routes and hut details etc overprinted on them like those of Didier Richard mentioned above.

Maps published by Kompass for Alpine districts in Austria and Italy often include a booklet giving basic tourist information regarding towns and villages which appear on specific sheets, as well as hut details and walks suggestions.

All these maps should be obtainable from Stanfords in London, who operate a mail order service, or from The Map Shop in Upton-upon-Severn. (See Appendix A.)

### Guides

In the introductory essay to each Alpine country, a selection of guidebooks is given, for as the present collection of walks covers the length of the Alps and concentrates on hut routes, there will be countless possibilities left for walkers to explore elsewhere that simply could not be covered in this book. So for each district, or mountain group, visited within these pages, I have given a note of those English-language guidebooks that cover the same area. Most of these are produced by Cicerone, the same publisher responsible for this guidebook, but a few others are published by West Col, Cordee or Inghams. Again, addresses are given in Appendix A.

## USING THE GUIDE

The layout of this guidebook is such that walks are grouped, first under the individual country, then under specific Alpine districts. At the beginning of each country's selection of walks, a short essay is given which summarises the character of the mountain districts under that country's heading, together with a note of other guidebooks that could usefully be employed for further exploration – as mentioned above.

As for the walks themselves, basic information is given at the head of the page, followed by a brief outline of what to expect, then the route description which culminates in specific details in regard to the hut, including the telephone number which could be useful if it is your intention to stay overnight.

Distances are given in kilometres, and heights in metres. To convert kilometres to miles, divide the distance given by 1.6; for metres to feet, divide the amount quoted by 0.3. These details are mostly taken from the recommended maps, but where these are not shown I have used an altimeter. In attempting to measure distances walked I have made the best estimate I could from cartographic readings. With numerous zigzags it's impossible to be exact.

Times quoted are approximations too. They make no allowances for rest stops or photographic interruptions, but are based simply on actual walking time. Inevitably they will be considered slow by some walkers, fast by others, but are offered as an aid to planning.

In route descriptions, 'left' and 'right' refer to the direction of travel, whether in ascent or descent. However, when used to describe the bank of a stream or glacier, 'left' and 'right' indicate the direction of flow, ie: downhill. Where doubts might occur a compass direction is also given.

The sketch maps which accompany each walk are based on the recommended mapping sheet quoted, and are offered as a route outline for orientation. They are not an alternative to a real map.

Finally, all the route and hut information contained in this book is given in good faith and in the firm hope that those who follow will gain as much enjoyment as I have, on the individual walks and in the actual huts visited. But I am fully aware that changes do occur from time to time, both to the landscape and to mountain huts, and it may be that you will discover paths that have been rerouted and certain landmarks altered. Huts may be improved, enlarged or rebuilt; some quoted as having no resident guardian may one day be fully staffed. Conversely, one or two that are manned today, with meals provided for visitors, may become less popular so there's no guardian and self-catering the only option.

Should you find changes that ought to be mentioned in order to update any future edition, I would very much welcome a note. A postcard giving details sent to me via the publisher would be much appreciated.

*Kev Reynolds*

*Signpost on the way to the Brechhornhaus*

*Glacier Blanc in the Ecrins Massif*

# THE FRENCH ALPS

The Alps of France extend roughly northward from the Mediterranean, running parallel with the Italian frontier, and culminating in the Mont Blanc massif where the borders of France, Italy and Switzerland coincide on the summit of Mont Dolent. Each of the mountain groups has its own distinctive appeal, its own scenic dimension that gives it a unique quality. The bare stony peaks of the Maritime Alps are very different, for example, from the bold snow- and ice-draped peaks of the Massif des Écrins; the tarn-dazzling pasturelands of the Vanoise in direct contrast to the aiguille-guarded Mont Blanc range, yet each will repay the explorations of the mountain walker.

## THE MARITIME ALPS

Rising behind Nice at the southwestern end of the whole Alpine range, the Maritime Alps have no permanent snowfields, and few summits rise much above 3000m. With deep valleys and surprisingly tortuous road passes linking one with another, picturesque medieval villages appear to hang suspended from gorge walls, or are perched on the top of remote and seemingly inaccessible crags. Many of the inner valleys are uninhabited, save for the occasional mountain hut which entices walkers to explore, and a number of splendid tarns lie scattered among the upper pastures. Since 1979 a large section of the Maritime Alps has been set aside as the Mercantour National Park. Although popular among local walkers and climbers, very few English-speaking enthusiasts stray into these mountains.

Guidebooks:   *Mercantour Park* by Robin Collomb (West Col), *Walking the Alpine Parks of France & Northwest Italy* by Marcia R Lieberman (Cordee/The Mountaineers).

## DAUPHINÉ ALPS

This extensive region includes several mountain groups, among them the Queyras and Massif des Écrins. The first of these forms part of the Cottian Alps which border the northernmost hills and mountains of the Maritime Alps. Again, few English-speaking activists are seen here, other than walkers tackling the multi-day Tour du Queyras, but the lush inner glens are very fine, while many of the peaks, though little-known to any but the most avid of mountain buffs, are excitingly attractive. Only one Queyras hut walk is included here, but with Monte Viso in sight for much of the way, that will provide a good hint of what the area has to offer. As for the Massif des Écrins, this dramatic block of high mountains is situated northwest of the Queyras. Boasting the southernmost 4000m summit in the Alps (Barre des Écrins: 4102m), this compact yet complex group, with huts in amazing locations, reveals some unforgettable scenery.

Guidebooks: *Tour of the Queyras* by Alan Castle (Cicerone Press), *Tour of the Oisans* by Andrew Harper (Cicerone Press), *Walking the Alpine Parks of France & Northwest Italy* by Marcia R Lieberman (Cordee/The Mountaineers), *Écrins National Park – a Walker's Guide* by Kev Reynolds (Cicerone Press).

## GRAIAN ALPS

Wedged between the Dauphiné Alps and the Mont Blanc range, the Graian Alps have at their hub the Vanoise National Park – a glorious region of glacier peaks turned upside down by a wealth of dazzling mountain tarns. This is walking country par excellence. In the early summer the high meadows are ablaze with flowers. Chamois, ibex and marmots are seen almost daily, and there's a good selection of mountain huts, many of which are owned by the National Park authorities. Although day walks are possible on the periphery, the most rewarding way of getting to know the Vanoise is by making a hut to hut tour of the region. Several possibilities exist, of varying lengths and degrees of difficulty.

Guidebooks: *Walking in the Tarentaise & Beaufortain Alps* by J W Akitt (Cicerone Press), *Walking the Alpine Parks of France & Northwest Italy* by Marcia R Lieberman (Cordee/The Mountaineers), *Tour of the Vanoise* by Kev Reynolds (Cicerone Press).

## THE MONT BLANC RANGE

With Chamonix at its base, the Mont Blanc range is understandably the busiest of all the mountain regions of France. Scenically dramatic, all the ingredients of an Alpine landscape are gathered here in abundance – towering aiguilles, huge snow domes, rock slabs, screes, glaciers, waterfalls, flower-starred pastures, forests and lush green valleys. Shared between France, Italy and Switzerland the Mont Blanc massif is surrounded by seven valleys, the linking of each providing the route of the classic Tour du

Mont Blanc. But numerous possibilities exist for day walks, and just a small selection of hut routes are offered here.

<u>Guidebooks:</u> *Chamonix-Mont Blanc: A Walking Guide* by Martin Collins and *Tour of Mont Blanc* by Andrew Harper (both published by Cicerone Press).

*Col de la Croix du Bonhomme*

FRANCE

GENEVA

CHAMONIX
20
19
Mt Blanc
18

CHAMBÉRY

Gr Casse
17    16
14  15
13

GRENOBLE

12
11   10
B des Écrins
9
8   7

BRIANÇON

6   Mte Viso

GAP

5   Pta Argentera
4   3
2   1

NICE

N

MARSEILLES

25

# WALK 1: REFUGE DE VALMASQUE (2221m: 7287ft)

| | |
|---|---|
| Valley base: | Casterino or St-Dalmas |
| Start: | Nat. Park entrance (1732m: 5683ft) |
| Distance: | 11km (7 miles) round trip |
| Time: | 2hrs up, 1½hrs down |
| Total ascent: | 489m (1604ft) |
| Map: | Didier Richard 9 'Mercantour' 1:50,000 |

*The Vallée de la Roya, flowing south from Col de Tende, marks the eastern limit of the Maritime Alps. To the west the Mercantour National Park runs against the Franco-Italian border, and within it lies some first-rate walking country. Several huts grouped within a comparatively small area are linked by accessible cols. The first of these is Refuge de Valmasque. Overlooking a small dammed lake at the head of the Valmasque valley, it is reached by a short but interesting walk from a narrow road which projects deep into the mountains from St-Dalmas-de-Tende. Walkers without their own transport can take a twice-daily bus from St-Dalmas railway station as far as Casterino (13km), and begin the walk there – in which case add 5km and a further 1½hrs to the overall route.*

About 3km upvalley from the hamlet of Casterino, the narrow jeep road forks at the entrance to the Mercantour National Park; vehicles should be parked here. At this point wander along a stony track, signposted to Refuge de Valmasque, soon looking steeply down to the Valmasque stream. Green mountains on the north side of the valley rise to the Italian frontier, while the track

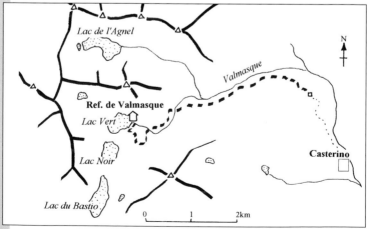

rises gently among larch, rowan and alder and curves south-west towards wilder country marked by jagged, rocky peaks. After about 40mins an alternative path slants off right ahead to explore Lac de l'Agnel. We remain on the track for a further 15mins to reach a barrier (2027m).

*Supply mule on its way to Refuge de Valmasque*

Now take a narrow path rising on the left. At first steeply, the angle soon eases across a small pasture with a fine stream flowing through. The path accompanies this stream upvalley, then rises to a higher level and crosses the stream below a cascade. At a junction of paths take the upper option and eventually gain a high, rocky terrace where you traverse to the right (north). The trail forks; the left branch leads to the Baisse de Valmasque via Lac Noir and Lac du Basto, the right-hand option is marked to the refuge. This latter trail contours over a hillside of bald slabs, passes a ruin, climbs a little to a second ruin, now with the hut in sight, and slopes down to the small barrage at the eastern end of Lac Vert. The hut is perched on a rocky knoll on the far side overlooking a wild and rocky landscape dominated by Cime Montolivo, Cime Chamineye, and Cime Lusiere. Above the latter rises the cone of Mont Clapier.

*Refuge de Valmasque belongs to the CAF (Section Nice). It has 54 places and a guardian is in residence from mid-June to the end of September; meals available. There is no phone at the hut. (Tel CAF, Nice: 04 93 62 59 99).*

Unless your plan is to make a cross-country journey to Refuge des Merveilles (see Walk 2), return by the same path as the upward route. Allow 1½hrs to the roadhead.

# WALK 2: REFUGE DES MERVEILLES (2111m: 6926ft)

| | |
|---|---|
| Valley base: | St-Dalmas or Tende |
| Start: | Lac des Mesches (1390m: 4560ft) |
| Distance: | 12km (7½ miles) round trip |
| Time: | 2¾hrs up, 2hrs down |
| Total ascent: | 721m (2365ft) |
| Map: | Didier Richard 9 'Mercantour' 1:50,000 |

*Refuge des Merveilles is one of the busiest of all huts in the Maritime Alps, thanks to the proximity of literally thousands of prehistoric rock engravings, a number of which are thought to have been chipped into slabs along the Vallée de Merveilles about 3000 BC. A search for some of these pictographs will add considerably to a visit to the Merveilles refuge, and time should be allowed for this. However, the hut approach in itself makes for a rewarding walk, for the scenery in the lower Vallée de la Minière is lush and pastoral, while the upper valley sparkles with tarns. If you plan to spend a night at the hut, you are advised to phone ahead to check that there's room – especially in the main season and at weekends, when space is at a premium.*

West of St-Dalmas-de-Tende in the Vallée de la Roya, a narrow road (summer bus service) extends for 10km to Lac des Mesches where there are five parking 'bays' on the west side. The walk begins by a notice board at parking bay number 1, where a path

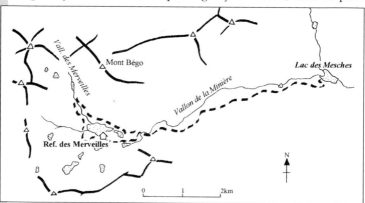

rises into larchwoods and after some long switchbacks joins a rough jeep track by a National Park information office. Just beyond, on the right-hand side of the stream, stands Refuge Neige de Merveilles (20mins).

Follow the track upstream on the south side of the Vallée de la Minière, soon overlooking an attractive lake. A little over an hour after setting out enter the Mercantour National Park and continue rising gently among larchwoods for another half-hour until you reach a small stone hut by a left-hand hairpin. A trail breaks away from the track at this point offering a shorter, but more demanding, ascent and is recommended. It climbs a short distance, then cuts to the right before resuming the climb alongside some cascades. Rising among slabs, gain height through increasingly rocky terrain until you cross a minor 'saddle' and come to a path junction. Bear left and soon rejoin the track, which you follow into a region of tarns leading to the hut.

*Lac Long and Refuge des Merveilles*

*Refuge des Merveilles has places for 75 and meals provision when it is manned – usually from mid-June to the end of September, and at weekends during school holiday periods. (Tel: 04 93 04 64 64) Located on the south bank of Lac Long, it is linked with Refuge de Valmasque (see Walk 1) by a trail which crosses the Baisse de Valmasque at the head of the Merveilles valley.*

To vary the return to Lac des Mesches, follow the track all the way (2hrs). This gives surprisingly fine views, especially in its upper reaches. But you should also allow a minimum of 2½hrs to explore part of the narrow Vallée des Merveilles northwest of the hut where many fine pictographs are to be found, then return along the north side of Lac Long to rejoin the track east of the refuge.

## WALK 3: REFUGE DE NICE (2232m: 7323ft)

| | |
|---|---|
| Valley base: | St-Martin-Vésubie |
| Start: | Pont de Countet (1692m: 5551ft) |
| Distance: | 9km (5½ miles) round trip |
| Time: | 2–2½hrs up, 1¾hrs down |
| Total ascent: | 540m (1772ft) |
| Map: | Didier Richard 9 'Mercantour' 1:50,000 |

*Located in a rocky cirque at the head of the Vallon de la Gordolasque – a long tributary of the important Vésubie – Refuge de Nice is suited equally to climbers and trekkers. Peaks that rim the cirque offer a variety of routes, while the summit of Mont Clapier (3045m) rewards with one of the finest panoramas of the whole Maritime Alps. Since the hut is also on the route of the long-distance GR52, it's well-used by trekkers, and by day visitors too who tackle the following route from the roadhead car park at Pont de Countet. It's a fine walk which exchanges the gentle* pastoral nature of the lower Gordolasque for the wild inner recesses of the mountains.

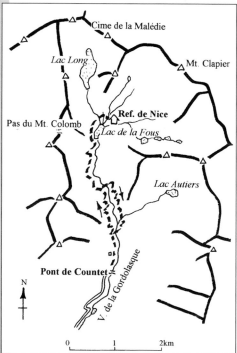

Vallon de la Gordolasque is gained by a serpentine road which climbs out of the Vésubie valley at Roquebillière to reach Belvédère village. Pont de Countet lies about 12km upvalley where there's ample parking space. The path to the Nice hut begins by the bridge and heads along the left (west) side of the stream, and soon passes a small shepherd's hut. Beyond this it weaves among huge boulders on which routes have been marked by a local climbing school, and about 20mins from the start comes to a junction of trails. The right-hand option offers an alternative way to the hut via the so-called Mur des Italiens, and has a spur to Lac Autiers – a recommended walk for another day.

Remain on the left of the stream where the path tacks to and fro up long switchbacks over scree, in order to rise above huge smooth slabs that form a mid-valley barrier. Eventually gain a

*Vallon de la Gordolasque, below Refuge de Nice*

high point above the slabs and slope down slightly to stream level, where the alternative Mur des Italiens path rejoins ours. This is a brief respite only, for the way resumes climbing among slabs with cairns provided where the trail is a little indistinct. After topping another high point, the path then eases into a marshy meadow below a barrage behind which (unseen as yet) lies Lac de la Fous. On the far side of the meadow the path rises again to another junction at 2173m. The left-hand trail here crosses Pas du Mont Colomb and offers a way to neighbouring Refuge de la Madone de Fenestre, but we veer right along GR52 and soon gain a track on the west bank of Lac de la Fous. The Nice hut can be seen on a knoll above the northeast shore. Keep well above the lake, and at the far end cross a stream and climb directly to the hut.

*Owned by the CAF, Refuge de Nice has 80 places and meals provision when the guardian is in residence. This is usually from mid-June to end of September. There's no telephone but enquiries should be made to the CAF in Nice (Tel: 04 93 62 59 59).*

Return to Pont de Countet either by the same route of approach, or descend by the steep, but straightforward, Mur des Italiens path.

# WALK 4: REFUGE DE COUGOURDE (2090m: 6857ft)

| | |
|---|---|
| Valley base: | St-Martin-Vésubie |
| Start: | Vallée du Boréon (1680m: 5512ft) |
| Distance: | 9km (5½ miles) in all |
| Time: | 2hrs to the hut, 1hr down |
| Total ascent: | 470m (1542ft) |
| Map: | Didier Richard 9 'Mercantour' 1:50,000 |

*The standard approach to this hut is interesting enough, since it rises through a charming valley with a clear stream for company much of the way. But what is suggested here is a diversion to visit first a lake in a magical setting before making a traverse round the mountain flank to the hut itself. Refuge de Cougourde is an odd-looking hut, like a converted railway carriage painted yellow. However, its location on the edge of meadowland under peaks that form the Franco-Italian border is delightful.*

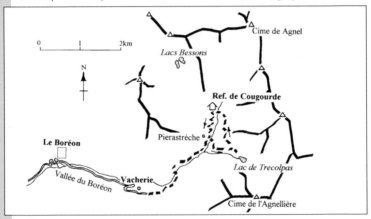

From Le Boréon hamlet, northeast of St-Martin, drive towards the head of the Vallée du Boréon (taxi possible). The tarmac road ends with plenty of parking spaces and picnic sites near the Vacherie du Boréon, but a broad track continues to an upper car park (*Parking Supérieure*) in the woods just above the vacherie. The walk begins here, by an information board. Initially follow a track through forest, but when it swings right in about 3mins, walk ahead on a stony path, then when it forks take the upper option. This leads to a forest clearing with a pool, a small building, and views to nearby cascades. Beyond this clearing the path twists uphill and comes to a bridge over the stream at 1838m.

Cross this and wander upvalley with the stream for company, and rocky peaks looming ahead. Reach a junction where the left-hand path goes to the Lacs Bessons, but continue ahead for another 3 mins

*Refuge de Cougourde*

to another junction on the north side of a dock-covered pasture below the little Pierastrèche cabin (1936m). The left-hand path is the direct route to the hut, but we bear right and recross the stream.

At first the path slants across the hillside among alpenroses, then twists more steeply up the south side of a broad spur dividing two stems of the upper Boréon valley. This is blocked by Cime de l'Agnellière and its consort of slabs and cliffs. Just below an obvious brief saddle there's another path junction. (Left to the hut, straight ahead to the lake.) Climb to the saddle, beyond which you'll find the lovely Lac de Trecolpas (2150m), then when you can tear yourself away, return to the junction and bear right. The path makes a traverse of rocks and scree below the Tête de Trecolpas, then among larch and alpenroses before negotiating yet more rocks. Finally cross a stream to gain Refuge de Cougourde, about 30mins from the lake.

*Refuge de Cougourde is owned by the CAF, with 42 places and simple meals service. It is staffed from mid-June to the end of September, but having no telephone, enquiries should be made via the CAF in Nice (Tel: 04 93 62 59 59).*

The downward path begins from the hut and descends steeply to the Pierastrèche junction where you rejoin the main trail used on the upward route.

## WALK 5: REFUGE DE GIALORGUES (2280m: 7480ft)

| | |
|---|---|
| Valley base: | St-Étienne-de-Tinée |
| Start: | St-Dalmas-le-Selvage (c1500m: 4921ft) |
| Distance: | 8km (5miles) to the hut |
| Time: | 3hrs up, 2hrs down |
| Total ascent: | 780m (2559ft) |
| Map: | Didier Richard 9 'Mercantour' 1:50,000 |

*Not being among the higher mountains of the Maritime Alps, and on the 'wrong' side of the Tinée valley, Refuge de Gialorgues does not have many visitors. Indeed, it is unmanned and locked, and prospective users should arrange to collect the key in advance – either from St-Dalmas or St-Étienne. And yet the scenery enjoyed on the approach to this hut is second to none, for as you progress through the Jalorgues glen, so the great battlements of the Ane massif (highest is Pointe Côte de l'Ane, 2916m) excite the imagination, and one could be forgiven for thinking you'd been transported to the Dolomites. The hut itself nestles among high rolling pastures under the southeastern crags of the massif, in a landscape conducive to lazy reflection.*

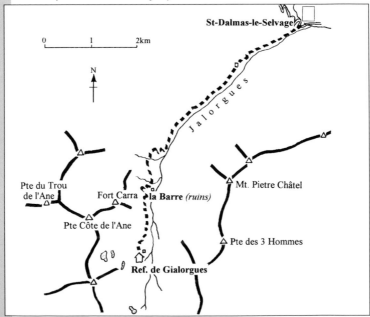

St-Dalmas-le-Selvage (gîte d'étape) is a time-worn village with a beautifully decorated church tucked in a side glen approached by a minor road cutting west from the Col de la Bonette road about 4km north of St-Étienne-de-Tinée. It gazes southwest into a lovely valley through which a jeep track pushes its way to the base of the Ane massif. Either walk along this track, or drive as far as the National Park boundary near the La Barre ruins where the track forks and crosses a stream about 5km from St-Dalmas. If you walk from this point it will take little more than 1¼hrs to reach the hut.

A signpost directs the path from the track (1980m), and twists easily up the hillside to cross the track again at a higher level by a sign for the Mercantour National Park. The way continues among larches before angling left. Gaining height with little effort, views downvalley grow in extent, while the crags of Fort Carra loom

*The unmanned Refuge de Gialorgues*

above. An upper pasture is reached, and the trail sneaks past a number of low ruins and grey stone walls. Ahead a stream escapes a high basin through a narrow cleft. The way eases towards it, guided by a line of well-made cairns, then enters a broad open basin of pastureland – marshy in its bed where the stream meanders through. The path rises over grass hillocks (more tall cairns) to a knoll where you come to two small huts. The first is a timber chalet used by a shepherd; the second is the stone-built Refuge de Gialorgues. Above to the north-west a small cirque is rimmed with fingers and towers of rock, while the walkers' pass of Col de Gialorgues lies 30mins to the southwest.

*Refuge de Gialorgues is CAF-owned. It can sleep 12, but as was mentioned above, it is unmanned and locked. Keys available at St-Dalmas or St-Étienne (Tel. CAF, Nice: 04 93 62 59 59). If you plan to stay overnight you should be self-sufficient with food and cooking equipment.*

Allow 45mins to return to the jeep track at la Barre, or 2hrs to St-Dalmas by the same route used on the approach.

## WALK 6: REFUGE DU BALIF VISO (2460m: 8071ft)

| | |
|---|---|
| Valley base: | Abriès or Ristolas |
| Start: | La Roche Ecroulée (1780m: 5840ft) |
| Distance: | 7km (4 miles) to the hut |
| Time: | 2½hrs up, 1¾hrs down |
| Total ascent: | 680m (2231ft) |
| Map: | Didier Richard 10 'Queyras' 1:50,000 |

*Although it rises on the Italian side of the border, Monte Viso (3841m) stands at the head of the Guil, a long and important valley that eventually opens to the Durance at Guillestre south of Besançon. It's not only a handsome mountain but, thanks to its position, it is visible from the summit of countless Alpine peaks, and its presence is thereby felt over a large area. Refuge du Balif Viso enjoys a grandstand view of this noble peak, and for much of the way to the hut, the mountain entices you on. The walk begins at the second parking area known as La Roche Ecroulée, named after the huge boulder which dominates the first one. This is found about 7km upstream of Ristolas, and is as far south as vehicles are allowed in the valley. An information office stands next to the car park.*

At the southern end of the car park, where a barrier prevents unauthorised vehicles from proceeding, a footpath signposted to the right gives 1½hrs to the Grand Belvédère du Viso. It rises through larchwoods and in 15mins emerges to an open meadow where the way forks. The right-hand path is an 'ecological trail', but we wander across the meadow to gain a first magical view of Monte Viso, before entering larchwoods once more. A well walked path leads through the woods, then out to birches by the stream and a bridge across the Guil. Now on the east bank the way briefly heads downstream, before cutting back up the hillside to join the road near a farm building. Once again Monte Viso towers at the head of the valley.

*Monte Viso on the Franco-Italian border*

Just before coming onto the road another path breaks to the right to contour along the hillside below road level. Either walk along the road as far as the Grand Belvédère, or take the footpath. The path certainly makes for more comfortable walking, and is most attractive where it crosses pastures and weaves among silver birch and larch, although in places it spills onto the road for a short distance. When the road twists left to climb in hairpins, the alternative path goes through a small gorge, then climbs out at the southern end onto the Grand Belvédère du Viso, a romantic name for a disappointingly flat area of roadhead at 2133m – although the view it commands is anything but disappointing.

Climb from the roadhead to a path junction and continue ahead, rising quite steeply over pastures for another 45mins where you intercept the route of GR58 and bear right. After crossing a few minor streams the path leads directly to the refuge.

*Refuge du Balif Viso was built to a modern design by the CAF in 1976. It is well-equipped and comfortable, has places for 40 and a full meals service from mid-June to mid-September when the guardian is in residence (Tel: 04 92 46 81 81).*

## WALK 7: REFUGE DES BANS (2076m: 6811ft)

| | |
|---|---|
| Valley base: | Vallouise |
| Start: | Entre les Aygues (1604m: 5262ft) |
| Distance: | 4km (2½ miles) to the hut |
| Time: | 1¾hrs up, 1¼hrs down |
| Total ascent: | 472m (1549ft) |
| Map: | Didier Richard 9 'Massif et Parc National des Écrins' 1:50,000 |

*This short and undemanding walk takes you towards the head of the Vallée de l'Onde west of Vallouise, the main resort and one of the best walking centres on the east side of the Écrins massif. From Vallouise to Entre les Aygues a narrow road pushes along the north bank of the river, passing the clustered hamlet of le Villard and an unmanned campsite (Pont des Places), with mountains crowding ahead within the National Park boundary. The roadhead of Entre les Aygues, as the name suggests, is at the confluence of streams: the Selle which flows from a glen opening to the south, and the Torrent des Bans coming from a narrow valley to the west. Heading this latter glen the rock peak of Les Bans (3669m) forms a barrier between the Bans (l'Onde) valley and that of the Vénèon, and the Refuge des Bans stands on a knoll at its feet.*

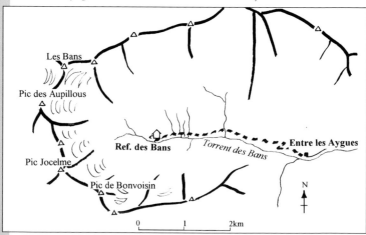

A signpost at the western end of the parking area near the *buvette* (refreshment hut) marks the start of the path, and gives a generous 2hrs for the walk. At first the path strikes ahead among larch and silver birch trees on the north side of a gravelly plain, and remains fairly level for about 10mins before rising gently in long switchbacks up the hillside. As height is gained, so the trees thin out to allow clearer views towards the head of the valley where the ragged ridge which closes it runs from les Bans over Pic des Aupillous to Pic Jocelme and Pic de Bonvoisin, their upper flanks draped with minor glaciers and snow patches. Topping a rise the refuge may be detected by those with keen eyesight. It stands end-on atop a rocky knoll some way ahead; at first you may imagine the white-painted shutters at its windows to be tiny patches of snow.

Midway along the valley cross a small, rough pasture with a stream coming down from the right, and with large boulders littering the upper pastureland slopes. Then you come to a pool on

*Vallée des Bans, at Entre les Aygues*

the left of the trail – look for tadpoles here. It's noted for them. Beyond this more streams need to be crossed, and after heavy rain or early snowmelt you may need to choose a crossing place with care. The trail angles below the hut on its south side, and is aided by fixed cables where it goes along ledges. The way is not difficult, but the cables may be useful in descent during inclement weather. Then the path cuts back to the right to gain Refuge des Bans. Views into the cirque are splendid.

*Refuge des Bans is a small hut provided by the CAF. It has just 30 places and a simple meals service on offer when the guardian is in residence during the summer. Booking is essential for an overnight stay (Tel: 04 92 23 39 48). Towards the end of the season, or in bad weather, the hut may be unmanned. If in doubt, enquire at the Vallouise tourist office.*

The return to Entre les Aygues is of necessity by the same path. Allow 1¼hrs for this.

# WALK 8: REFUGE DU PRÉ DE CHAUMETTE (1790m: 5873ft)

| | |
|---|---|
| Valley base: | Vallouise |
| Start: | Entre les Aygues (1604m: 5262ft) |
| Distance: | 16km (10 miles) to the hut |
| Time: | 7hrs one way |
| Total ascent: | 1205m (3953ft) |
| Descent: | 1030m (3379ft) |
| Map: | Didier Richard 9 'Massif et Parc National des Écrins' 1:50,000 |

*A glance at the route summary above should be sufficient to underline the fact that this is quite a tough walk, and is emphasized by the fact that it is also possible to approach this refuge by a stroll of little more than an hour! However, that approach is from the western side of the range, from a road projecting north from Les Borels, while the route described below forms part of the long-distance Tour de l'Oisans (GR54). There are two cols to cross; the first, Col de l'Aup Martin (2761m) is the highest encountered on the GR54, while Pas de la Cavale is just 26m lower. The hut lies almost a thousand metres below that, on pastures near the head of the Vallée de Champoléon, and is a welcoming place with good facilities.*

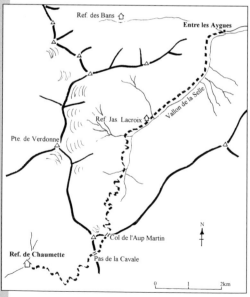

From the roadhead at Entre les Aygues above Vallouise the path (signposted) descends to the gravel plain, crosses a footbridge and then winds among trees and bushes before entering the narrow wedge of the Vallon de la Selle. For much of the way through this glen the trail maintains an easy gradient on the west side of the stream, passes Refuge du Jas Lacroix and crosses another stream issuing from the Chanteloube corrie. You then climb to a high pastureland basin rimmed by a skyline of rocky peaklets spilling great aprons of scree. The path goes along the right-hand side of these pastures, then up to the next natural terrace before tackling the screes leading to the first col. The scree consists of compacted

shales and grit, and in places the path is little more than a line of embedded footprints in it – rather like crossing a steeply-angled snowfield. Col de l'Aup Martin is reached in 4¼–4½hrs. Views are very fine; off to the right the next col, Pas de la Cavale, can be clearly seen.

*Refuge du Pré de Chaumette*

The path now contours round the head of a glen draining to the left, in the process of which you negotiate a ledge directly beneath a cascade. Pas de la Cavale (2735m) is gained in about 15mins from the previous col, and you then continue down a raking path, broad at first, but as the gradient steepens, so it becomes more narrow and slightly exposed across a band of rocks. Below these the path zigzags down to the green pastures of the Vallée de Champoléon – the hut in sight for much of the way.

*Refuge du Pré de Chaumette was built by the CAF in 1980 to replace a former hut. With 60 places, showers and a full meals service during the summer months when it is manned, the hut is well-appointed and comfortable (Tel: 04 92 55 95 34).*

To return by the same path allow 6–6½hrs. The shortest way out is to descend through the valley to Les Borels and work a way from there to the Gap–Grenoble road. GR54 (Tour de l'Oisans) continues northwest from here via three cols to Refuge de Vallonpierre (Walk 9) and la Chapelle-en-Valgaudémar in 8½hrs.

## WALK 9: REFUGE DE VALLONPIERRE (2280m: 7480ft)

| | |
|---|---|
| Valley base: | Valgaudémar |
| Start: | Ref. du Pré de Chaumette (1790m: 5873ft) |
| Distance: | 13km (8 miles) to hut |
| Time: | 4¾hrs |
| Total ascent: | 1253m (4111ft)    Descent: 763m (2503ft) |
| Map: | Didier Richard 9 'Massif et Parc National des Écrins' 1:50,000 |

*Refuge de Vallonpierre is a simple little stone-built hut idyllically set on the north shore of a small tarn. For walkers based in the Valgaudémar, one path approaches it via Refuge du Clot (Ref. Xavier-Blanc), another starts at a parking area below Chalet-Hotel du Giobernay. These approaches are shorter than that described below, but this particular walk is suggested as a way of linking this hut with Refuge du Pré de Chaumette along the route of the Tour de l'Oisans (GR54). It's a magnificent trek, with three cols to cross and an ever-evolving set of landscapes in view.*

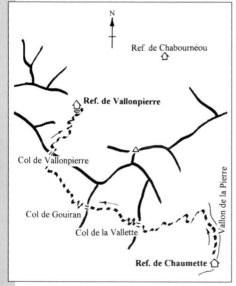

GR54 sets off NNE into the Vallon de la Pierre, a corrie headed by Pointe de Verdonne and le Sirac, their cliffs rising out of a rough boulder-pocked pasture. The path is a good one and it gains height steadily at first, then in long zigzags to mount the western slopes. The first col of the day can be seen almost an hour before you reach it, and as progress is made, hands are needed on a few brief scrambling sections, followed by thin ledges – quite safe but demanding caution. Col de la Vallette (2668m) is gained about 2¼hrs after setting out; views show steeply-plunging mountainsides, curving ridges with long scree chutes, green meadows and the twisting scar of the continuing path leading to the next pass, Col de Gouiran, to the northwest.

The path angles to the right, then zigzags down a very steep slope where for about 10mins caution is called for, especially with a large rucksack; balance is essential and a trekking pole would be helpful. Eventually the way eases and you reach a green meadow with a small pool. Soon the trail rises again and twists up to Col de Gouiran (2597m) in a little under an hour from the previous col. Like its predecessor this is a bare, windswept saddle looking onto bare mountains, and when you leave, the path descends to the northwest round the head of a corrie, crossing little streams and slithering on grit, before twisting up an eroded hillside to the third and final pass, Col de Vallonpierre (2607m), gained about 3¾hrs after leaving Chaumette.

*Refuge de Vallonpierre*

This is on a very narrow ridge, and the descent from it is steep, the path slender in places and with a couple of nasty steps, but not as bad as the descent from Col de la Vallette. Views which have been impressive throughout, become even better as you go down to Lac de Vallonpierre and the hut, reached about an hour from the col.

*Refuge de Vallonpierre (CAF) is built of mottled stone with a corrugated iron roof; 40 places, meals service when the guardian is in residence. (Tel: 04 92 55 27 81)*

Follow GR54 north down to la Chapelle-en-Valgaudémar in 4hrs, or take a contouring path NNE to Refuge de Chabournéou in a little under 2hrs.

## WALK 10: REFUGE DU GLACIER BLANC (2550m: 8366ft)

| | |
|---|---|
| Valley base: | Ailefroide |
| Start: | Pré de Madame Carle (1874m: 6148ft) |
| Distance: | 4km (2½ miles) to the hut |
| Time: | 2hrs up, 1–1½hrs down |
| Total ascent: | 676m (2218ft) |
| Map: | Didier Richard 9 'Massif et Parc National des Écrins' 1:50,000 |

*Some of the finest high mountain views in the eastern Écrins are revealed on the walk to, and from, this hut. Located above the east bank of the glacier which flows from the Barre des Écrins, Refuge du Glacier Blanc looks south to Mont Pelvoux, from whose north flank flows the Glacier Noir – named for the discoloration of the ice by its surface rubble. Not surprisingly the hut is much in demand by climbers tackling an assortment of major peaks, as well as by day visitors who make the strenuous approach in order to experience the majesty of its surroundings.*

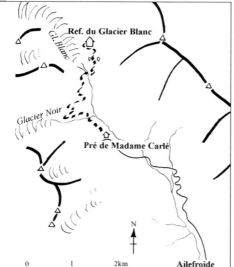

Pré de Madame Carle is the name given to a broad open meadow at the head of the Vallouise about 5km upstream from the climbing centre of Ailefroide. There's a Chalet-Refuge, information building and a huge parking area served by bus from Vallouise resort. From the car park the path used on this walk can be seen climbing in switchbacks up the hillside ahead, just left of prominent glacial slabs. It begins to the right of the Chalet-Refuge and at first leads through spacious larchwoods, then across a more open glacial plain to a bridge over a stream coming from the Glacier Noir (Black Glacier) whose moraines are seen pushing valleywards from the left-hand glen. The path soon slants left and rises towards Glacier Noir, but in 30mins it divides (signpost). Turn right and climb in numerous zigzags, rising above the slabs which appeared from below to be supporting the Glacier Blanc (White Glacier).

In a little over an hour from the car park the gradient slackens among whale-back slabs with the glacier now seen head-on, streams pouring from its snout. The refuge can be seen to the north, about 250m above, on a rocky knoll to the right of the glacier. Cross below the icefall and use a footbridge over the torrent, then bear left towards the Glacier Blanc. Waymarks soon direct the path to the right, rising in tight zigzags up a series of grit-covered

*Refuge du Glacier Blanc*

ledges and minor gullies. Eventually gain an upper terrace where you head almost due north, and pass a spur path cutting right to the former Refuge Tuckett (named after pioneer F.F. Tuckett), now used as a small museum of sorts. The main path continues between pools, then climbs up the left-hand side of the knoll on which the hut is set (brief scrambling involved), before cutting back to the hut itself.

*Refuge du Glacier Blanc is a substantial stone-built hut, CAF owned and with 135 places. It is manned throughout the summer season when a full meals service is available (Tel: 04 92 23 50 24). Booking is essential to ensure a bed. From the hut Mont Pelvoux, Pic Sans Nom, l'Ailefroide and Barre des Écrins can all be seen, while Montagne des Agneaux towers over it from the northeast.*

The return to Pré de Madame Carle is of necessity by the same route.

## WALK 11: REFUGE DU CARRELET (1909m: 6263ft)

| | |
|---|---|
| Valley base: | La Bérarde |
| Start: | La Bérarde (1713m: 5620ft) |
| Distance: | 4km (2½ miles) one way |
| Time: | 1hr up, 45mins down |
| Total ascent: | 196m (643ft) |
| Map: | Didier Richard 9 'Massif et Parc National des Écrins' 1:50,000 |

*Although this is one of the shortest and easiest walks in the book, there are two opportunities to extend it to other huts situated further upvalley. La Bérarde in any case has so much to offer as a base for a walking holiday, that this particular outing merely serves as a taster. As the highest settlement in the Vénéon valley, La Bérarde is primarily a climbing centre. Although little more than a hamlet, it has a large campsite, gîte d'étape, a couple of small hotels, restaurants, a basic grocery, information office/bureau des guides, and a CAF Centre d'Alpin. It sits at the junction of two valleys: the Étançons to the north, and the upper Vénéon in which the Carrelet refuge is located.*

From the centre of La Bérarde by the tourist office, walk past the large CAF building and follow a good path heading upvalley to the left of the Vénéon stream, a milky blue river which betrays its glacial origins. It's a pleasant, easy valley walk with l'Ailefroide in view to the southeast for much of the way. The rocky glen is tamed a little with juniper and wild raspberries and, later, alpenroses.

There's a section where the path cuts across the foot of steep screes, while the large flat plain where the hut is set (the Plan du Carrelet) is open and sunny at the confluence of the Vénéon and Chardon glens. As you approach the hut there are pine, birch and a few rowan trees to soften the otherwise raw nature of the valley.

*Refuge du Carrelet*

*Refuge du Carrelet is an austere-looking building. Privately-owned but open to all, it has 60 places, and is open from mid-June to mid-September when a full meals service is offered (Tel: 04 76 79 25 38).*

Of the two other options in the upper Vénéon valley, the first is **Refuge du Temple-Écrins** (2410m: 100 places, meals service) which sits on a high grassy shelf below Pic Coolidge, with impressive views. To gain this hut continue upvalley beyond Refuge du Carrelet for about 10mins where there's a signposted trail junction. Bear left, cross a stream and climb to another stream crossing. Beyond this the way zigzags steeply to gain the high shelf on which the hut is set. (1½hrs from the trail junction in the valley.)

The other alternative hut approach continues through the valley beyond the Temple-Écrins junction, crossing several side streams as it does, and with the Glacier de la Pilatte seen ahead, plastered on the face of Les Bans. A little under an hour from the Temple-Écrins junction, cross the Vénéon to its west bank. From here the trail zigzags to gain height, joining another path where you bear left. Another side stream is crossed by footbridge, thereafter the way rises again, and eventually gains **Refuge de la Pilatte** (2577m: 120 places, meals service) about 3hrs from the Carrelet hut – fantastic views.

## WALK 12: REFUGE DU CHÂTELLERET (2225m: 7300ft)

| | |
|---|---|
| Valley base: | La Bérarde |
| Start: | La Bérarde (1713m: 5620ft) |
| Distance: | 5km (3 miles) one way |
| Time: | 2hrs up, 1½hrs down |
| Total ascent: | 512m (1680ft) |
| Map: | Didier Richard 9 'Massif et Parc National des Écrins' 1:50,000 |

*Despite the fact that this is a fairly undemanding walk, it is drawn to some of the most dramatic scenery in the Alps. The hut sits at the head of the charming Étançons glen beneath the huge south face of La Meije, and gazes downstream at a landscape almost Himalayan in appearance. Wherever one looks, impressive peaks jostle for attention, mountaineers' mountains on which some of the great names of the Victorian age played out their*

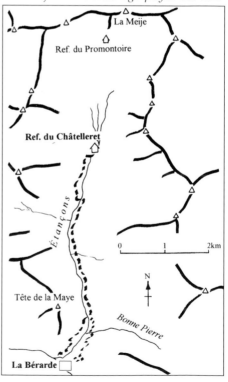

*adventures. Interesting to note that when Whymper descended this glen in 1864 he was singularly unimpressed, describing it as "a howling wilderness, the abomination of desolation ... suggestive of chaos, but of little else." In truth it is a magnificent valley. Try it for yourself.*

At the entrance to La Bérarde near the road-head a bridge spans the Étançons stream. A few paces from this on the downstream side a signpost signals the path to the Châtelleret hut. It twists uphill with several separate braidings, and in about 20mins or so another path breaks off to the left to climb to the viewpoint of Tête de la Maye (highly recommended for another day). Continue ahead, still gaining height across the hillside, then slope downhill briefly to cross a footbridge over the stream. Another path breaks off to the right at this point, heading for the Vallon de Bonne Pierre, the steep little glen seen to the east where the Roche Faurio sends out an extravagant ridge. Ignore this option, but bear left and continue upstream among silver birch, alpenrose and bilberry, and shortly join an alternative path rising from La Bérarde.

The way now leads through an utterly charming part of the valley, more or less on the level for a while among alpenrose and juniper, with waterfalls cascading from cliffs that wall the valley to both left and right. Then you rise easily between rocks and boulders, turn a corner and gain the first view of La Meije ahead. It's an awesome sight. Continuing to gain height without effort, you then cross to the west bank of the stream (the hut now seen ahead), make a few zigzags, cross a few minor streams, then once more over the Étançons by another footbridge to gain the hut.

*Refuge du Châtelleret is a grey, barrack-like hut with 90 places, staffed between mid-June and mid-September when meals are available (Tel: 04 76 79 08 27). In the mid-50s an earlier refuge (built 1882) was described as being little more than a broken-down, three-*

*The Étancons valley below Refuge du Châtelleret*

*walled hovel built against a huge boulder. The present hut shows considerable improvement!*

To vary the return to La Bérarde, descend by the same path used on the approach, but then follow the alternative left bank trail joined near the entrance to the Bonne Pierre glen. A little rougher and steeper than the main path, it leads to La Bérarde chapel.

## WALK 13: REFUGE DE L'ORGÈRE (1935m: 6348ft)

| | |
|---|---|
| Valley base: | Modane |
| Start: | Modane (1058m: 3471ft) |
| Distance: | 5.5km (3½ miles) one way |
| Time: | 2½–3hrs |
| Total ascent: | 877m (2877ft) |
| Map: | Didier Richard 11 'Massif et Parc National de la Vanoise' 1:50,000 |

*The approach to this hut marks the first stage of the magnificent 10–12 day Tour of the Vanoise, a hut-to-hut circuit of the Vanoise National Park which starts and ends at Modane in the Maurienne (the valley of l'Arc) to the east of Grenoble. This particular section of that longer walk climbs from the Maurienne through forest and across brief open pastures, then emerges to the mouth of the Orgère glen, dominated by the graceful Aiguille Doran. Using the hut as a base a number of fine expeditions are possible, and unless your plan is to tackle the Tour of the Vanoise, or one of its variants, it would be worth booking in for two or three nights.*

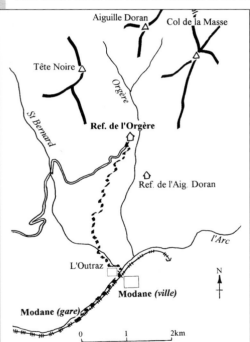

Beginning at Modane railway station (served by main-line trains via Chambéry) wander upvalley along the main road towards Modane *ville*. Shortly after passing a supermarket turn left on a minor road signposted to le Bourget. This takes you beneath the railway line and into the village of L'Outraz. Follow red-white waymarks ahead at a staggered crossroads, continue

50

uphill between houses and bear right by a small chapel. The road soon becomes a tree-lined track. When it forks bear right over a bridge. Winding uphill among trees the track narrows to a footpath.

Climbing through the forest you will come to many trail junctions. Mostly the way to take is obvious – the path is part of the GR5 which makes a traverse of the French Alps from the Lake of Geneva to the Mediterranean. Signposts or waymarks appear wherever doubts could arise, with Orgère on most of the signs. Eventually emerge from the trees to a lovely open meadow by the solitary stone chalet of Pierre Brune (about 2½hrs), from which good views are had to the east through the Haute Maurienne. Across the meadow come to a track where you bear right for a few paces, then join a continuing trail rising to the left. (About 5mins further along the track stands another hut; the privately owned

*Refuge de l'Orgére*

**Refuge de l'Aiguille Doran** with 40 places and meals provided from mid-May to mid October.) The path re-enters forest, then con-tours round the hillside to a fork just below a minor road. Go up to the road, leaving GR5, and just ahead stands Refuge de l'Orgère.

*Refuge de l'Orgère belongs to the Vanoise National Park and is one of the 'portes du parc'. It has 56 places and restaurant service when it is manned. This is from mid-June to mid-September (Tel: 04 79 05 11 65). Advanced booking advised.*

A nature trail runs along the eastern side of the valley, while a more demanding trail makes a high traverse of the western side. There's a route over Col de la Masse to Refuge du Fond d'Aussois, or a circuit to be made of the Tête Noire. Alternatively follow the Tour of the Vanoise to Plan Sec where there's another privately-owned hut.

## WALK 14: REFUGE DE L'ARPONT (2309m: 7575ft)

| | |
|---|---|
| Valley base: | **Termignon or Aussois** |
| Start: | **Termignon (1304m: 4278ft)** |
| Distance: | **7km (4 miles) one way** |
| Time: | **3–3½hrs** |
| Total ascent: | **1005m (3297ft)** |
| Map: | **Didier Richard 11 'Massif et Parc National de la Vanoise' 1:50,000** |

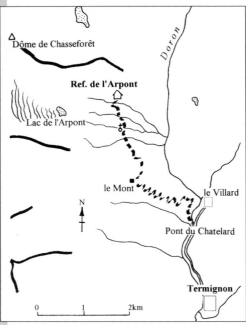

*Located on a grassy shelf high above the west bank of the Doron gorge, and with tongues of the 11km-long Glaciers de la Vanoise glinting from the upper ridge, Refuge de l'Arpont is a fine place in which to spend a night. Ibex are often spied grazing nearby. Cascades shower over high cliffs, and from a bluff behind the hut La Grande Casse and La Grande Motte are both on display. The hut is visited by walkers tackling the GR5, and by both the Tour of the Vanoise and the shorter Tour des Glaciers de la Vanoise, but the approach described below is the direct route from Termignon in the Maurienne, upvalley from Modane, by which it is served by bus. It's quite a tough walk, in that the trail which climbs out of the valley makes few concessions, and gains something like 700m in less than 3km.*

From Termignon wander along a narrow surfaced road (D83) heading northwest beside the Doron river towards le Villard and la Fontanelle. After about 2km come to the Pont du Chatelard and a small parking area at about 1347m. Cross to the west bank of the river where you soon join a path which begins the steep climb to a group of farm buildings at le Mont. It is a steep climb too, twisting in numerous tight zigzags to the west, then northwest, up the hillside a little south of the Doron gorge – a dramatic cleft through which the river is fed by a whole series of streams falling from the icefields above the Arpont hut.

On gaining the farm buildings and ruins at le Mont (2038m; 2½hrs) join the GR5 and bear right through thickets of alder and with occasional views down into the gorge. As the way progresses you come to the first alpenroses, while Pointe de la Réchasse gives the impression that it's blocking the valley ahead. Footbridges lead the path across streams that have dug channels through the rock,

waterfalls spray above the trail and you pass a few ruined hutments, the Chapelle St-Laurent and a small farm, with the hut now in view on a spur jutting from the Dôme de

*Refuge de l'Arpont*

Chasseforêt. This is gained by slanting up a final easy slope at 2309m.

*Refuge de l'Arpont commands a fine view to the south. Owned by the National Park authority it has 95 places, a full meals service and kitchen facilities. It is manned from the end of May to mid-September (Tel: 04 79 20 51 51).*

Above the hut to the southwest lies the little Lac de l'Arpont at the foot of the Glacier de l'Arpont. A 2hr round-trip to this tarn is worth making, if it is your intention to spend a night here. Other routes from Arpont lead down-valley along GR5 to the privately-owned Refuge du Plan Sec, and upvalley to either Refuge du Col de la Vanoise, Refuge d'Entre Deux Eaux or Refuge du Plan du Lac (see Walk 15).

## WALK 15: REFUGE D'ENTRE DEUX EAUX (2120m: 6955ft)

| | |
|---|---|
| Valley base: | Termignan or Aussois |
| Start: | Bellecombe (2307m: 7569ft) |
| Distance: | 5km (3 miles) to the hut |
| Time: | 1½–1¾hrs up, 1hr down |
| Total ascent: | 124m (407ft) |
| Map: | Didier Richard 11 'Massif et Parc National de la Vanoise' 1:50,000 |

*Thanks to the provision of a shuttle bus service (navette) in summer between Termignan and the Torrent de la Rocheure, several mountain huts situated near the head of the Doron gorge are made easily accessible. These are Plan du Lac, la Femma, Entre Deux Eaux and la Leisse. In addition one could mention the hut at Col de la Vanoise and the Refuge de l'Arpont (see Walk 14). By use of the shuttle the particular walk described below could be shortened to just 15 or 20mins, but that would defeat the object. Instead, transport is left at the Bellecombe bus stop (plenty of car parking space – no private vehicles beyond it) high above the east bank of the Doron gorge, followed by a short walk to the attrac-*

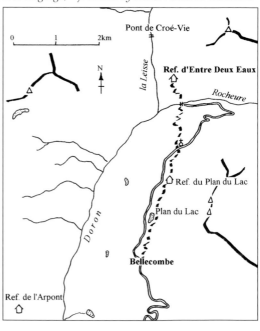

*tive tarn at Plan du Lac. An unfor-gettable panora-ma makes this one of the great sites of the Vanoise National Park. As for Refuge d'Entre Deux Eaux, this is still recognisable from descriptions penned by Janet Adam Smith (in Mountain Holidays) after she first visited in 1935. A one-time dairy farm, it retains its charac-ter and provides a very special ambience.*

Leave the Bellecombe parking area at its northern end on an obvious path to the right of the road. It rises easily through a narrow defile to an open grassy plain in which the main feature is a beautiful tarn reflecting La Grande Casse in its clear waters. Off to the left (west) the Glaciers de la Vanoise crown the long mountain ridge walling the opposite bank of the unseen Doron gorge. A few minutes north of the tarn come to the Refuge du Plan du Lac (2364m, PNV owned, 60 places, meals provided). There is a bus stop nearby, and an orientation table on a col just beyond the hut that will help to identify the numerous peaks in view.

Continue north of the hut, over the col and down to the Chapelle St-Barthélémy. Cross the road and follow the path over rolling grassland, before

*Plan du Lac and the Grande Casse*

descending more steeply through lush vegetation to regain the road near its terminus by a bridge over the Torrent de la Rocheure, which drains a glen off to the right. It is up this glen that the Refuge de la Femma is to be found (about 2hrs from the bridge). Cross the bridge and wander uphill to reach Refuge d'Entre Deux Eaux.

*Privately-owned but open to all, Refuge d'Entre Deux Eaux has 60 places, self-catering facilities, restaurant service and showers. Open in summer only (Tel: 04 79 20 50 85). One part of the building is two-storey, the other is a single-storey conversion; both have plenty of character.*

A short distance to the north the hump-backed Pont de Croé-Vie carries GR55 which links Refuge de la Leisse and Refuge du Col de la Vanoise. The first is easily gained from Entre Deux Eaux in 2–2½hrs, the latter in 2½hrs.

## WALK 16: REFUGE DE LA LEISSE (2487m: 8159ft)

| | |
|---|---|
| Valley base: | Val d'Isère or Tignes |
| Start: | Lac de Tignes (2093m: 6867ft) |
| Distance: | 12km (7½ miles) one way |
| Time: | 4–4½hrs up, 3½hrs down |
| Total ascent: | 665m (2182ft) |
| Descent: | 271m (889ft) |
| Map: | Didier Richard 11 'Massif et Parc National de la Vanoise' 1:50,000 |

*The ski resorts of Lac de Tignes and Val Claret are situated just outside the Vanoise National Park a short distance from Val d'Isère, their cableways strung across the hillsides as marked and unwelcome adornments – in summer at least. By contrast the inner Vanoise is a pristine region where chamois and ibex roam, and only rough trails twist among meadows of flowers. On the approach to Refuge de la Leisse such contrasts are noteworthy, especially when on the descent from Col de la Leisse you enter a new world, seemingly wild and untamed. GR55 passes this way, as does the route of the Tour of the Vanoise, for the Leisse hut provides welcome accommodation for trekkers midway between Val d'Isère and Pralognan.*

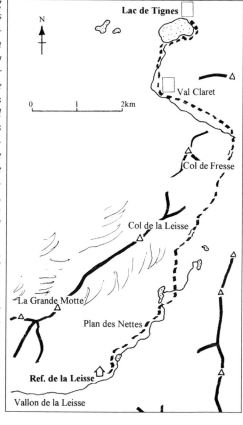

Situated above the dammed Lac du Chevril high in the Isère valley, Lac de Tignes is reached by bus from the railhead at Bourg St Maurice in the Tarentaise (limited accommodation in summer). As an alternative, stay in Val d'Isère and follow GR5 through the Vallon de la Tovière and across the Pas de la Tovière to Lac de Tignes, thereby adding 6km (2¼hrs) to the walk.

Now go to the southern end of the lake and continue to the head of the valley where the modern buildings of Val Claret look dreadfully out of place. Just beyond the high-rise blocks a car park is situated to the left of a tunnel entrance. Here the GR55 is marked with a signpost. The waymarked path rises to the southeast on its way to Col de Fresse, at first over grassland, then through a cleft beside a stream before crossing more open pastures. Beyond Col de Fresse it curves southwest to enter the National Park with Grande Motte and its glaciers dominating the view ahead. The landscape becomes increasingly barren, with cairns leading the way to Col de la Leisse (2758m). This is gained after a series of

*Refuge de la Leisse*

false cols, and there is no discernible loss of height as you pass through a trough until the way slopes down a series of natural terraces into a wild region below the cliffs of La Grande Motte.

Pass along the eastern side of Lac des Nettes, then descend to the Plan des Nettes where the path eases along the right-hand shore of another tarn with a barrage at its southern end. From here the trail goes down a short slope to the hut.

*Refuge de la Leisse is another National Park hut, with 48 places and full restaurant service, self-catering facilities and showers. Manned during the high summer season (Tel: 04 79 20 50 85), a winter room is permanently open. The hut actually consists of three tent-shaped buildings overlooking Vallon de la Leisse. The Entre Deux Eaux hut (Walk 15) lies just 2hrs away downstream, while Refuge du Col de la Vanoise is reached in 3½hrs via Pont de Croé-Vie (see Walk 17).*

## WALK 17: REFUGE DU COL DE LA VANOISE (2517m: 8258ft)

| | |
|---|---|
| Valley base: | Pralognan |
| Start: | Les Fontanettes (1644m: 5394ft) |
| Distance: | 11km (6½ miles) round trip |
| Time: | 5½hrs in all |
| Total ascent: | 873m (2864ft) |
| Map: | Didier Richard 11 'Massif et Parc National de la Vanoise' 1:50,000 |

*Probably the most popular destination for walkers based in Pralognan, this is a fine circular outing with tremendous high mountain scenery on show, and a busy hut with refreshments at the halfway point. Refuge du Col de la Vanoise (formerly known as Refuge Félix-Faure after a President of France who visited the site in 1897), is situated just below a saddle in full view of the Grande Casse. Glaciers, screes and a mountain tarn add character to the scene, but the whole walk is full of notable features and it's invidious to single out specific highlights.*

The walk begins above Pralognan at the Les Fontanettes parking area where there's a bar-restaurant and a chairlift. If you walk to it from Pralognan, allow an hour to reach Les Fontanettes by a

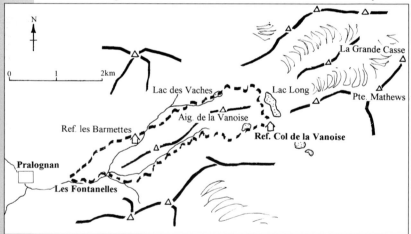

steep path which begins near the upper end of the main street. An alternative is to ride the Mont Bochor cable-car, whose valley station is found opposite the tourist office. Should you take this option, however, you'll need to descend from the upper station to join the uphill footpath, and at the end of the day it will be necessary to walk all the way down to Pralognan.

A signpost at the parking area marks the start of the path to Refuge du Col de la Vanoise. This rises through woods to the left of a ski piste and comes onto a dirt road where you bear left. Winding uphill heading northeast reach the privately owned **Refuge les Barmettes** (2030m: 22 places, restaurant service).

Col de la Vanoise, above the refuge

Above this cross the Glière stream on a bridge, and continue uphill, now between drystone walls, and enter the National Park. The hillside is adorned with alpenroses and honeycombed with marmot burrows. On coming to a junction of paths with a signpost, veer right and before long you'll come to the shallow Lac des Vaches, from whose southern shore the blade-like Aiguille de la Vanoise presents a formidable wall. Flat-slabbed stepping stones enable you to cross the lake towards huge moraine walls and glaciers flowing from La Grande Casse. The trail now climbs steeply and passes above a second lake, Lac Long, to gain the hut.

*Refuge du Col de la Vanoise consists of more than one building. Manned from mid-June to mid-September, this CAF-owned hut can sleep 154 in its dormitories; meals service and kitchen facilities on offer (Tel: 04 79 08 25 23).*

Rather than return to Pralognan by the same path, an alternative descent, giving a circular walk, is recommended for strong walkers. This goes down the south side of Aiguille de la Vanoise to the Lac des Assiettes (often dry in summer), then descends steeply through a wild valley. Follow waymarks back to Les Fontanettes – reached in about 2½hrs from the hut.

# WALK 18: REFUGE DU CROIX DU BONHOMME (2443m: 8015ft)

| | |
|---|---|
| Valley base: | Les Contamines-Montjoie |
| Start: | Les Contamines (1164m: 3819ft) |
| Distance: | 12km (7½ miles) one way |
| Time: | 5hrs up, 3½hrs down |
| Total ascent: | 1314m (4311ft) |
| Map: | Didier Richard 8 'Mont Blanc Beaufortain' 1:50,000 |

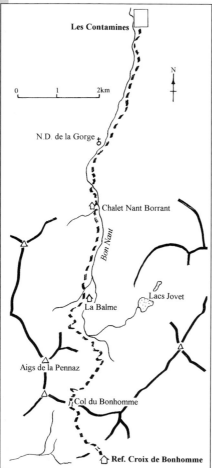

*The Tour du Mont Blanc is perhaps the best-known long-distance walk in the Alps. With outstanding scenery throughout, it's a rewarding tour that attracts walkers from as far away as the USA, Australia and New Zealand. The Croix du Bonhomme hut is on the route of the TMB, and is much-visited during the main trekking season. It sits just below a col southwest of Mont Blanc, on a grassy hillside high above the Vallée des Glaciers. Although nowhere difficult, the route to it traverses some wild country that will no doubt have snowfields lying even in midsummer, and as conditions can change abruptly walkers should be equipped with weatherproof clothing.*

Summer mornings see laden trekkers wandering upvalley from Les Contamines on the east side of the Bon Nant river to the church of Notre Dame de la Gorge, where the path suddenly steepens through a wooded ravine. The way here is an ancient one dating from Roman times (2000 years ago), and some of the paving is of Roman origin. About 1½hrs from the start reach the attractive Chalet du Nant Borrant (1460m: 30 places, meals provision) set among meadows. Beyond this the valley opens out with pastures grazed by bell-clattering cows as you walk along a track to the **Chalet-Restaurant de la Balme** (1706m: 80 places, meals provided). Ahead the Aiguilles de la Pennaz form a gatepost to the saddle of Col du Bonhomme, and after leaving la Balme a well-used trail rises to a bluff topped by an electricity pylon. After this enter a charming pastureland sliced with streams, andwhen the path forks take the right-hand option, cross a torrent and climb to a large cairn. With Col du Bonhomme in sight it's possible you'll have to cross snowfields. The path has several braidings which regroup below the col.

In a little over 4hrs Col du Bonhomme (2329m: 7641ft) is reached. On it a small wooden shelter can be very welcome if a cold wind is blowing and you need to pause to

*Col de la Croix du Bonhomme*

regain your breath while plotting the onward route. Most of the day's work is now over, and there's only another 150m of height to gain before dropping down to the hut. In good visibility and with no patches of ice to negotiate the next col should be gained without difficulty, although in mist it may demand concentration. The trail veers left from Col du Bonhomme, and rises among more rocky terrain, often with old snow lying and minor streams to cross, and about 40mins later you come onto Col de la Croix du Bonhomme (2479m) with its dominant lofty cairn and a new landscape to ponder. A short distance away to the south (about 10mins walk) stands the hut.

*Refuge du Croix du Bonhomme is owned by the CAF. It can sleep about 70 and has a simple meals service when the guardian is in residence – usually between mid-June and mid-September.*

## WALK 19: REFUGE DE BELLACHAT (2151m: 7057ft)

| | |
|---|---|
| Valley base: | Chamonix |
| Start: | La Flégère (1894m: 6214ft) |
| Distance : | 9km (5½ miles) one way |
| Time: | 4¾hrs to the hut, 1¾hrs down |
| Total ascent: | 705m (2313ft) |
| Descent: | 448m (1470ft) |
| Map: | Didier Richard 8 'Mont Blanc Beaufortain' 1:50,000 |

*First climbed in 1760 by H.B. de Saussure (who inspired the first ascent of Mont Blanc 26 years later), the easy Brévent (2525m: 8284ft) is one of the finest of all viewpoints from which to study the northwest flank of the Mont Blanc massif. Nowadays a cablecar swings visitors to the summit from Chamonix via Planpraz, but a very fine balcony walk traverses the mid-height slopes of the Aiguilles Rouges range, of which the Brévent is but a part, crosses the summit and descends very steeply to the valley near Les Houches. On the way down it passes the Refuge de Bellachat – a magnificent location for a hut and one that more than repays with its views the cost of a night spent there.*

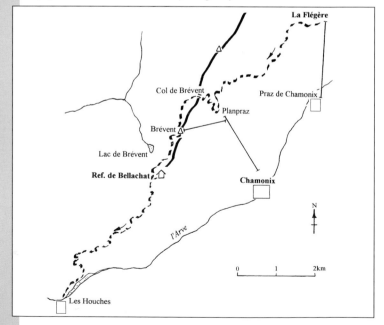

Whilst the *Grand Balcon Sud* begins at Col des Montets, the walk may be joined at the halfway point by taking the cablecar from Les Praz de Chamonix to La Flégère. From there a path is signposted to Planpraz. The way soon forks and you take the upper branch – this is used by the classic Tour du Mont Blanc. About 10mins after leaving La Flégère descend through a narrow gully safeguarded with handrails. Thereafter the trail rises a little, then contours among alpen-

*The Mont Blanc massif from below Refuge de Bellachat*

roses towards the grassy bowl of la Charlanon. Over a track veer right at another fork and climb to a junction of paths where the continuing route is signposted again to Planpraz and Brévent.

The ski industry has scarred the hillside with bulldozed pistes at Planpraz, making this a sorry sight. Ski-tows and chairlifts lace the slopes, but once again alpenroses provide a splash of colour in early summer. Above the Planpraz restaurant turn right on a broad track rising to Col de Brévent – an alternative trail avoids the col altogether and rejoins the main route north of the summit of Le Brévent. The col (2368m) rewards with very fine views, not only to Mont Blanc, but northwest to Pointe d'Anterne and the Rochers de Fiz across the Passy nature reserve. Here the GR5 comes in from the right, but the TMB path swings left and makes its way without difficulty to the summit of Le Brévent where there's an orientation table, restaurant and cablecar station – all with a stunning panorama. Chamonix lies nearly 1500 vertical metres (5000ft) below. Retrace your steps to a well-made path cutting left, signed to Bel Lachat. It first descends in zigzags, then along a stretch known as the Grand Balcon from where you can see across the lovely Lac du Brévent. Then, about 1hr from the summit a short spur path breaks left to the Bellachat refuge.

*Refuge de Bellachat is privately owned, has 30 places and restaurant service during the period when it is manned – usually end of June to end of September.*

The 1¾hr descent to Les Houches is steep but straightforward.

## WALK 20: REFUGE DU COL DE BALME (2191m: 7188ft)

| | |
|---|---|
| Valley base: | Chamonix or Argentière |
| Start: | Le Tour (1453m: 4767ft) |
| Distance: | 9km (5½ miles) round trip |
| Time: | 2hrs up, 2–2½hrs down |
| Total ascent: | 738m (2421ft) |
| Map: | Didier Richard 8 'Mont Blanc Beaufortain' 1:50,000 |

*Trekkers tackling the Tour du Mont Blanc as well as the Walker's Haute Route from Chamonix to Zermatt all cross Col de Balme on the frontier between France and Switzerland, and will know this hut for its tremendous view into the Chamonix valley, dominated by the Aiguille Verte and Drus, with Mont Blanc presiding over all. TMB walkers usually approach this col from the Swiss side, while those on the Haute Route follow the path described below. This hut walk makes an easy ascent from the little village of Le Tour, then returns by way of the Col des Posettes*

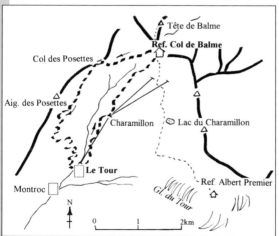

*and Ardossières chalets, thereby creating an oval-shaped circuit.*

At the head of the Chamonix valley Le Tour is renowned for having the highest snowfall of any village in France; it was also the birthplace of E d w a r d W h y m p e r ' s great guide, Michel Croz (1830–65), who took part in the first ascent of the Matterhorn, but who died on the descent. From Le Tour a gondola lift offers an easy way to Col de Balme. Our route goes along the right-hand side of the gondola lift station and straight ahead on a broad track. Before long a signed footpath breaks away and rises without difficulty to Charamillon and the intermediate lift station. At a junction of paths continue ahead and, gaining height without undue effort, you will reach Col de Balme and the unmarked

Franco-Swiss frontier. The view back to Aiguille Verte, Mont Blanc and the Vallée de l'Arve is justifiably famous. As R.L.G. Irving once wrote: "If that view does not thrill you you are better away from the Alps."

*Refuge du Col de Balme: privately owned, open throughout the year, 25 places, full meals service. Services may be paid for in either French or Swiss francs.*

From Col de Balme you could either continue down into Switzerland to the village of Trient (2hrs), take another path south to the Albert Premier hut on the edge of the Glacier du Tour (2hrs),

*Refuge du Col de Balme*

or make an easy climb to the viewpoint of Tête de Balme to the north (¾hr). To descend to Le Tour the following route is recommended.

Leave the hut descending on a waymarked path towards Col des Posettes. The path is used by TMB walkers and slopes gently down a grassy hillside with a glorious panorama almost every step of the way. At Col des Posettes there's a choice of routes. One follows the ridge over Aiguillette des Posettes then descends to the road below Col des Montets – a very fine scenic route, but on this occasion it is recommended to take the path veering left (southwest) and marked to Ardossières. Rise easily to Chalet de Balme and the deserted Ardossières hutments, then cut left and descend by way of countless zigzags among lavish alpine flowers, before twisting to the right and, dropping through woodland, come eventually to Le Tour.

# THE SWISS ALPS

To generations of travellers the Alps simply meant Switzerland, and no European Grand Tour was complete without at least a visit to its glaciers. Despite its modest size, it has the greatest number of 4000m (13,000ft) peaks of all Alpine countries, and arguably the best-maintained and most comprehensive system of waymarked mountain paths in Europe. In addition the public transport system is second to none, and the hillsides are dotted with countless Alpine farms doubling as restaurants – to the benefit of the walker. Needless to say, the majority of its huts are set in idyllic locations.

## THE PENNINE ALPS

Sharing a common boundary with Italy, the Pennines extend eastward from Col Ferret (on the edge of the Mont Blanc massif) to the Simplon Pass. It's a tremendous range of ice-sculpted peaks and snowfields, whose valleys all drain northward to the fertile Rhône. The best-known resort is, without question, Zermatt – thanks to the Matterhorn which towers nearby. But there are plenty of others that are worth considering as a base for a walking holiday; among them Saas Fee, Zinal and Arolla. Day walks, and multi-day tours and circuits are plentiful, and many huts are accessible without the need for technical skills.

Guidebooks:  *The Valais* and *Chamonix to Zermatt: the Walker's Haute Route* – both by Kev Reynolds (Cicerone Press), *The Grand Tour of Monte Rosa, Vol 2* by C J Wright (Cicerone Press).

## THE BERNESE ALPS

Renowned for the trio of peaks (Eiger, Mönch and Jungfrau) that gaze north at Interlaken, the Bernese Alps rival the Pennines for scenic grandeur. Although their summits are not quite as high as those south of the Rhône, the icy heart of the range gives birth to the Grosser Aletschgletscher, Europe's longest glacier, which bulldozes its way Rhônewards. Despite this glacial heartland, across the north flank of the Bernese Alps a whole series of valleys are linked by way of walkers' passes, while some of the best hut routes lead into wild and comparatively remote country.

Guidebooks:  *The Bernese Alps* and *The Alpine Pass Route* – both by Kev Reynolds (Cicerone Press).

## THE CENTRAL SWISS ALPS

The Vierwaldstättersee, or Lake of Lucerne, lies virtually in the centre of Switzerland, while to the south and east of its many-fingered shores the line of Alpine ranges extends from the eastern limit of the Bernese Alps. The first of these is the Uri Alps, accessed from the south by the lovely Göschener Tal from whose upper reaches several huts may be reached. This valley flows out to the Reuss, on the far side of which the Uri Alps continue with more fine hut walks. Bordering the east bank of the Lake of Lucerne, however, rise the Glarner, or Glarus Alps; attractive mountains, splendid valleys, but very few visitors. For all its ease of accessibility, this is very much a forgotten land that is well worth discovering.

Guidebook: *Central Switzerland* by Kev Reynolds (Cicerone Press).

## THE LEPONTINE ALPS

Switzerland's only canton lying south of the Alpine watershed is Ticino (Tessin), a pear-shaped projection into Italy that, unsurprisingly, shares the language of Italy, has Italian-styled buildings, and whose mountains are even bathed in the warm sunshine of Lombardy. Little-visited by walkers from the UK, the Lepontine Alps – the Alps of Ticino – consist of granite peaks rising from deep, chestnut-wooded valleys in which the most charming and romantic of villages nestle. Through the inner glens pour crystal streams that lie here and there in deep green pools that invite a mid-walk bathe. Some of the huts are situated in high open pastures, others in stony country among the larger peaks. Each one is worth seeking out, for the views – though totally different from those of the Pennine Alps 'next door' – are full of surprises.

Guidebook: *Walking in Ticino* by Kev Reynolds (Cicerone Press).

## THE SILVRETTA, BERNINA AND BREGAGLIA ALPS

The common denominator linking these three groups is the Engadine, that vast trench-like valley slanting across southeast Switzerland, whose tourist 'capital' is St Moritz. Its southern projection is Val Bregaglia which spills down to the Italian Lake Como, while bordering the northern flank of the Lower Engadine, before that section of valley enters Austria, rise the Silvretta Alps – mountains shared with the Austrian provinces of Vorarlberg and Tirol. Switzerland's only National Park is sited in the Lower

Engadine, and a hut walk is described through one of the Park's heavily wooded valleys. This forms a direct contrast to hut walks in the Bernina and Bregaglia Alps. The first offers magnificent glacier scenery, the second wild and dramatic rock walls.

<u>Guidebook:</u> *Walks in the Engadine, Switzerland* by Kev Reynolds (Cicerone Press).

*Cabane de Moiry*

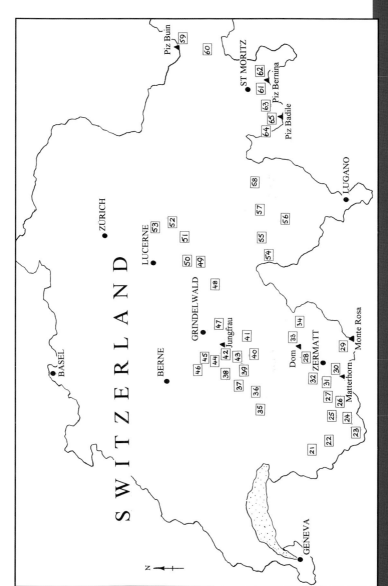

SWITZERLAND

N

BASEL

ZURICH

BERNE

LUCERNE

53
52
51
50 49
48

GRINDELWALD

47 Jungfrau
45 42 41
46 44 43 40
38 39
37 36
35

Dom 33
34
28 29
32 31 ZERMATT 30
27 26 Matterhorn, Monte Rosa
25 24
22 23
21

GENEVA

Piz Buin 59
60

ST MORITZ
61 62 Piz Bernina
63 65 Piz Badile
64

LUGANO

58
57
56
55
54

69

# WALK 21: CABANE DU MONT-FORT (2457m: 8061ft)

| | |
|---|---|
| Valley base: | Le Châble, Val de Bagnes |
| Start: | Le Châble (821m: 2694ft) |
| Distance: | 9km (5½ miles) one way |
| Time: | 6–6½hrs up |
| Total ascent: | 1636m (5367ft) |
| Map: | LS 1326 'Rosablanche' 1:25,000 |

*Although it's possible to reach Cabane du Mont-Fort by much shorter and easier ways, the walk described here is highly recommended, despite its length and steepness. First the alternatives. From Verbier (bus or cableway from Le Châble) a 3-hour walk via Clambin is an attractive option; from Verbier by cableway to Les Ruinettes followed by a good path in 1½hrs, or from the higher Les Attelas in 45mins. From the hut you gaze southwest to the Mont Blanc massif, south to the Grand Combin and west to the Dents du Midi. And the long walk to it is full of variety.*

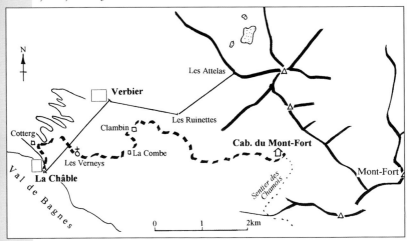

From the north side of the river at Le Châble waymarks direct you from the side of Café-Restaurant La Ruinette up through the village among houses and dark timber granaries to Cotterg. Here a signpost points right to Chapelle les Verneys. On coming to the hamlet of La Fontenelle a narrow path breaks away by a wooden cross to edge alongside an orchard and onto a track easing round the hillside to the chapel and farm buildings of Les Verneys. Just

70

beyond these a path strikes uphill into forest, gaining height steeply at times, and about 25mins from Les Verneys brings you to a junction of paths. Follow signs to Verbier and Les Ruinettes and ascend the right-hand side of what becomes a distinctive combe.

*Evening light on Mont Blanc from Cabane du Mont-Fort*

Crossing a dirt road take an upper track veering left. Using footpath short-cuts come to a pair of wooden buildings (La Combe) where the path forks. Take the lower option into forest, and at the first junction bear right on a trail which climbs to the chalets of Clambin (3hrs 45mins) – tremendous views.

Here a track is signposted to Les Ruinettes and Mont-Fort. The ascent continues, mostly through forest, but emerging at last to rewarding views of Grand Combin and the Mont Blanc massif. On coming to a track by a chairlift turn right. This becomes a path, crosses another track, and then merges into a dirt road heading right for about 250m. At this point a narrow path goes up onto an earthen causeway alongside a *bisse* (an irrigation channel). Follow the *bisse* round the hillside with Grand Combin in view most of the way, and so gain the hut which is set on a spur below the Monts de Sion, to the west of Mont Fort.

*Cabane du Mont-Fort has 80 places and offers a full meals service; manned during the ski-touring season, and from July to the end of September. It is one of the stages on the Chamonix-Zermatt Walkers' Haute Route, and has several walker's passes accessible from it. Sunset views are especially fine  (Tel: 027 778 13 84).*

Descent to the Val de Bagnes could be eased by cableway. Better still take a full day to walk southeast along the Sentier des Chamois (watch for ibex) to Col Termin, and descend from there to Fionnay via the *lac* and Cabane de Louvie in 5½hrs (Walk 22).

## WALK 22 CABANE DE LOUVIE (2207m: 7240ft)

| | |
|---|---|
| *Valley base:* | **Fionnay or Le Châble** |
| *Start:* | **Cab. du Mt-Fort (2457m: 8061ft)** |
| *Distance:* | **9km (5½ miles) in all** |
| *Time:* | **4hrs to hut, 1½hrs to Fionnay** |
| *Total ascent:* | **222m (728ft)** |
| *Descent:* | **1189m (3901ft) to Fionnay** |
| *Map:* | **LS 1326 'Rosablanche' 1:25,000** |

*Dominating Val de Bagnes, the Grand Combin is a huge block of snow, ice and rock which, from some angles at least, gives a good impression of a Mont Blanc lookalike. Set upon a high terrace on the sunny side of the valley, Cabane de Louvie enjoys a privileged view of the mountain – a full-frontal view that is even more impressive when seen from the tarn above and behind the hut. Cabane de Louvie may be reached in two*

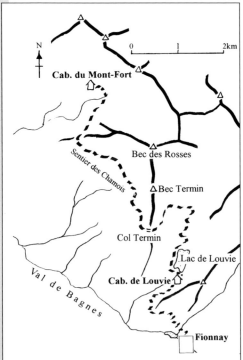

*hours from Fionnay in Val de Bagnes by an extremely steep path, but the approach suggested here makes one of the finest excursions in all the Alps. The Combin massif is on show almost every step of the way from Cabane du Mont-Fort as you wander the aptly named 'Sentier des Chamois' to Col Termin, while the descent to the Lac and Cabane de Louvie adds colour and foreground splendour to the scene.*

From the Mont-Fort hut descend to a major path junction and take the right-hand option which forks soon after, at which point you bear left, descending to a dirt road. Leave this at the second hairpin and follow a path cutting across screes, then climbing at a steady angle. The trail becomes a magnificent belvedere with the Combin massif full ahead, and the Mont Blanc range far off to the right. In places the path, which is exposed here and there, is protected with fixed chains and cables, although in normal summer conditions the route should be safe enough. As you advance towards Col Termin, keep alert for the possible sighting of ibex, chamois or marmots – a herd of ibex has been seen on each of my wanderings along this

path. After about 1¾–2hrs you should reach Col Termin (2679m), an obvious saddle on a shoulder of Bec Termin.

A direct route descends to Lac de Louvie, but it is better to cross the col on a path signposted to Col de Louvie and Prafleuri. The way descends a little, then makes an undulating traverse of a steep mountainside, with Lac de Louvie seen below. About 20mins from Col Termin leave the main path and descend steeply on a trail which brings you to the marshy Plan de la Gole. After crossing a couple of streams the way divides. The upper trail resumes a lengthy

*Lac de Louvie and Grand Combin above Cabane de Louvie*

traverse of hillside, but we bear right and take the lower option, soon passing a small shelter. Beyond this descend to the beautiful Lac de Louvie, wander along its right-hand shore, bear left at the southern end and pass through a cleft to reach Cabane de Louvie.

*Cabane de Louvie belongs to the local Val de Bagnes commune. It has 54 places and is manned from the beginning of July to mid-September, when meals are available (Tel: 027 778 17 40).*

The path to Fionnay continues beyond the hut and makes a tortuously steep descent via hundreds of tight zigzags – fixed chains in places. Allow about 1½ hours for this.

# WALK 23: CABANE DE CHANRION (2462m: 8077ft)

| | |
|---|---|
| **Valley base:** | Fionnay, Val de Bagnes |
| **Start:** | Mauvoisin (1841m: 6040ft) |
| **Distance:** | 20km (12½ miles) round trip |
| **Time:** | 4hrs up, 2½hrs down |
| **Total ascent:** | 801m (2628ft) |
| **Map:** | LS 1346 'Chanrion' 1:25,000 |

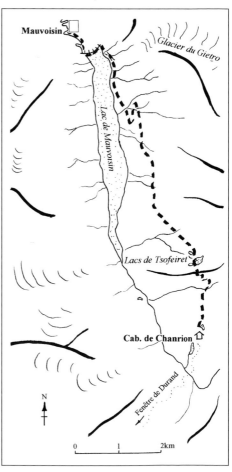

*Anyone relying on Whymper's classic Scrambles Amongst the Alps for a lead in regard to this hut, would never set out. He called the chalets of Chanrion where he spent the night of 5 July 1865, "a foul spot, which should be avoided." Today's Chanrion hut is, however, a fine one, its situation idyllic, the walk to it delightful. It's set in a lovely basin of pastureland at the very head of the Val de Bagnes, the Grand Combin massif rises to the west, Pointe d'Otemma to the east, while the Fenêtre de Durand provides a way across the border into Italy to the southwest. For walkers, climbers, and (in the spring touring season) skiers, it makes an attractive base. One night at the very least ought to be spent there.*

The tiny hamlet of Mauvoisin below the huge dam wall at the roadhead is served by Postbus, but if you have your own transport there's a car park near the dam. Walk to the head of the barrage and cross to the east side where a track strikes south alongside the reservoir. Passing through a couple of tunnels it then begins to rise up the hillside where streams drain the Giétro Glacier in cascades. When the track ends a path continues and crosses several more streams as it works a way up to the Tsofeiret pastures and a cluster of tarns. This is a splendid region of grass, flowers, lakes and striking views across the valley to the eastern face of the Grand Combin.

The path goes up to a low crest, the so-called Col de Tsofeiret (2642m: 8668ft), where the descent at first is steep and exposed and potentially hazardous. However, fixed chains provide some security, although caution is necessary. From the left screes fan down from the long and narrow Glacier de Brenay, but beyond these the route is straightforward. Alpine flowers brighten a wilderness of rocks and moraine debris before you return to grass once more. The hut is set among grass bluffs and with more tarns nearby.

*Cabane de Chanrion*

*Cabane de Chanrion is owned by the Geneva Section of the SAC; 100 places, guardian in residence in the spring ski touring season (the hut forms a stage on the classic Haute Route) and from July to September. Meals service (Tel: 027 778 12 09).*

The Fenêtre de Durand (2797m: 9177ft) makes an obvious destination for a walk from here. A good path heads up the left (west) bank moraines of a shrinking glacier to the pass which forms the Swiss-Italian border – noted for its alpine plants (2½hrs). In the distance the Gran Paradiso can be seen floating above the hinted Valle d'Aosta. From the hut return to Mauvoisin either by the route of approach (2½–3hrs), or by way of a good track/dirt road down the west side of the valley (2–2½hrs).

# WALK 24: CABANE DES DIX (2928m: 9606ft)

| | |
|---|---|
| Valley base: | Arolla |
| Start: | Arolla (1998m: 6555ft) |
| Distance: | 6km (3½ miles) one way |
| Time: | 3½–4hrs |
| Total ascent: | 950m (3117ft) |
| Map: | LS 1346 'Chanrion' 1:25,000 |

*Situated on a rocky knoll on the west bank of the Cheilon Glacier below the north face of Mont Blanc de Cheilon, the Dix hut is reached by two major routes; the first rises from Val d'Hérémence and takes a track along the west bank of the dammed Lac des Dix, then on moraines and rocks without treading glacier ice in about 3hrs from Le Chargeur. The second, and most 'sporting' approach route comes from Arolla at the head of Val d'Hérens, wanders over pastures beside Pigne d'Arolla, crosses a blocking ridge by the Pas de Chèvres with descent by two steep ladders to the Glacier de Cheilon, and crosses the glacier by a marked route directly to the hut. This is a classic hut walk with inspiring scenery all the way.*

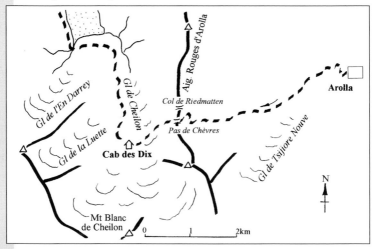

From the village square walk up the road for a short distance, then bear left on a path leading to the Grand Hotel Kurhaus. Beyond this the way is marked by signpost over steep grass slopes to join a broad track. From the track views are very fine to Mont Collon and Pigne d'Arolla and their accompanying glaciers. Pass a group of derelict huts and continue to gain height steadily heading southwest. A wooden bridge takes the track over a stream (2512m), but soon after this you break away left on a trail which rises below a lateral moraine banking the Tsijiore Nouve Glacier.

On reaching a rough bowl of rock-strewn pastureland the path forks (2780m). The right-hand trail climbs to the higher Col de Riedmatten, the left-hand option is the one to take for the Pas de Chèvres. The ascent is straightforward, and the pass – the lowest point on the ridge – is naturally paved with flat boulders. The view to the pyramid-shaped Mont Blanc de Cheilon is dramatic, while looking back Mont Collon is the best feature, although

the stiletto tip of the Matterhorn can also be seen.

Descend with care the two iron ladders on the west side, then over rocks to the dry Cheilon Glacier. The route across the glacier to the hut, which is in view at the left-hand end of the Tête Noire, is usually clearly marked and well-trodden. On the far side a path climbs directly to the hut.

*Cabane des Dix is one of the largest and busiest of SAC huts with 150 places, restaurant service and a guardian from mid-March to mid-May, and July until mid- September (Tel: 027 281 15 23).*

*Mont Blanc de Cheilon, from the route to Cabane des Dix*

Either return to Arolla by the same route in 2–2½hrs, or go down a clear path heading north to Lac des Dix, then take a track alongside the reservoir as far as the barrage at the northern end (2hrs). Le Chargeur is served by Postbus by which you can travel to Evolène, Les Haudères and Arolla.

## WALK 25: CABANE DES AIGUILLES-ROUGES (2810m: 9219ft)

| | |
|---|---|
| Valley base: | Arolla |
| Start: | Arolla (1998m: 6555ft) |
| Distance: | 10 km (6 miles) in all |
| Time: | 2–2½hrs up, 1¾hrs down |
| Total ascent: | 812m (2664ft) |
| Map: | LS 1326 'Rosablanche' & 1327 'Evolène' 1:25,000 |

*Arolla makes a good centre for a walking holiday. With a southerly back-drop of ice-clad mountains, a steep rock wall to the east, and with forest and pasture rising to the stony Aiguilles-Rouges to the west, this little resort nestles in an impressive alpine basin. Two of the shorter and more popular walking destinations are the chalets of Pra Gra and the tiny circular tarn of Lac Bleu. By following the route described below to the Cabane des Aiguilles-Rouges, we pass the Pra Gra hamlet, then descend to and beyond Lac Bleu, making a 10km trip with either a bus ride back to Arolla at the end of the day, or a return through woods from the tarn.*

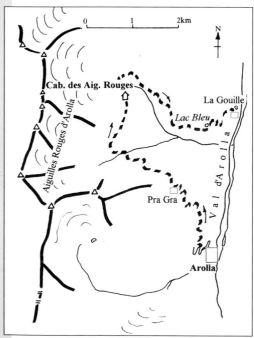

From the square by the post office in Arolla walk up the surfaced road, passing the Centre Alpin just above the village, and at the second hairpin bend above that take a track off to the right which winds steadily uphill across steep pastures. The way takes you above a small huddle of alp huts and, with footpath short-cuts, comes onto a hillside shelf a little to the right of Pra Gra, an attractive group of alpine chalets and cattle sheds where local farmers spend the summer months grazing their cattle and making cheeses. Mont Collon and Pigne d'Arolla provide a scenic backdrop.

Continue along a broad path well to the right of the chalets, heading north across pastures to gain a wide plateau. On gaining this the trail swings left among boulder slopes and gravel beds cut with streams in the base of the Ignes corrie. Several tiny glaciers hang against the ridge of the Aiguilles-Rouges high above. The trail turns right (north) to cross more boulder slopes and scree, and when you come to a short exposed section, a fixed chain provides assistance – which could be useful early in the season when the trail can be icy. Towards the end of the northward trend the path rises to the hut, which is seen on a rib of rock and scree below the Glacier des Aiguilles-Rouges.

*Cabane des Aiguilles-Rouges is owned by the Academic Alpine Club of Geneva. 80 places, and full meals service during the summer period (July and August) when there's a guardian in residence (Tel: 027 283 1649). Views to the east show the needle-like Aiguille de la Tsa on the Bertol-Veisivi ridge, and southeast to Mont Collon.*

Continue above the hut for a short distance following paint marks on rock, then descend steeply, at first heading east to cross a stream, then south-eastward on a good path. Although

*Cabane des Aiguilles-Rouges*

steep for much of the way, the route is now clear to Lac Bleu. The continuing path goes past the nearby huts of Louché and through pinewoods to La Gouille on the Arolla–Les Haudères road (Postbus stop). Alternatively bear right at the tarn on a woodland path leading directly back to Arolla.

## WALK 26: CABANE DE MOIRY (2825m: 9268ft)

| | |
|---|---|
| **Valley base:** | **Grimentz** |
| **Start:** | **Barrage de Moiry (2249m: 7379ft)** |
| **Distance:** | **7km (4 miles) one way** |
| **Time:** | **2½hrs to the hut** |
| **Total ascent:** | **576m (1890ft)** |
| **Map:** | **LS 1327 'Evolène' 1:25,000** |

*Built originally in 1924, the Cabane de Moiry enjoys a privileged near-view of the Moiry glacier's icefall. Following his visit to the region in 1864, the great Victorian pioneer, A.W. Moore, described this as "a tremendous ice-fall of great height and very steep." It certainly is that,*

*and visitors to the hut are able to study its complex maze of séracs from a position of safety, and watch as an occasional ice tower crashes into the depths below. The hut sits on a prominent spur of rock on the eastern (true right) bank of the glacier near the head of Val de Moiry, a tributary of the lovely Val d'Anniviers, and is reached by way of a path that runs up a crest of lateral moraine, from which it's possible to gaze directly into blue lines of crevasse.*

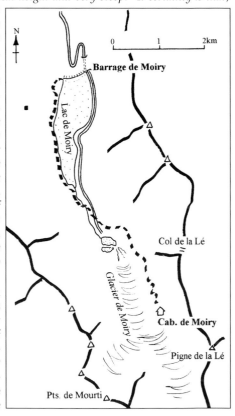

The only village in Val de Moiry is Grimentz, a typically Valaisian collection of handsome, dark-timbered chalets heavily bedecked with flowers. This lies some way        below        the

*Moiry Glacier, below Cabane de Moiry*

barrage blocking the northern end of the Moiry reservoir, and only a vague hint at the delights of the upper valley are suggested from its windows. From Grimentz it would take about 2hrs to reach the barrage on foot, but it's also served by the ubiquitous Postbus during the summer, thus saving time that can be better spent higher, and walkers with their own transport are able to drive to the southern end of Lac de Moiry where there's considerable parking space. If the walk is begun there, the hut may be reached in about 1½hrs.

Assuming you begin at the barrage, cross the dam wall to its western side and follow the track which rises above the reservoir. A path soon breaks away, slopes down towards the lake and heads south along the shoreline. At the southern end of the lake continue to a metal bridge enabling you to cross a glacial stream. Over the bridge bear right on a track, then take a footpath leading up to the road. Cross this and remain on the continuing path as it winds over boulder-littered grassland and eventually comes to the lateral moraine walling the east side of the Glacier de Moiry – "a noble ice-stream, comparable to any other in the Alps" is how A.W. Moore described it. Now the path follows the moraine crest for a while before descending left, then climbing steeply in zigzags to gain the hut.

*Cabane de Moiry belongs to the Montreux Section of the Swiss Alpine Club and is usually manned from the end of June to the end of September when meals are available (Tel: 027 475 45 34). There are 95 places in its dormitories.*

The icefall referred to above is seen immediately to the south. Above this the glacier eases in a swathe between the Pointes de Mourti and Pigne de la Lé, while projecting from the latter peak a high ridge divides the Moiry glen from Val de Zinal.

# WALK 27: CABANE DU PETIT MOUNTET (2142m: 7028ft)

| | |
|---|---|
| Valley base: | Zinal |
| Start: | Zinal (1675m: 5495ft) |
| Distance: | 5km (3 miles) to the hut |
| Time: | 1¾hrs |
| Total ascent: | 467m (1532ft) |
| Map: | LS1327 'Evolène' 1:25,000 |

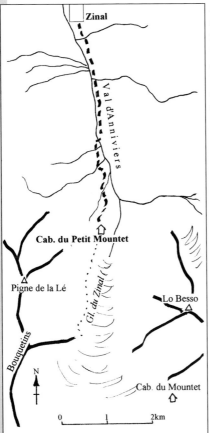

As the highest village in Val d'Anniviers, Zinal's location is ideal as a base for a walking holiday, although thanks to the steepness of the valley walls, many of the outings here are quite tough. Several SAC huts are accessible from the village: the Tracuit, set high on the northwest ridge of Tête de Milon (a spur of the Weisshorn); the unmanned Cabane d'Ar Pitetta in a glorious cirque below the Weisshorn; Cabane du Mountet in full view of the Ober Gabelhorn, and the privately-owned Petit Mountet, perched on a wall of moraine overlooking the Zinal Glacier. This last-named is the easiest to reach, but the walk to it, although short, has plenty of awe-inspiring scenery to contemplate on the way. It makes an almost perfect site for lunch, seated at a bench in the sunshine with views to the head of the valley a short distance away, where motionless cascades of ice and snow inspire admiration.

From the heart of Zinal wander upvalley past the old timber chalets and *mazots* that extend the village, and after the last of the buildings, when the road gives out, continue ahead on a track which brings you to a bridge spanning the river. Cross to the west bank and wind uphill on a broad, clear track. About 45mins from Zinal, and just before coming to a white-walled hut, turn off the track on a narrow path branching to the right. Five minutes later come to a path junction. Continue straight ahead. The trail now becomes increasingly attractive, with views across the valley to the great cirque of Ar Pitetta topped by the Weisshorn (which shows a very different face to that

seen by walkers above Zermatt), while the lovely Zinalrothorn is effectively blocked by the lesser peak of Lo Besso.

The way sneaks through lush vegetation, then descends into the narrow gully-like ablation trough that is trapped between moraine wall and mountainside. A stream runs through this trough, and after crossing it you then mount the slope of moraine to the crest, on which sits Cabane du Petit Mountet.

*Cabane du Petit Mountet is privately owned but open to all during the main summer season. Dormitory accommodation, restaurant service. Advanced booking is essential if you plan to stay overnight. (Check at the Zinal tourist office for information.)*

*The path to Cabane du Petit Mountet*

An interesting extension to this walk leads further along the moraine crest. In one place the path is interrupted by crags, but a metal ladder fitted to the rock helps overcome this obstacle. The moraine crumbles too, so caution is advised, but about 1hr from the hut you should reach the so-called Plan des Lettres, a grassy bluff at about 2465m, with a stunning high mountain panorama to enjoy.

# WALK 28: TÄSCH HUT (2701m: 8862ft)

| | |
|---|---|
| Valley base: | Zermatt |
| Start: | Sunnegga (2288m: 7507ft) |
| Distance: | 16km (10 miles) |
| Time: | 3¼hrs up, 2¾hrs down |
| Total ascent: | 885m (2904ft) |
| Map: | 'Zermatt Wanderkarte' 1:25,000 |

*The shortest and most direct way to reach this hut is by taxi from Täsch to Täschalp, then on foot for 1½ hours on an easy track. The following walk is much longer and more rewarding, though, and it makes a splendid day out. It follows a high path from Sunnegga above Zermatt, to the classic viewpoint of Ober Sattla, descends steeply to Täschalp, then makes the final winding ascent to the hut. At every stage there are fine views to enjoy; from Sunnegga the Matterhorn dominates, at Tufteren it is the alp hamlet that gladdens the eye, from the high trail there's the deep Mattertal, with Weisshorn soaring above it and Bietschhorn far ahead on the other side of the Rhône Valley, while at Ober Sattla a mountaineer's tick-list of peaks is on display.*

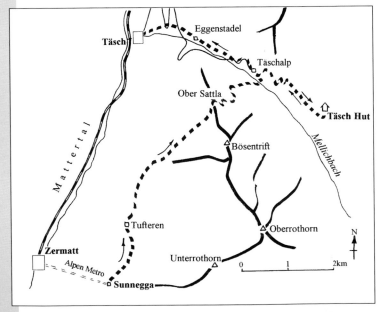

Take the Alpen-Metro (Sunnegga Express) from Zermatt to the top station, descend to crosstracks and continue downhill for another 50m before turning right on a broad path. This follows a gentle contour to the alp hamlet of Tufteren (*refreshments*) in about 30mins. Leave the main track here in favour of a more narrow trail rising ahead. When it forks continue rising across the hillside. About 15mins from Tufteren it forks again, and once more you continue ahead for a further 15mins until the way divides. Both options go to Täschalp; the left-hand trail is lower and easier, but the right-hand alternative is favoured, for this climbs to the Ober Sattla viewpoint.

*The Alps in bloom*

At first it goes through a grassy trough, then over rocks before resuming a steady rise across pastures. The gradient steepens and becomes exposed in places (one fixed cable section) until you gain the high point of Ober Sattla (2686m: 8812ft 2½hrs). After enjoying the magnificent panorama, descend by a steep, twisting path to Täschalp (*refreshments*), which is reached in a little under an hour.

The track to the Täsch Hut passes between a small stone-built chapel and a cattle shed, then slants up the hillside in long twists. About 40mins from the chapel the way forks. Bear right and, rising at a regular gradient, the track makes a few more twists before arriving at the hut.

*Situated at the foot of the Alphubel's west ridge, the Täsch Hut has 60 beds, is open at Easter and from the end of June to the end of September when meals are available (Tel: 027 967 39 13). A herd of chamois can often be seen near the hut, while the best views are to Weisshorn, Zinalrothorn and Ober Gabelhorn.*

Descend by the same track to Täschalp, and continue down-valley by a series of marked paths to reach Täsch in 2hrs 45mins. Return to Zermatt by train.

# WALK 29: MONTE ROSA HUT (2795m: 9170ft)

| | |
|---|---|
| **Valley base:** | **Zermatt** |
| **Start:** | **Rotenboden (2815m: 9236ft)** |
| **Distance:** | **12km (7½ miles) round trip** |
| **Time:** | **2½hrs up, 2–2½hrs down** |
| **Total ascent:** | **254m (833ft) to the hut** |
| **Map:** | **'Zermatt Wanderkarte' 1:25,000** |

*From its perch upon the western edge of the Plattje – an island of rock in a sea of glaciers – the Monte Rosa Hut commands a spectacular view along the Gorner Glacier to the Matterhorn, while above it folds of ice and snow lead the eye in a confusion of white shapes towards Liskamm and the 'twins', Castor and Pollux. The first hut to be built on this site was named after François Bétemps who paid for its construction, and it is from here that the normal ascent route to Monte Rosa begins. This hut approach crosses the Gorner Glacier, and although the way is marked with stakes there are crevasses, so caution and good conditions are essential.*

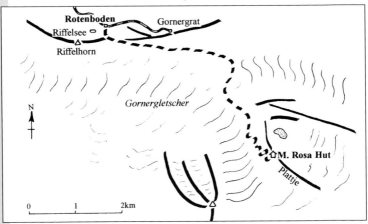

The walk begins at Rotenboden, the final station on the Gornergrat railway before Gornergrat itself. Try to get a seat on the right-hand side of the carriage from Zermatt for the best views. On leaving Rotenboden go down the path towards the Riffelsee and bear left on a crossing path just above the tarn. You then cross a low ridge to the east of the Riffelhorn and find yourself on a shelf directly above the Gorner Glacier. Monte Rosa – like a huge iced gateau – is seen to the left, then fin-like Liskamm, followed by Castor and Pollux, with Breithorn directly opposite your viewpoint. The Matterhorn stands well to the right, a pyramid of rock in a dazzling world of ice and snow.

A good path makes a long slanting traverse of the south-facing slopes of the Gornerli, an undemanding belvedere that eventually brings you down to a grass-and rock-covered bluff at the very edge of the glacier – another tremendous viewpoint that is worth walking to even if you've no intention of going as far as the hut.

A marker pole indicates the point at which you get onto the glacier, and a line of stakes leads the way roughly southeastward.

*The Monte Rosa Hut*

*Do not stray from the marked route.* The Matterhorn remains a significant feature in what is otherwise a predominantly arctic landscape, but it does not lie, of course, on our route. On the second half of the glacier crossing there are usually plenty of crevasses to work a way round and across, and normal safety precautions are advised. On leaving the ice a marked route leads over moraines and up bands of rock, sometimes quite steeply, before reaching the hut about 2½ hours from Rotenboden.

*The Monte Rosa Hut can sleep 150, and has a resident guardian from mid-March to mid-May and from July to mid-September when meals and drinks are available (Tel: 027 967 21 15). The situation is magnificent.*

Return to Rotenboden by the same route, allowing 2–2½ hours, or follow well-marked paths all the way down to Zermatt (an extra 3 hours).

## WALK 30: HÖRNLI HUT (3260m: 10,696ft)

| | |
|---|---|
| Valley base: | Zermatt |
| Start: | Schwarzsee (2583m: 8474ft) |
| Distance: | 15km (9 miles) round trip |
| Time: | 2hrs up, 3¾ or 3½hrs down |
| Total ascent: | 677m (2221ft) |
| Map: | 'Zermatt Wanderkarte' 1:25,000 |

*The Matterhorn is unarguably the most easily-recognised of all mountains, and the most powerfully magnetic attraction for visitors to Zermatt. Whether it is your intention to climb the mountain or simply to get close enough to it to absorb some of its atmosphere, the steep walk to the Hörnli Hut is a must, while from the terrace in front of the hut you can sit with a drink and gaze across the glaciers at the numerous other 4000m peaks which rim the head of the Mattertal. Add to this a return to Zermatt through pastures and alp hamlets, and a memorable day is guaranteed.*

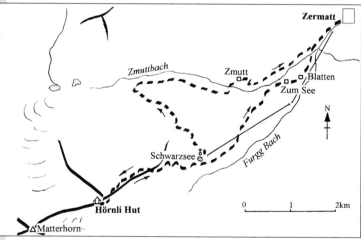

Begin by riding the two-stage cable-car to Schwarzsee. Once there the path is broad and obvious, and with the Matterhorn soaring above you it's impossible to lose the way. It leads above the Schwarzsee tarn and winds up a spur onto a stony shoulder. Before long a steel ladder takes you onto a catwalk built out from the rockface. Above this the way climbs on, then over a fairly level section across a slope of shale, at the end of which the ascent resumes, and although there's nothing difficult or outwardly dangerous about it – except perhaps under icy conditions – fixed ropes have been placed here and there. Eventually the path cuts onto the east flank of the mountain to tackle the final 100m switchback section to gain the hut.

*The trail to the Hörnli Hut*

*The Hörnli Hut stands next to the Berghaus Matterhorn, formerly known as the Belvedere Hotel, whose terrace is a classic viewpoint. The Matterhorn rears directly above, severely foreshortened from this aspect and, with stones clattering down, is revealed as a disintegrating pile of rubble! Dormitories here can sleep 170, and the hut is manned from July to mid-September. Meals and drinks are available (Tel: 027 967 27 69).*

Descend to the Schwarzsee tarn (1½ hours) and follow a broad path curving left round the base of the Matterhorn. About 30mins from Schwarzsee the path forks by a bench seat. Now leave the main path and go ahead on a narrow trail among alpenrose, bilberry and juniper, pass a brief marshy area and then go downhill alongside a stream to Stafelalp (*refreshments*). Bear right along a track to the alp buildings of Biel, then left at the next fork to cross the Zmuttbach gorge to Zmutt hamlet (*refreshments*). It's just an easy stroll from there down to Zermatt. (2hrs 15mins from Schwarzsee)

An alternative descent to Zermatt takes a steep path to the right of Hotel Schwarzsee. Going beneath the cableway it enters forest and comes to Hermettji (*refreshments*), continues down to Zum See and Blatten (*refreshments at both*) and finally into Zermatt. This is a shorter descent than that via Stafelalp and Zmutt, but it can be wearing for tired knees.

# WALK 31: SCHÖNBIEL HUT (2694m: 8839ft)

| | |
|---|---|
| Valley base: | Zermatt |
| Start: | Zermatt (1606m: 5269ft) |
| Distance: | 23km (14 miles) round trip |
| Time: | 6–6½hrs up, 3hrs down |
| Total ascent: | 1518m (4980ft) |
| Map: | 'Zermatt Wanderkarte' 1:25,000 |

*Generally reckoned to be one of the best of all walks from Zermatt, this is not only visually spectacular, but also quite long and demanding, if tackled as a one-day round trip. Better still, make it a two-day outing with a night spent at the hut, which sits on a moraine bank overlooking a chaos of glaciers with the Dent d'Hérens and Zmutt Ridge of the Matterhorn directly opposite.*

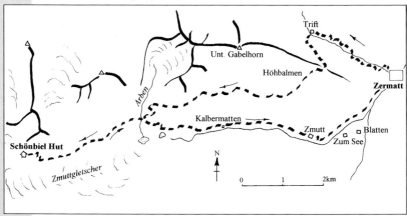

From Zermatt's church square walk towards the Matterhorn, and 1min later bear right on a cobbled path signposted to Herbrigg, Hubel, Edelweiss and Trift. When it forks take the right branch to climb above the last houses, and bear right again at the next path junction. Through meadows dotted with *mazots* join another path rising from Zermatt and follow this into the Trift gorge. The way then climbs in zigzags to Pension-Restaurant Edelweiss (*refreshments*), and continues through the gorge to reach Hotel du Trift (2hrs *refreshments*).

Bear left, cross a footbridge just beyond the hotel and wind up a grassy hillside to turn a spur where a tremendous panorama of

4000m glacier-clad mountains is gained. With the Matterhorn now ahead, come to a junction known as Höhbalmen (2665m: 8743ft) where there's a bench seat. Ignore the left-hand path which descends to Zermatt via Hubel, and follow the main trail curving to the right with a view to the head of the Zmutt Glacier and the Dent d'Hérens. Eventually the path descends into the Arben glen and reaches another junction.

Turn right and wander upvalley. Before long cross a stream of glacial meltwater – you may need to leap the various braidings to avoid wet feet. After this the way goes onto a moraine wall

*The Schönbiel Hut and the Matterhorn*

edging the Zmutt Glacier, follows the crest for a while, then climbs a final steep slope to gain the hut.

*The Schönbiel Hut is owned by the Monte Rosa Section of the Swiss Alpine Club. It can sleep 80, and has a guardian from July to mid-September. Meals and drinks available. Very fine views across converging glaciers to the Dent d'Hérens and Matterhorn. Dent Blanche rises to the north (Tel: 027 967 13 54).*

Return to Zermatt along the outward path as far as the Arben glen, then continue down-valley on a clear trail to the solitary building of Kalbermatten (*refreshments*). After this comes the hamlet of Zmutt (*refreshments*) and a final, easy stroll to Zermatt. Allow at least 3 hours from the hut.

## WALK 32: ROTHORN HUT (3210m: 10,531ft)

| | |
|---|---|
| Valley base: | Zermatt |
| Start: | Zermatt (1606m: 5269ft) |
| Distance: | 12km (7½ miles) round trip |
| Time: | 4½hrs up 2–2½hrs down |
| Total ascent: | 1604m (5262ft) |
| Map: | 'Zermatt Wanderkarte' 1:25,000 |

*Tucked against steep crags at the base of the Zinalrothorn's southeast ridge, high above the Trift glen, the Rothorn Hut makes a challenging destination for a day's walk. It overlooks a wild glacial cirque, with a fine collection of 4000m peaks seen to the south and southeast. The hut is used as a base for climbs on a number of neighbouring peaks, and visits by walkers are few. Don't let that put you off. The route to it is quite straightforward, but it is both steep and interesting, and there are two opportunities to stop for refreshment on the way. Early accounts of climbing the Rothorn contain some disparaging references to the 'infernal' moraines below the hut, but these comments are a little unfair, for they are usually reserved for the descent after a tiring climb. Endless though the cone may appear on the way to the hut, it's an access ramp speckled with alpine plants, and it provides a steadily unfolding panorama to be appreciated.*

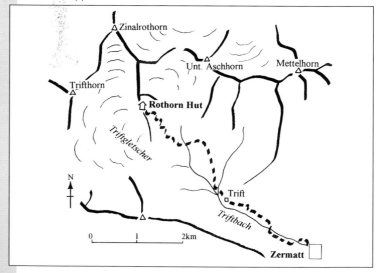

The route first ascends the narrow Trift gorge above and to the west of Zermatt, and the way into this is described under the Schönbiel Hut route (Walk 31). An initial 45 minute approach leads to the Pension-Restaurant Edelweiss (*refreshments*) in the

*Above the Trift gorge en route to the Rothorn Hut*

mouth of the gorge, and a further hour or so will bring you to Hotel du Trift (*refreshments*) in a rough basin of boulder-strewn pasture just above the gorge.

About 3mins beyond the hotel the path forks. Continue ahead, winding into an upper basin where another path (to the Mettelhorn in 2¾hrs – recommended for another day) breaks away to the right. Here the basin is rimmed with glaciers. The trail to the Rothorn Hut edges the right-hand side above a rock tip, then comes to a little plain below the Trift Glacier. Cross a stream flowing from the right, then go straight up the obvious moraine cone walling the glacier ahead. It's a long, fairly steep ascent, and about 200m (650ft) from the top, the hut can be seen for the first time. This will be reached about 4½ hours after leaving Zermatt.

*The Rothorn Hut looks across the Trift Glacier to the topmost triangle of the Matterhorn seen above two intervening ridges, while to the southeast Monte Rosa and wave upon wave of snowpeaks form the Swiss-Italian border above the Gorner Glacier. The hut belongs to the Oberaargau Section of the SAC and has room for 84 in its dormitories. It is manned between mid-July and mid-September, when meals and drinks are provided (Tel: 027 967 20 43).*

Descend to Zermatt via the same path used on the upward route, allowing 2–2½ hours for this. Alternatively bear right immediately before Hotel du Trift on the Hohbalmen path, and descend from there via Hubel – add 2 hours from Trift.

# WALK 33: MISCHABEL HUT (3340m: 10,958ft)

| | |
|---|---|
| **Valley base:** | Saas Fee |
| **Start:** | Hannig (2340m: 7677ft) |
| **Distance:** | 7km (4¼ miles) round trip |
| **Time:** | 3–3½hrs up, 2hrs down |
| **Total ascent:** | 1029m (3376ft) |
| **Map:** | Kümmerley & Frey 'Wanderkarte Saastal' 1:40,000 |

*Saas Fee is set in open meadows at the base of a glorious amphitheatre of glacier-hung mountains, among which the Dom reigns supreme as the highest mountain entirely within Swiss territory. But the Dom is one of several great peaks which form the so-called Mischabelhorner upon whose flank rests the object of this walk. There are in fact two Mischabel Huts, one built just above the other, perched more than 1500m (4900ft) above Saas Fee near the base of the east-northeast ridge of the Lenzspitze, and approached by a notoriously steep path. By judicious use of the Hannig gondola lift, some of the effort is taken from it, although the steepest sections are just below the huts and are therefore unavoidable. None of this should deter the fit walker – with a good head for heights – although it is definitely not a good route to tackle on the first day of a holiday.*

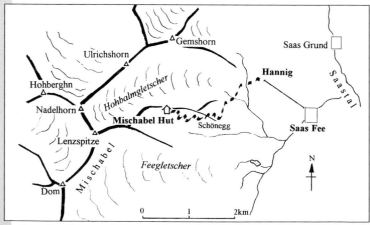

Leaving the gondola station at Hannig, bear left on a good path which soon turns a spur and angles down into a shallow corrie. After crossing the first of two streams come to the junction of Spissen. Continue ahead and cross a second stream where the path forks. Go straight ahead, rising over an old grass-covered moraine, then slanting up the hillside beyond to yet another path junction (Schönegg). Continue uphill to gain a very fine view of Allalinhorn, Alphubel and the tumbling Fee Glacier.

The gradient is now very steep as the trail picks a way up the bare mountainside and becomes increasingly rocky as you progress. Waymarks are blue and white, but under good summer conditions the route is clearly seen. Gaining height on broken ledges there are many fixed cable sections which can be useful on the descent, and southerly views are sufficient to excuse plenty of rests. For some time Allalinhorn and Alphubel, with their unmistakable snow crests, are the main features on show, but with height gain, so the summit fin of the Rimpfischhorn shows above the Feejoch. A final pull brings you to the huts, the second of which is the main one.

*The Mischabel Hut path*

*Owned by the Academic Alpine Club of Zurich, the Mischabel Huts have 120 places; staffed July to end-September; meals available (Tel: 027 957 13 17). Clearly this is not a walker's, but a climber's hut, and is used as a base for climbs on most, if not all, of the neighbouring Mischabel peaks. The outlook is stunning.*

The descent is necessarily the same as the ascent, at least as far as Schönegg. Caution is advised on the upper rocky section, and you should be especially careful to avoid knocking stones onto others below. From the Schönegg junction there's an option of continuing steeply down to Saas Fee, as opposed to cutting across to Hannig for the gondola. In this case allow about 3 hours from the hut.

## WALK 34: BRITANNIA HUT (3030m: 9941ft)

| | |
|---|---|
| Valley base: | Saas Fee |
| Start: | Plattjen (2570m: 8432ft) |
| Distance: | 6.5km (4miles) |
| Time: | 2¾–3hrs in all |
| Total ascent: | 516m (1693ft) |
| Map: | Kümmerley & Frey 'Wanderkarte Saastal' 1:40,000 |

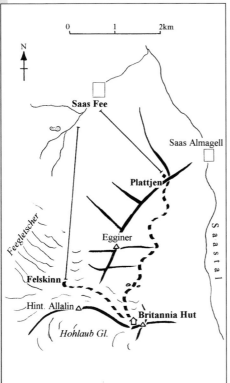

*From the top station of the Plattjen gondola lift a well-made path skirts the steep east flank of mountainside which contains Saas Fee's glacial cirque, and makes a dramatic walk high above the bed of the Saastal. It's a true belvedere of a path, a little exposed in places, but equipped with fixed cable at its narrowest point, which leads to a chaos of moraines below a small glacier. The final hut approach leads up this ice slope, while the continuing walk uses a popular trail along the upper edge of the glacier to Egginerjoch and the Felskinn cableway, for a convenient return to Saas Fee. From the Britannia Hut itself, a short (10min) ascent of the Klein Allalin is recommended for a survey of the glacial world in which it is set.*

The Plattjen top station lies just below a minor saddle on the north shoulder of the Mittaghorn, and the path rises at once to cross it. Views from this point include the huge Mischabel wall to the west towering above Saas Fee, to the north the Bernese Alps across the unseen depths of the Rhône Valley, and in the northeast the Fleschhorn-Lagginhorn-Weissmies complex across the Saastal. The trail swings to the right and picks a way across a boulder-tip before easing into a more comfortable traverse. Saas Almagell can be seen toylike almost 1000m (3281ft) below, the milky Mattmark reservoir ahead. About a half-hour from Plattjen the way cuts into the stony Meiggertal, which is little more than a scoop of hillside where ibex are sometimes seen, crosses another clutter of rocks and boulders and rises to a saddle adorned with cairns – Heidenfriedhof (2764m: 9068ft). From here the Britannia Hut comes into view.

Skirting to the right under the cliffs of Egginer, the path slopes down to moraines bulldozed by the Chessjen Glacier, twists up a moraine rib, then drops into a raw basin brightened only by a few pools. Beyond this you come to the foot of the Chessjen icefield where painted rocks direct the way up to the hut (2hrs).

*Built largely by donations from British members of the Swiss Alpine Club (ABMSAC), but owned by the Geneva Section of the SAC, the Britannia Hut is staffed from late February until the end of September: 134 places, meals service (Tel: 027 957 22 88). To the left (east) of the hut rises the rocky viewpoint of the Klein Allalin.*

*The Britannia Hut*

Either return to Plattjen by the same path (2hrs), descend to Saas Almagell by a steep trail below the Chessjen Glacier (2½hrs), or follow the much-used track heading northwest from the hut along the upper edge of the glacier to the Egginerjoch, and briefly down to the Felskinn cablecar station (45mins) for the descent to Saas Fee.

# WALK 35: GELTEN HUT (2008m: 6588ft)

| | |
|---|---|
| Valley base: | Lauenen or Gstaad |
| Start: | Lauenen (1241m: 4072ft) |
| Distance: | 16km (10 miles) round trip |
| Time: | 3½hrs up, 2½–3hrs down |
| Total ascent: | 767m (2516ft) |
| Map: | LS 1266 'Lenk' 1:25,000 |

*The Wildhorn massif presents a formidable blocking wall at the head of the Lauenental south of the consciously-chic resort of Gstaad. But there's a world of difference between Gstaad's boutiques and the ice-sheets of the Wildhorn-Arpelistock ridge, while the thunderous spout of the Geltenschuss, together with the reed-fringed Lauenensee and neatly trimmed hillsides, invests the Lauenental with an air of refreshing beauty. Above the valley, and below the icefields, the Gelten Hut not only has the high mountains as a backdrop, but it enjoys a splendid outlook over the whole valley. The walk to it from*

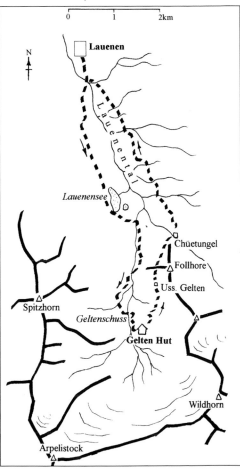

*Lauenen is one to delight all who love unsullied mountain scenery. It is, arguably, one of the finest hut walks in the Bernese Alps.*

South of Lauenen a road-then-track leads through meadows and past chalets to gain the shores of the Lauenensee tarn in about an hour. At the southern end of this a track rises among trees, but you soon break away on a marked trail climbing steeply through forest before emerging to the pastures of Feisseberg, a nature reserve. Flowers fill the meadows in early summer, the Geltenschuss bursts from its cleft ahead, and a corn-

*The Geltenschüss en route to the Gelten Hut*

flower-blue stream scurries valley-wards. The trail heads for the waterfall, then swings right to climb the southwest slopes in long switchbacks, crosses a stream and, climbing still, ducks behind a cascade. Alpenroses colour the hillsides as the way veers to the right alongside the Geltenbach which has bored great holes and swirls in the limestone. Crossing the stream to its left-hand side the path then rises over a final grassy bluff to reach the rustic, shingle-walled hut.

*Built by the local Oldenhorn Section of the SAC (based in Gstaad), the Gelten Hut can sleep about 87 in its dormitories. It is staffed for about five weeks in mid-summer, when meals are provided (Tel: 033 765 32 20). Summits accessible from here include Wildhorn, Geltenhorn, Arpelistock and Spitzhorn.*

Rather than return to Lauenen by the same path (2–2½hrs), take the trail which snakes over a knoll northeast of the hut, and continues along the ridge heading north. You then traverse green hillsides to an isolated hut (Ussere Gelten), go round the flank of the Follhore before descending steeply – in one place with the aid of a steel ladder – to the alp hamlet of Chüetungel. At the stream there's a junction of paths. Bear left on a narrow trail which crosses rough pastures, then cuts across rocky crags with a steep and exposed drop below – there are fixed cables in the worst places. Eventually the way eases, goes through forest and across more pastures, past solitary alp huts and farms on a marked trail that spills down into the valley. A road then takes you along the final stretch to Lauenen.

## WALK 36: WILDHORN HUT (2303m: 7558ft)

| | |
|---|---|
| **Valley base:** | Lenk |
| **Start:** | Iffigenalp (1586m: 5203ft) |
| **Distance:** | 6km (3½ miles) to the hut |
| **Time:** | 2½hrs up, 2hrs down |
| **Total ascent:** | 717m (2352ft) |
| **Map:** | LS 1266 'Lenk' 1:25,000 |

*The small resort of Lenk nestles among pastures at the head of the Ober Simmental. Modest wooded hills rise on either side, but to the south the long Oberland wall is marked by the Wildstrubel massif whose icefields leak numerous streams. West of the Wildstrubel, stark rocky peaks contain a wilder country, and it is in one of these hidden corries that the Wildhorn Hut is found among bare slabs and screes. The approach walk from Iffigenalp provides an insight to this wild country, and passes among lively streams, a tarn set in a deep well, grassy bluffs and crags starred with alpine flowers in summer. A fine outing.*

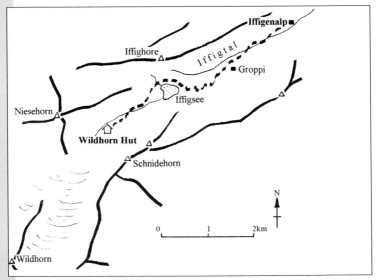

Iffigenalp, where the walk begins, is located about 8km (5 miles) south of Lenk in a tributary glen, the Iffigtal, drained by the Iffigbach. A narrow service road leads to it. This is served by bus during the summer months, but it is also accessible to private vehicles. Please note that above Färiche the road is single-track only, and a timed system restricts access to fifteen minutes every hour. There's a large car park at Hotel Iffigenalp.From the hotel car park follow a clear track upvalley towards the Iffigsee. Crossing the stream on two occasions, the track narrows to footpath before reaching the alp hut of Groppi. Passing to the right (north) of the hut the way soon rises up a long grassy cone, at the top of which the path eases, and you go through a rocky defile to emerge above the dazzling blue Iffigsee. This is set within a deep well, but the attractive northwest shoreline is accessible and popular with picnic parties.

*Iffigsee, on the way to the Wildhorn Hut*

The way to the hut continues above the northern shore to a path junction. Bear left and descend to a solitary building above the lake. Thereafter the trail climbs over grass-covered knolls heading southwest, and although it is a little vague on the ground in places, the direction is obvious. Soon enter a desolate hanging valley draped with long screes. Rising steadily through this valley the hut becomes visible on a bluff at mid-height. The final approach is up a rocky slope mellowed with alpine plants.

*Owned by the Moléson Section of the SAC, based in Fribourg, the Wildhorn Hut is manned from the end of June until the beginning of October. Meals are usually available, but self-catering is also possible. There are places for 100 in its dormitories (Tel: 033 733 23 82).*

Trekkers could use this as an overnight base whilst making a high crossing to the Gelten Hut at the head of the Lauenental, by way of a pass north of the Niesehorn. Alternatively, a ridge-walk north of that pass links with a trail descending to Lenk.

# WALK 37: FRÜNDEN HUT (2562m: 8406ft)

| | |
|---|---|
| Valley base: | Kandersteg |
| Start: | Oeschinensee (1682m: 5518ft) |
| Distance: | 12km (7½ miles) round trip |
| Time: | 3hrs up, 2–2½hrs down |
| Total ascent: | 969m (3179ft) |
| Map: | LS 1248 'Murren' 1:25,000 |

*Pictures of the Oeschinensee appear on numerous Swiss calendars, and not surprisingly it is one of the most popular sites for visitors to Kandersteg. Served by chairlift, followed by an easy stroll, this almost circular lake lies trapped in a deep well of mountains. Daubs of snow and ice are plastered on the upper slopes of the Blümlisalp massif, the western shores of the lake are fringed with trees and grass, while cliffs soar steeply from the eastern end. High above the southern shore, on a rocky knoll below the Fründen Glacier, sits the Fründen Hut, from whose door a goodly selection of climbs are possible. This approach to it is by a steep zigzag path which, though not difficult under dry conditions, will certainly require care to descend when wet.*

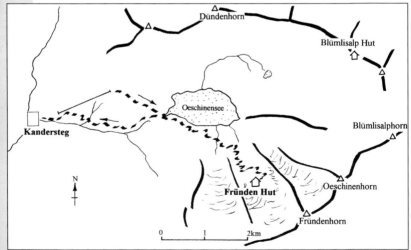

From the upper terminus of the chairlift take a broad, well-trodden track heading east between meadows. This, and a variety of narrow footpaths breaking from it, will take you to the Oeschinensee, at the western end of which there are plenty of temptations to sit with a cold drink and enjoy the view – if you don't mind the crowds, that is.

Cross the little flood plain at the end of the lake and follow a path meandering south-eastwards among trees and shrubs. It soon begins to rise, quite gently at first, then more steeply, and as the walk progresses so you find fixed cables protecting exposed sections, or where the way could be difficult when wet. There is only one trail to take, so you can't really get lost. Two fast-flowing streams are crossed on plank footbridges, and above these the landscape turns more rugged and barren. The gradient becomes more severe, but then eases with the aid of numerous zigzags which seem endless, although at each turn there is something to admire. Then you swing left to ascend the final few metres of a rocky stretch, and there is the hut with a glacier seemingly just behind it.

*The Fründen Hut sits high above the Öeschinensee*

*The situation is spectacular, with ice-cliffs, séracs and crevasses nearby, the lake far below and big mountains rimming each horizon. The Fründen Hut has 90 places and is staffed from June to October when meals are available (Tel: 033 675 14 33). It is owned by the Altels Section of the SAC. There's an interesting route which links the hut with the Doldenhorn Hut to the west, but this is for adepts only.*

For the return to Kandersteg it is necessary to descend by the same path used on the ascent as far as the Oeschinensee, then either walk back to the chairlift and ride down, or take the obvious service road from the lake, and desert this for alternative tracks or footpaths as and when they appear.

# WALK 38: BLÜMLISALP HUT (2837m: 9308ft)

| | |
|---|---|
| Valley base: | Kandersteg |
| Start: | Oeschinensee (1682m: 5518ft) |
| Distance: | 7km (4miles) one way |
| Time: | 3½–4hrs |
| Total ascent: | 1155m (3789ft) |
| Map: | LS 1248 'Mürren' 1:25,000 |

*Of the two walkers' routes to the Blümlisalp Hut, this is the shorter and more often used. The other, which is offered as a descent option, climbs steeply from Griesalp at the head of the Kiental and is used by the fairly tough, long distance Alpine Pass Route. Walkers based for a few days at Kandersteg, however, are urged not to ignore the following possibility. It has contrasting features: the popular Oeschinensee, a seemingly remote basin of alpine pasture, and a lunar landscape of moraine ribs, glacial debris and shrinking icefields. The hut itself stands on a bank of moraine above the Hohtürli pass which links the Kandertal and Kiental valleys.*

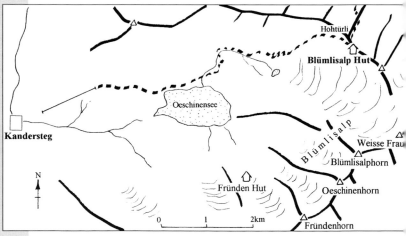

Purists who shun the chairlift and choose to walk from Kandersteg should add an extra hour or so to the route, but since the approach is quite long enough for most walkers, we begin at the top station of the chairlift which allows time to visit the Oeschinensee first. Go round the west and north shores of the lake on a good path rising among trees. For a while it hugs steep cliffs, but then comes to the alp chalets of Unter Bergli (1767m).

From the upper buildings the trail climbs steeply on what is almost a stairway with fixed ropes in places, to gain a rock step above the Oeschinensee's deep bowl. There you come to Ober Bergli, set in a landscape of boulders.

Cross the stream and rise out of the basin towards moraine tips, above which can be seen the retreating glaciers that still adorn various peaks of the Blümlisalp massif. Climbing a series of zigzags you gain the crest of lateral moraine formed by the Blümlisalp Glacier, and wander up to a rocky shelf giving into an upper region of screes. A switchback route twists up to the Hohtürli (2778m), while another trail rises a further 56m to the hut.

*The Blümlisalp Hut*

*Owned by the Blümlisalp Section (Thun) of the SAC, the Blümlisalp Hut is well equipped and comfortable, with 138 places and staffed between end-June and mid-October when meals are available (Tel: 033 676 14 37). An extensive panorama looks onto a wild scene of rock and ice, with plunging screes and a maze of ridges, while to the west peaks and ridge systems form a divide between Kandersteg and Adelboden.*

The normal descent reverses the upward path in about 3hrs 15mins to Kandersteg, but for a more challenging way, cross the Hohtürli and follow a waymarked route (fixed ropes in places) down to Griesalp in the Kiental. This may be reached in 2½hrs. Dormitory accommodation is available in that small hamlet. From Griesalp either take the Postbus through the Kiental to Reichenbach and catch a train from there to Kandersteg, or spend another long day or so walking all the way.

# WALK 39: BALMHORN HUT (1955m: 6414ft)

| | |
|---|---|
| Valley base: | Kandersteg |
| Start: | Kandersteg (1176m: 3858ft) |
| Distance: | 7km (4 miles) to the hut |
| Time: | 3½hrs up, 2hrs down |
| Total ascent: | 779m (2556ft) |
| Map: | LS 1267 'Gemmi' 1:25,000 |

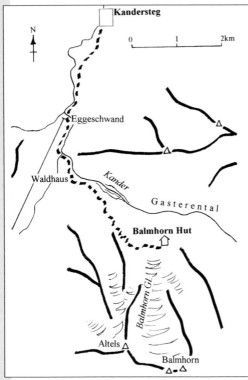

*The Gasterntal (also spelt as Gasterental) is a splendid, fjord-like valley at the head of the Kandertal. Waterfalls cascade down the huge slab walls while the river, the Kander, spreads itself in assorted braidings through the valley flats. There are no villages in the Gasterntal, just two or three rustic inns and a few farms, and the only vehicles allowed to intrude are those with special permits. In this valley nature rules supreme. Overlooking the entrance from the high southern wall stand the twin-like peaks, Altels and Balmhorn, both more than 3600m high and draped with glaciers on their north-facing slopes. Below the Balmhorn's glacier stands the hut which is the object of this walk. The route to it is steep in places, and there's one short stretch where the path crosses directly below the glacier's ice cliffs which, on occasion, break away and avalanche across the trail or create the hazard of stonefall. A notice warning of this danger is positioned on the path as you approach.*

Walk out of Kandersteg heading upvalley along the road as far as Eggeschwand, the valley station of the Sunnbüel cable-car. Bear left through the car park and follow a path through the Chluse gorge where the Kander bursts in a fury of spray. Emerging at the entrance to the Gasterntal join a narrow service road, but leave this soon after on a track leading to Hotel Waldhaus. Remain on the track heading deeper into the valley, and after about 600m as you cross an open meadow you should find a sign indicating the start of the path to the hut.

The path branches right and leads among trees on the way to the foot of steep cliffs. Here the climb begins in earnest, making a way up the mountainside with fixed cables or sections of ladder as aid where the route demands. A degree of caution is necessary as there's invariably some exposure to take into consideration. But eventually the gradient eases as you enter at mid-height a glacial cirque with the hut seen to the east on a grassy promontory. The blue-white séracs of the Balmhorn Glacier are ominously poised above you. The warning sign is reached soon after, and from here until just before reaching the hut, you should proceed warily but with speed across moraines, streams and glacial debris.

*The Balmhorn Hut*

*The Balmhorn Hut belongs to Section Altels of the Swiss Alpine Club. Usually manned at weekends in summer only, the hut can sleep 34. No meals provision, so take your own food if you plan to stay the night (Tel: 033 822 38 08).*

Of necessity the return to Kandersteg follows the same path used on the way to the hut, but given sufficient time, it would be worth spending a day exploring the Gasterntal. Better still, link this route with Walk 40 to the Lötschenpass Hut.

# WALK 40: LÖTSCHENPASS HUT (2690m: 8825ft)

| | |
|---|---|
| **Valley base:** | **Kandersteg or Ferden** |
| **Start:** | **Selden (1552m: 5092ft)** |
| **Distance:** | **5km (3 miles) to the hut** |
| **Time:** | **3½–4hrs up** |
| **Total ascent:** | **1138m (3734ft)** |
| **Map:** | **LS 1268 'Lötschental' 1:25,000** |

*Located on a ridge between the Balmhorn and Hockenhorn, the Lötschenpass is known as the oldest glacier pass in the Bernese Alps, for it was used for centuries as a link between the Kandertal/Gasterntal on the north side, and the secluded Lötschental on the south which drains*

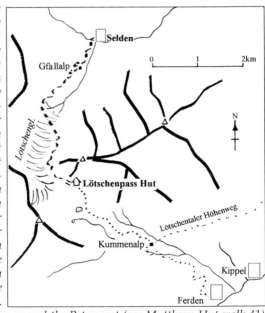

*down to the important Rhône Valley. Though it has long lost any significance as a route of trade, its crossing today makes a first-class outing for strong mountain walkers. The hut on the summit enjoys spectacular views and is a great place in which to either spend a night or enjoy lunch with the noble Bietschhorn dominating the view south.*

*Walkers who have crossed the Petersgrat (see Mutthorn Hut walk 41) could reverse this route on their return to Kandersteg.*

Take the morning minibus from Kandersteg railway station to the hamlet of Selden in the Gasterntal, and cross the river by a Himalayan-style suspension bridge to the south bank. The Lötschenpass trail then climbs the hillside on the west (right-hand) side of the Leilibach stream. It's a steep route in places, but having gained about 300m above the river, you reach Gfällalp (1847m) where you can buy refreshments and enjoy a grandstand view up the length of the Gasterntal to the gleaming Kanderfirn glacier at its head.

*The Bietschhorn, from the tarn below the Lötschenpass*

Above Gfällalp the trail slants southwestward away from the Leilibach, rising steadily towards the Lötschengletscher, which is reached about 2½hrs from Selden. The glacier is crevassed, but so long as it is dry (ie: not snow-covered) the route across is usually accomplished without difficulty – the way is marked with poles and crevasses should be clearly seen and avoided. It brings you to the eastern side where you climb a series of rock terraces by a thin path that could be troublesome for anyone suffering vertigo. Otherwise it is safe enough, and it leads directly to the Lötschenpass and the hut.

*The Lötschenpass Hut is privately owned and has 40 places. Manned from June to end-October, meals are usually available (Tel: 027 939 19 81). It is sometimes visited as a diversion from the classic Lötschentaler Höhenweg, one of the great walks of the district.*

Below the hut on the south side lies a small tarn from which the Bietschhorn across the depths of the Lötschental looks very fine, as does the range of the Pennine Alps seen across the Rhône Valley to the south. A path descends below the tarn to Kummenalp, from which Ferden and Kippel in the bed of the Lötschental may be reached (2¼hrs from the hut). A return to Kandersteg could then be achieved by walking down-valley to Goppenstein and taking a train through the Lötschberg Tunnel. Alternatively walk down to Kandersteg from the pass by reversing the upward route in about 4½ hours.

# WALK 41: MUTTHORN HUT (2901m: 9518ft)

| | |
|---|---|
| Valley base: | Kandersteg |
| Start: | Selden (1552m: 5092ft) |
| Distance: | 10km (6 miles) to the hut |
| Time: | 4½hrs up |
| Total ascent: | 1349m (4426ft) |
| Map: | LS 1248 'Mürren' 1:25,000 |

*The Mutthorn Hut occupies an arctic site on a glacial saddle between the Gasterntal (or Gasterental) and the Lauterbrunnen Valley. Whichever way it is approached entails crossing a glacier, and although the route described here is perhaps the easiest, it should only be attempted by mountain walkers equipped with rope and ice axe and experience of movement on crevassed icefields. That being said, it makes a splendid introduction to the ice world of the Alps and, if the suggested descent to the Lötschental is taken, is part of an exhilarating two-day crossing of the Petersgrat – a remnant of the great ice-sheet that once covered much of the Bernese Alps.*

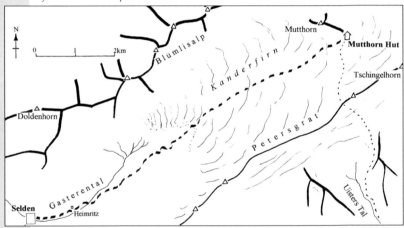

It takes about 2½ hours to walk from Kandersteg to Selden in the Gasterntal, but it's preferable to use the minibus which leaves Kandersteg railway station and delivers you to the Selden inns fresh for a day's effort on the Kanderfirn glacier. (Private vehicles are not allowed in the Gasterntal.) From the hamlet wander upvalley on the continuing track which ends at the Heimritz farm. A clear path remains on the left side of the valley and rises into a higher section bright with natural rock gardens and shrubberies of dwarf pine and juniper before crossing the Kander stream to join another path. (If the stream is high after prolonged bad weather, or heavy snow-melt, it will be better to cross at Selden and use the south bank trail to this point.)

*Approaching the Kanderfirn en route to the Mutthorn Hut*

Continue up valley, making height towards ice cliffs at the snout of the Kanderfirn. Passing through a belt of alpenroses the trail then zigzags up a rock barrier to the glacier. The path edges the glacier, then climbs grit-strewn terraces before easing onto the ice. Although it is not heavily crevassed, all normal precautions should be taken as you work your way up the gently-ascending Kanderfirn, keeping right of centre. The hut is not visible until shortly before you reach it, but you make for the right-hand end of the Mutthorn rock projection which appears in the centre of the broad saddle at the head of the glacier. The hut is on a rock platform overlooking the Tschingelfirn which tumbles northeastward into the secluded upper reaches of the Lauterbrunnental.

*Owned by the Weissenstein Section of the SAC the Mutthorn Hut has 100 places and a guardian in residence from the end of June until mid-September, when meals are usually available. The hut is supplied by helicopter (Tel: 033 853 13 44).*

Descent by the same route to Kandersteg would take about 4 hours, but by crossing the Petersgrat south of the hut, and descending through the steep little Uisters Tal to Fafleralp in the Lötschental, makes a first-rate outing of about 3 hours, and is highly recommended. Return could then be made to Kandersteg by crossing the Lötschenpass whose path descends first to Selden in the Gasterntal.

## WALK 42: ROTTAL HUT (2755m: 9039ft)

| | |
|---|---|
| Valley base: | Stechelberg or Lauterbrunnen |
| Start: | Stechelberg (910m: 2986ft) |
| Distance: | 6km (3½ miles) to the hut |
| Time: | 5hrs up, 3hrs down |
| Total ascent: | 1845m (6053ft) |
| Map: | LS 1248 'Mürren' & 1249 'Finsteraarhorn' 1:25,000 |

*Reached by a long and extremely steep path, with two fixed-rope scrambling sections, the Rottal Hut enjoys a privileged outlook across the head of the Lauterbrunnen Valley to the Breithorn, Tschingelhorn, Blümlisalp and Gspaltenhorn, each rising above a cascade of ice. Nearer to hand gleam the Gletscherhorn, Ebnefluh, Mittaghorn and Grosshorn, while the Jungfrau is a contortion of rock, snow and ice immediately above to the northeast – but this otherwise graceful mountain is seriously foreshortened from here. Ibex can often be spied near the hut, and both dawn and dusk can be quite magical. The route to the hut, however, is not for the faint-hearted, and should only be attempted by fit walkers with a good head for heights. An early start is advisable; there could be some danger from stonefall, and there's a steep snow slope to negotiate.*

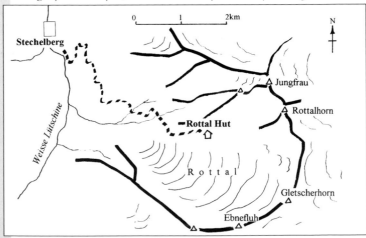

From Stechelberg at the Lauterbrunnen Valley roadhead (bus from Lauterbrunnen) wander along a paved footpath heading upvalley to the left of the Weisse Lütschine river. The way soon eases between meadows, and after about 8mins you take a path on the left by a side-stream. This is signposted to Stufenstein and the Rottal Hut and it climbs steeply with a number of zigzags before making a long rising traverse southward with the Breithorn appearing directly ahead. On coming to an alp hut at 1585m, veer left to enter a broad gully steepening wedge-like ahead. Go through a fenced enclosure and bear right to cross the stream issuing from the gully. The steep ascent resumes, now with the Rottal Glacier's icefall seen above.

The trail heads up to a line of steep, near-vertical crags, eases along their base, then reaches a gully with a fixed chain hanging down it. If there are others on the cliffs above, shelter from stonefall until they've moved on. Climb the gully with the aid of fixed ropes and/or chains, and on emerging at the top, you'll find a clear path winding up an old moraine, then along the moraine crest itself heading east with the hut now in view. The way leads

*On the approach to the Rottal Hut above the Lauterbrunnental*

to a short but steep snow slope headed by a wall of rock. Cross the snow along its upper edge, then scale a small cliff with another fixed rope for assistance. At the top of this take a final short stroll to the hut.

*Owned by the Interlaken Section of the SAC, the Rottal Hut can sleep 46 in its dormitories. Although there's a resident guardian during the main summer period, there is no regular meals provision, so take your own supplies (Tel: 033 855 24 45).*

There is no alternative descent route for walkers to take, so you'll have to retrace the upward path all the way to Stechelberg (3hrs). Although it's a tiring descent, it is scenically spectacular throughout.

## WALK 43 SCHMADRI HUT (2263m: 7425ft)

| | |
|---|---|
| Valley base: | Stechelberg or Lauterbrunnen |
| Start: | Stechelberg (910m: 2986ft) |
| Distance: | 15km (9 miles) round trip |
| Time: | 5hrs up, 2½hrs down |
| Total ascent: | 1353m (4439ft) |
| Map: | LS 1248 'Mürren' 1:25,000 |

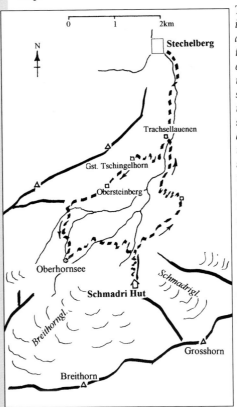

*The route suggested below is not the shortest available to this hut, but it is the most varied and interesting, with a steadily unfolding series of landscapes, views to a thundering waterfall, a visit to several mountain inns and a lovely mountain tarn on the way. The hut itself is small and basic and with no permanent warden, so if you plan to spend a night there, take your own supplies. It sits on the edge of a small meadow at the very head of the Lauterbunnen Valley in the midst of a wild scene of glaciers and moraines. Ibex and chamois often graze the meadow close to the hut.*

Heading upvalley from the roadhead at Stechelberg the path rises gently, crosses first the river, then a track. Signposts direct the way through meadows to Berghaus Trachsellauenen (*refreshments*), beyond which you turn right at a crossing track. When it ends a footpath continues in forest, and after taking the right-hand option at a junction, climbs on, then over pastures to reach Gasthaus Tschingelhorn (*refreshments*). About 20mins later come to Berghaus Obersteinberg (*refreshments*), about 2½hrs from Stechelberg. From here a good path continues round the edge of a deep basin, crosses a glacial

*The view from the Schmadri Hut*

torrent and winds over old moraines below the Tschingelfirn to gain the Oberhornsee tarn. To the south both Tschingelhorn and the curious rock peak of the Lauterbrunnen Wetterhorn look very fine, while to the northeast the Jungfrau is reflected in the water.

Go down to a little plain below the tarn and wander downstream for about 20mins. Cross the stream on a footbridge and climb a steep vegetated moraine, which is crossed at about 2125m, then descend into a tight little hanging valley with the rubble-strewn Breithorn Glacier seen off to the right. Over the drainage stream cross a stony plain to a path junction. Take the upper route to ascend another steep moraine wall with séracs of the Vordere Schmadrigletscher hanging above to the left. The hut is found at the top of this moraine on the edge of meadow and marsh in a small ablation valley.

*The Schmadri Hut was built by the Academic Alpine Club of Bern, and has 12 places. It is fully equipped, but not having a resident guardian it is essential to take all your own food. Magnificent wild mountain scenery is on show (Info. tel: 033 855 23 65).*

Return to Stechelberg by descending the moraine wall, then cutting right on a thin trail which crosses the mountainside above the Schmadri Falls, goes to a lone farm, then descends to the valley bed. From there wander down to Trachsellauenen and Stechelberg.

## WALK 44: ROTSTOCK HUT (2039m: 6690ft)

| | |
|---|---|
| *Valley base:* | **Mürren** |
| *Start:* | **Mürren (1638m: 5374ft)** |
| *Distance:* | **12km (7½ miles) round trip** |
| *Time:* | **2¾hrs up, 1½hrs down** |
| *Total ascent:* | **502m (1647ft)** |
| *Map:* | **LS 1248 'Mürren' 1:25,000** |

*Unlike most of the other mountain huts visited in this book, the Rotstock Hut is located on a working alp farm with cattle and pigs nearby, and the atmosphere reflects the nature of its surroundings. The hut is owned by the Stechelberg Ski Club, but is open to all in the summer, and as it is accessible from Mürren, it is well-used. The circular walk offered here is mostly pastoral, while major peaks of the Bernese Alps are never far away, guaranteeing more fine views.*

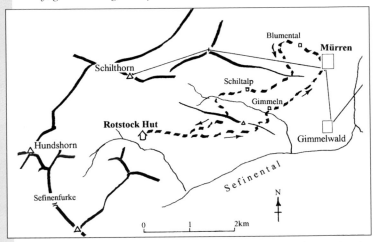

A short distance south of the Allmendhubel funicular station in Mürren a steep tarmac footpath goes up the side of a bakery, rises above the village and soon passes between meadows adorned with timber chalets and haybarns in a pastoral basin known as the Blumental. Just beyond Pension Sonnenberg (*refreshments*) come to a junction of tracks. Continue directly ahead, and 5mins later you'll reach Pension Suppenalp (*refreshments*) and another junction. Ignore the left-hand trail descending to Mürren and follow a clear path winding up a hillside spur beneath the

Schilthorn cableway. Over the spur the trail eases across pasture-land and reaches the alp hutments and farm of Schiltalp. Walk ahead along the farm track for about 2mins, then fork left on a narrow path which crosses rough pastures on the way to the Schiltbach stream. Using a footbridge cross the stream and climb a second vegetated spur, at first among alder scrub, then among flowers, and on gaining the ridge fine big mountain views reward your efforts.

Slant down the south side of the spur over a hillside pocked with marmot burrows, and at a junction of paths marked as Oberläger (2050m) wander ahead across more pastureland, soon with the buildings of Poganggenalp and the red-shuttered Rotstock Hut coming in sight. The trail, which also climbs to the Sefinenfurke, leads directly to it.

*The Rotstock Hut has 52 places and a full meals service. Owned by the Stechelberg Ski Club it is wardened from June to October (Tel: 033 855 24 64).*

Beyond the hut the Sefinenfurke (2hrs) is an interesting crossing used by walkers tackling the Alpine Pass Route on the stage leading from Mürren to Griesalp at the head of the Kiental. South of the hut lies the deep cleft of the

*The Gspaltenhorn from the trail to the Rotstock Hut*

Sefinental which provides a challenging route out to the Lauterbrunnental, but for a return to Mürren it is better to retrace the outward route as far as the Oberläger path junction. Continue ahead on a trail which contours across an increasingly steep hillside before making a sharp descent, partially on steps and with tight zigzags, to Spielbodenalp and, just beyond it, the hamlet of Gimmeln. From there an easy track leads down to Mürren.

## WALK 45: SCHILTHORN HUT (2432m: 7979ft)

| | |
|---|---|
| **Valley base:** | Mürren |
| **Start:** | Mürren (1638m: 5374ft) |
| **Distance:** | 3.5km (2 miles) to the hut |
| **Time:** | 2–2½hrs |
| **Total ascent:** | 794m (2605ft) |
| **Map:** | LS 1248 'Mürren' 1:25,000 |

*The ascent of the Schilthorn has been a popular excursion for visitors to Mürren since the middle of the 19th century, but it has never been more popular than it is today, thanks to the cable-car which ferries hundreds of tourists to the summit in winter as in summer. On the crown of the mountain there's a revolving restaurant and a bizarre 'Touristorama' which takes the form of a cinema showing clips of the James Bond movie 'On Her Majesty's Secret Service' that was filmed there. The Schilthorn Hut is situated not on the summit, but on a minor ridge projecting from the mid-height peaklet, Birg, with a first-rate view of the big Oberland peaks to the southeast. The approach from Mürren is uncomplicated, and with various options for continuing the walk from it.*

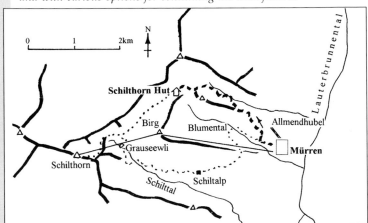

At the Allmendhubel funicular station in Mürren, a signpost directs the way to Allmendhubel, Schilthorn Hut and Schilthorn. This climbs steeply above a bakery and leaves the village to enter the pastoral basin of the Blumental. At a junction of paths bear right, then take the upper option at the next two junctions to ascend the north flank of the lower Blumental, eventually gaining a major crosstrack. Continue ahead and come onto a grass-covered ridge marked as Allmendhubel (this is about 5mins from the upper funicular station of the same name). Maintain direction and join a broad stony track which rises through a cleft in the hills

*The Blumental above Mürren en route to the Schilthorn Hut*

known as the *Kanonrohr* – the 'Cannon Barrel'. Through this you enter a basin of pastureland and skirt the north side of the curious Muttlerenhoren. Round this you come into the stony lower reaches of the Engital, at the head of which stands the Schilthorn. Soon after entering this glen, you'll find the Schilthorn Hut standing just to the left.

*The Schilthorn Hut was built by the Mürren Ski Club. It has 40 places, a restaurant service, and is manned from July to September, and from December to April (Tel: 033 855 11 67 or 033 855 25 12).*

The easiest return to Mürren is via the same route used on the approach – allow 1–1½ hours. A better option is to continue to the head of the Engital to a 2599m saddle overlooking the Grauseewli tarn. At a junction of paths descend to the southern side of the tarn on a trail which continues into the Schilttal. When it forks bear left (the other option goes to the Rotstock Hut), and wander down to Schiltalp, where a continuing path leads back to Mürren by way of the Blumental. For this route allow another 2½ hours. A third option is to make the ascent of the Schilthorn. There are no difficulties in good summer conditions, although the way is quite steep towards the top. A path twists up the southeast ridge from the saddle at the head of the Engital, and where the trail is thin near the summit, fixed cables have been provided (2hrs from the hut).

## WALK 46: LOBHORN HUT (1955m: 6414m)

| | |
|---|---|
| Valley base: | Isenfluh, Lauterbrunnen or Mürren |
| Start: | Isenfluh (1081m: 3547ft) |
| Distance: | 5km (3 miles) to the hut |
| Time: | 2¾hrs up, 1½hrs down |
| Total ascent: | 874m (2867ft) |
| Map: | LS 1228 'Lauterbrunnen' 1:25,000 |

*Reached by a narrow road served by Postbus leading out of Lauterbrunnen, Isenfluh mimicks Mürren's exalted position on a shelf overlooking the Lauterbrunnen Valley a little south of its confluence with the Lütschental. From the village, as from Sulwald above it, views of Eiger, Mönch*

*and Jungfrau are spectacular, while similar views are obtained from the Lobhorn Hut. Above the hut, at the head of the little Fürtal glen, rise the five prongs, or fingers, of the Lobhörner.*

Take a well-signed path to Sulwald which rises out of Isenfluh through steep meadows and between farm buildings, then enters the Gufer forest. The path continues to wind ever-upward with several junctions where the way to Sulwald is clearly indicated, and about 1¼hrs from the start you emerge to open pastures at the hamlet of scattered chalets and haybarns of Sulwald. Views from here are extensive, and guaranteed to stop you in your tracks.

Take a narrow roadway leading past the top station of the

Isenfluh cableway, and then slant up to the right through more meadows on a path now marked to Sulsalp and the Lobhorn Hut. Once again enter forest and climb to a clearing above the alp of Kühbodmen (Chüebodmi). Do not take the path which descends to that alp, but continue uphill, soon exchanging forest for a slope of meadow with white limestone ribs jutting from it. An obvious saddle can be seen ahead, while the hut may be spied on a hilltop above and to the right of the saddle. The southward panorama includes Wetterhorn, Eiger, Mönch, Jungfrau, and the great shaft of the Lauterbrunnental. At one point both the lofty summit of the Jungfrau and its roots embedded in the Lauterbunnental can be seen in one glance – a difference in altitude of 3248m (10,656ft). The path is narrow as it passes through the saddle and enters the Fürtal with the smooth rockface of the unfortunately-named Ars peak above to the left. At the Sulsalp farmhouse branch right, go over a bluff to the Sulsseeli tarn, pass round its right-hand (east)

*The Lobhorn Hut*

shore and about 2mins later break away right to reach the hut.

*The Suls-Lobhorn Hut belongs to the SAC's Lauterbrunnen Section, a small rustic building with 24 places and a guardian from mid-June to the end of October. Refreshments available (Tel: 033 855 12 07). Since it faces across the Lauterbrunnental to Eiger, Mönch and Jungfrau, views are magical.*

The hut makes an interesting excursion from Mürren and Lauterbrunnen, and a return to the valley could easily be made via the Soustal and Grütschalp. Given time, however, the viewpoint of Bällehöchst (2095m) north of the hut is worth visiting. This is reached in about 1½ hours from the Sulsseeli tarn on a good path.

# WALK 47: SCHRECKHORN HUT (2530m: 8301ft)

| | |
|---|---|
| Valley base: | Grindelwald |
| Start: | Pfingstegg (1391m: 4564ft) |
| Distance: | 15km (9 miles) round trip |
| Time: | 4½hrs up, 3½hrs down |
| Total ascent: | 1139m (3737ft) |
| Map: | LS 1229 'Grindelwald' 1:25,000 |

*In 1977 the old chalet-style Strahlegg Hut – traditional base for moun-taineers tackling routes on the Schreckhorn, Lauteraarhorn, Finsteraarhorn etc in the heart of the Bernese Alps – was destroyed by an avalanche. A replacement was built in 1981 at the foot of the south-west ridge of the Schreckhorn, making the approach from Grindelwald a little shorter than formerly was the case. This approach takes the walker into an icy world of glaciers and dazzling mountains, among them the very highest of the Bernese Alps. It is both strenuous and, in places, exposed, but ladders, fixed cables and metal pegs give aid over the more difficult sections. As a walking route it is scenically spectacular, but with a serious edge to it.*

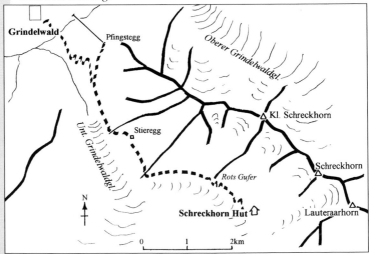

Take the cablecar from Grindelwald to Pfingstegg (*refreshments*) to save a 600m climb at the outset. On leaving the cablecar station a path heads to the right immediately behind the restaurant, and curves round the steep flank of mountainside which forms the entrance to the Unterer Grindelwald Glacier's gorge. On the opposite bank cliffs support the Eiger's Mittelegi Ridge, while the glacier below is shrinking back into a tremendous cirque backed by the gleaming Fiescherwand. There's only one junction along

this trail, offering an alternative way down to Marmorbruch, and is suggested for the return to Grindelwald. Our path cuts along the upper edge of the gorge and is a little exposed in places, but a little over an hour from Pfingstegg you turn a bend and come to an open

*Negotiating the Rots Gufer below the Schreckhorn Hut*

meadow where Restaurant Stieregg (*refreshments*) faces across a turmoil of glaciers to the towering ice wall of the Fiescherhorn – the Fiescherwand.

Continue along the path which grows thinner and less busy, and picks a way over moraine debris towards the icefall of the Obers Eismeer, which is seen close-to from a second patch of pasture. To the left of the icefall the cliffs of the Rots Gufer are safeguarded by a variety of aids, but it remains an exhilarating scramble. A fall could have serious consequences, and many inexperienced walkers turn back at this point.

Above the Rots Gufer the trail resumes across streams and old snow patches, passes the remains of the long-derelict Schwarzegg Hut and forks. Bear left for the final climb to the Schreckhorn Hut.

*The Schreckhorn Hut is owned by the Basel Section of the SAC; 90 places, guardian from July to September, meals provided (Tel: 033 855 10 25).*

Descend by the same route to Stieregg and on towards the Pfingstegg cableway, but at the single path junction bear left and go down through woodland to Marmorbruch and Grindelwald. The path is signposted all the way.

## WALK 48: LAUTERAAR HUT (2392m: 7848ft)

| | |
|---|---|
| Valley base: | Meiringen or Innertkirchen |
| Start: | Grimsel Hospice (1980m: 6496ft) |
| Distance: | 10km (6 miles) to the hut |
| Time: | 4–4½hrs up, 3hrs down |
| Total ascent: | 483m (1585ft) |
| Map: | LS 1230 'Gutannen' & 1250 'Ulrichen' 1:25,000 |

*In the early years of the 19th century Louis Agassiz, the famous Swiss geologist, embarked on a detailed study of glaciers during which he made a base on a rock island in the middle of the Unteraar Glacier. An overhanging rock sheltered the cave-like camp which became known as the Hôtel des Neuchatelois. As a centre for scientific enquiry it was visited by a number of eminent scientists, some of whom stayed for days at a time. This was replaced by the building of the Pavilion Dollfus on the north bank of the glacier, and the same site is now occupied by the Lauteraar Hut. The scenery on the walk to it is, in many ways, more akin to that of the Karakoram than the Swiss Alps, with an avenue of rock and ice-girt mountains soaring from a rubble-strewn glacier. Vegetation is in short supply, but there's an undisputed grandeur in the sheer ruggedness of the landscape, while the coming together of two tributary glaciers a short way to the west adds a sense of mystery.*

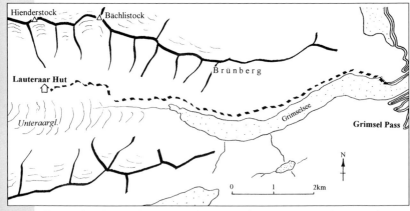

From the Grimsel Hospice (Postbus from Meiringen) cross the dam wall blocking the murky Grimselsee and follow a path which at first leads high above the north bank of the reservoir. The trail goes through a tunnel and out across steep, shrub-

124

covered slopes heading west. It passes below cascades, and bare crags popular with climbers, the path brushing past alpenroses before sloping down to the grey silt plain between the western end of the reservoir and the snout of the Unteraar Glacier.

About two hours from the dam wall you reach the snout of the stone-covered glacier where the continuing route is marked with cairns, poles and paint marks. It keeps to the northern half of the glacier where you come upon a huge pile of rocks making a *chorten*, complete with prayer flags when I was last there.

After about an hour on the Unteraar Glacier, note a shallow indent in the right-hand mountain wall with grass-covered slabs at its western end. Marker poles now direct the way off the glacier, followed by a trail of waymarks heading upvalley. Rising steadily you cross a few streams and on topping the grassy knoll see the Lauteraar Hut just ahead, with a confluence of ice-fields and an impressive backdrop of mountains.

*Lauteraar Rothorner, seen from the path to the Lauteraar Hut*

*The Lauteraar Hut is an important base for mountaineers tackling a variety of peaks at the heart of the Bernese Alps. Owned by the Zofingen Section of the SAC, it can sleep 50 and is staffed from mid-June to the end of September; meals not always available (Tel: 033 973 11 10).*

The return to the Grimsel Hospice for walkers is, of necessity, by the same route, and will take in the region of 3 hours.

## WALK 49: DAMMA HUT (2438m: 7999ft)

| | |
|---|---|
| Valley base: | Göschenen or Andermatt |
| Start: | Göscheneralpsee (1797m: 5896ft) |
| Distance: | 10km (6 miles) round trip |
| Time: | 3hrs up, 1½hrs down |
| Total ascent: | 652m (2139ft) |
| Map: | LS 1231 'Urseren' 1:25,000 |

*Accessible from Andermatt via the narrow confines of the Reuss gorge, the Göschener Tal is one of the most beautiful valleys in the Central Swiss Alps. In its lower reaches it is green and pastoral, its meadows dotted with chalets and with patches of woodland spilling into meadows bright with flowers. Further upvalley a barrage holds back the Göscheneralpsee reservoir, while soaring above that is the ice-caked Winterberg massif. The little Damma Hut is lodged on a spur project- ing from that mountain mass, while two other huts are also accessible from it: the Bergsee on the opposite side of the lake, and the Chelenalp which is reached through the lovely glen of the Chelenalptal. On this walk a complete circuit is made of the Göscheneralpsee, while the Damma Hut itself is reached by a short but steep path through the little Dammareuss glen.*

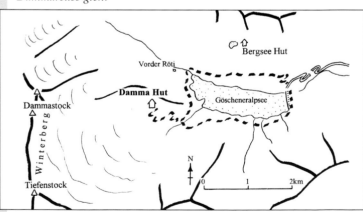

The road through the Göschener Tal ends below the dam wall. This may be reached by Postbus from Göschenen, but there are also parking spaces. A signpost indicates the start of the path to all three huts, and the way climbs easily among shrub-covered slabs, soon gaining the first of many viewpoints from which to study the Winterberg mountains ahead. Glaciers hang from their upper slopes and spill into a cirque which drains by way of the Dammareuss. After about 1km the path forks, with the right-hand option climbing to the Bergsee Hut. Ignore this and continue ahead, now slanting down towards the western end of the lake with the Chelenalptal stretching beyond it to a blocking amphitheatre carved by the retreating Chelengletscher.

*The Damma Hut*

The alp hut of Vorder Röti (1813m) can be seen on the opposite bank of the Chelenalp stream at the entrance to this upper valley, and at a path junction near a bridge spanning the stream bear left, cross the bridge, then heading south work a way among alpen-roses and alder scrub, climbing a rocky slope to the entrance of the Dammareuss glen. When the trail divides continue ahead with the glacial torrent to your left. The trail rises over rock slabs with plenty of waymarks and excellent views, and after making a rising westward traverse, it then swings north and climbs steeply to gain the hut.

*The Damma Hut has 23 places and is staffed from mid-July to the end of August, and at other summer weekends. Meals not always provided (Tel: 041 885 17 81). It is owned by the Pilatus Section of the SAC.*

Return to the barrage by descending to the Dammareuss glen, then cross the stream by footbridge and follow the continuing path which skirts the south side of the reservoir all the way back to the roadhead.

## WALK 50: CHELENALP HUT (2350m: 7710ft)

| | |
|---|---|
| Valley base: | Göschenen or Andermatt |
| Start: | Göscheneralpsee (1797m: 5896ft) |
| Distance: | 15km (9 miles) round trip |
| Time: | 3½hrs up, 4hrs down |
| Total ascent: | 575m (1886ft) |
| Map: | LS 1231 'Urseren' 1:25,000 |

*Near the head of the Chelenalptal, which forms the upper reaches of the Göschener Tal, the Hinter Tierberg spills its ice in a cascading glacial tongue to a moraine tip above rough meadowland where marmots burrow among the alpenroses. On the north flank of the glen sits the Chelenalp Hut – sometimes spelt Kehlenalp. It's a sunny but secluded site with a fine outlook across the glen to the Winterberg massif, while above it the steep mountainside rises to a ridge linked with the Sustenhorn. Few summits tackled from this hut are on the big-peak collector's tick-list, but there are some challenging cross-country routes linking one hut with another – always with serious glacier crossings except that which makes a high traverse to the Bergsee Hut – while the scenery on the approach route described below is enough to gladden the eye of any mountain walker.*

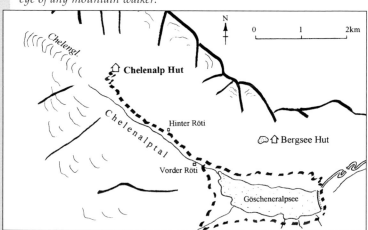

The trail which leads from the eastern end of the Göscheneralpsee reservoir to the alp hut of Vorder Röti has been described in Walk 49 – to the Damma Hut. It's a pleasant walk with fine views all the way, especially where the Winterberg ridge is reflected in a number of small pools trapped among granite slabs above the reservoir. It takes about 1½hrs to reach Vorder Röti from the Postbus terminus, but instead of crossing the Chelenreuss (the stream draining the Chelenalptal), stay on the north bank where

*The Chelenalp Hut*

the path crosses rough flower-filled meadows with minor streams snaking through, and with marmots often seen romping between the boulders. As the way progresses upvalley, so you pass the small hut of Hinter Röti (1941m) tucked below a boulder pile.

Approaching the head of the valley the way becomes increasingly stony, and littered with rust-red rocks. A similar stain discolours the tongue of the Chelengletscher. After about 6km the trail reaches a large granite slab upon which there's a sizeable cairn; this is Point 2127.8m. Here the path swings to the right and climbs steeply for more than 200m to gain the hut.

*The Chelenalp Hut belongs to the Aarau Section of the SAC, and has 65 places. The hut is usually manned at weekends between June and the end of September, when meals may be available (Tel: 041 885 19 30).*

The shortest descent is made by following the approach path all the way to the barrage at the end of the dam. However, a preferable alternative branches south at the entrance to the Chelenalptal, crosses a footbridge near Vorder Röti, and after going a short way into the Dammareuss glen, crosses the glacial torrent there on another footbridge, and works a way round the south side of the Göscheneralpsee.

## WALK 51: TRESCH HUT (1475m: 4839ft)

| | |
|---|---|
| Valley base: | Andermatt |
| Start: | Oberalp Pass (2044m: 6706ft) |
| Distance: | 14km (8½ miles) in all |
| Time: | 4hrs to hut, 2¼hrs to Wiler |
| Total ascent: | 434m (1424ft) |
| Descent: | 1733m (5686ft) |
| Map: | LS 1212 'Amsteg' 1:25,000 |

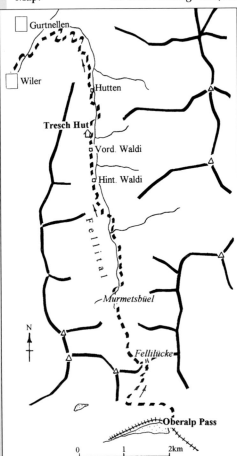

*The Fellital is one of those quiet little Alpine backwaters seldom visited by climbers, walkers or general tourists, and as a consequence it receives little, if any, publicity. Perhaps this is in its favour, for the glen is full of simple charms, unspoilt and undeveloped, although in the past it was known locally for its crystals. This narrow valley flows north from above the Oberalp Pass, and drains into the Reuss gorge near Gurtnellen. At its head the saddle of Fellilücke provides easy access to walkers from the south, while about two-thirds of the way downstream the little stone-built Tresch Hut nestles on the edge of woodland in a quite delightful spot.*

The Oberalp Pass is served by train between Andermatt

and Disentis, and the walk begins at the station. From there cross the road near Gasthaus Piz Calmut and wander down a narrow road between buildings as far as a stream where the trail to the Fellilücke is signposted. Initially heading up steep grass slopes, it

then uses rock steps to gain the first in a series of natural terraces. Cairns and waymarks guide the continuing route to the Fellilücke (2478m: 8130ft), which is reached in about 1½hrs from the Oberalp Pass.

The descending trail swings left round the head of the wild-look-

*The Fellilücke above the Tresch Hut*

ing Fellital, and then slopes down a little left of centre over patches of snow, rocks and, invariably, regions of avalanche debris, before easing into an oasis of grass and meandering streams shown on the map as Murmetsbüel (2010m: 6594ft). Beyond this lie more rock obstacles, but the trail is cairned and waymarked as it dodges from one side of the stream to the other, passes a few alp buildings and descends through a natural garden of alpenrose, juniper, bilberry, dwarf pine and numerous alpine flowers. About 2½hrs from the Fellilücke you'll reach the hut.

*The Tresch Hut belongs to the Albis Section of the SAC. It has 40 places, and basic snack meals are available when it's wardened, which is often at weekends between spring and autumn (Tel: 041 887 14 07). A 3½hr route to the Etzli Hut climbs through the hanging valley to the east and crosses the Portilücke. (Recommended)*

Continue below the hut, again crossing and recrossing the stream where the path dictates. At Hutten (1264m: 4147ft) there are a few small huts, a cattle byre and a bridge. Do not cross the stream here but remain on the left bank. Eventually come to a road at Felliberg. This leads to another road at a hairpin where you continue ahead, pass beneath the main Gotthard highway by a tunnel, and so gain the old valley road. About 150m upvalley take a footpath leading across the Reuss, then wander upstream to Wiler for the train back to Andermatt.

# WALK 52: WINDGÄLLEN HUT (2032m: 6667ft)

| | |
|---|---|
| Valley base: | Bristen (Maderanertal) |
| Start: | Golzern (1423m: 4669ft) |
| Distance: | 3km (2 miles) to the hut |
| Time: | 2hrs up, 3½ or 1½hrs down |
| Total ascent: | 609m (1998ft) |
| Map: | LS 1192 'Schächental' 1:25,000 |

*Born among the glaciers of Clariden and the Chammliberg, the Maderanertal is a true gem of a valley bordered by lofty mountains and watered by the racing Chärstelenbach torrent which drains into the Reuss south of Altdorf. There is no resort as such, but there's accommodation to be had in the small village of Bristen, with plenty of walking opportunities nearby. This route to the Windgällen Hut is one of the best. Though short, virtually every step of the way is a delight of steep flower-filled hillsides, big crowding mountains, and teasing distant summits. The hut occupies a shelf of grassland at the foot of the ragged limestone towers of the Windgällen massif, and the preferred descent towards the head of the valley uses a path once described by Baedeker (in pre-politically-correct days) as a "beautiful return route via the Stäfeln, practicable even for ladies."*

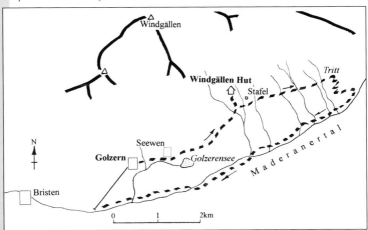

The valley station of the Golzern cableway lies about 2km upstream of Bristen and is served by Postbus. The 600m uplift takes just five minutes, and from the top station a well marked path leads between meadows to the hamlet of Seewen and, beyond it, to a small tarn, the Golzerensee – a popular destination for family picnics. Immediately on leaving Seewen another path, more narrow than the last, branches left and slants uphill with the sharp peak of the Grosse Düssi seen ahead. Rising through

*The Windgällen Hut*

meadows and patches of forest, it then cuts steeply among alpenroses, across minor streams and with plenty of alpine flowers starring the hillsides through the high weeks of summer.

Above the treeline you come to a tall, tapering cairn standing just above the path and commanding yet another fine panorama. From here the hut can be seen for the first time. Just beyond the cairn the trail forks and you bear left for the final steep climb which accompanies a small stream for some of the way, to gain the hut about 15mins from the trail junction.

*The Windgällen Hut was built by the Academic Alpine Club of Zürich; 48 places plus 38 in a neighbouring building, staffed in summer, meals provision (Tel: 041 885 10 88); well-placed for climbers tackling rock routes on the soaring crags above it.*

Descent by the same path to Golzern will take no more than 1½hrs, but a much better, and longer, way branches left (east) at the trail junction near the tall cairn. The path, which is marked to Alp Stafel, Tritt and Hotel SAC, passes just below the Stafel alp and gradually slants downhill to the Tritt viewpoint, beyond which a steep zigzag descent takes you to the head of the Maderanertal where cascades spray down the mountain walls. From there wander downstream to Balmenegg (SAC hotel), Balmenschächen and the cableway station. A tremendous walk of about 3½hrs.

## WALK 53: GLATTALP HUT (1896m: 6220ft)

| | |
|---|---|
| Valley base: | Muotathal or Schwarzenbach |
| Start: | Schwarzenbach (955m: 3133ft) |
| Distance: | 17km (10½ miles) round trip |
| Time: | 4½hrs up, 2–2½hrs down |
| Total ascent: | 1141m (3743ft) |
| Map: | LS 1173 'Linthal' 1:25,000 |

*On the north side of the mountains walling the Klausenpass, the pastoral Bisistal marks the upper reaches of the Muotatal, whose waters flow out to the Lake of Lucerne at Brunnen. The hamlets of Dürenboden and Schwarzenbach have limited accommodation, but there are more possibilities down-valley at Muotathal. The valley is served by Postbus, and has abundant walking opportunities, as have adjacent glens. This circular route is a little devious, but is designed as an introduction to the valley, while a more direct approach to the Glattalp Hut is possible from Sahli at the roadhead (2hrs). An even quicker way to the hut uses the Sahli-Glattalp cableway.*

From Schwarzenbach walk up the valley road for a little over 1km where a rock on the right-hand side bears a sign for Waldialp. Waymarks now lead over grass slopes and in another 30mins reach the huts of Vordersten Hütten, and a farm track. This rises gently to the south, passes more huts (Steinhütte, 1390m: 4560ft) and thereafter descends to a small, sunken tarn. At

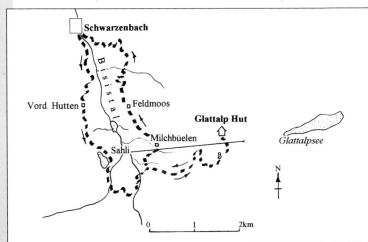

the southern end the track forks. Continue ahead, bear left over a concrete bridge and go left again at Ruosalp (1550m: 5085ft) where there's a junction of tracks. After a few paces take the upper track, then left to a large cattle byre. When the track ends at a stream descend on a narrow path, eventually reaching a wooden bridge at 1384m (4541ft).

Across the bridge the faint path contours along the hillside, but when you come to a major path you then join the Sahli-Glattalp trail. This takes you straight up the hillside to a sloping pastureland, which you skirt along the right-hand edge. At the eastern end of the pasture the continuing path can be seen making a rising traverse of the headwall. Along this traverse the way forks, the two branches regrouping a little higher. (The right-hand option is the 'sporting' route, being narrow, steep and exposed in

*In the Bisistal en route to the Glattalp Hut*

places.) Above this you ease alongside a stream with a fine example of limestone pavement on the left, but after passing another small tarn the path forks once more. Take the left-hand trail and 15mins later gain the hut.

*Owned by the SAC's Mythen Section, the Glattalp Hut has 60 places and is wardened usually between July and the end of September – but check first (Tel: 041 830 19 39) or else take your own food in case meals are not available.*

Descend by the same path of ascent as far as a track (lovely views ahead to the Waldibach Falls, claimed by Baedeker to be the finest in Central Switzerland), then wander uphill to the alp of Milchbüelen. Beyond the alp buildings lies an inner pasture with a fine stream flowing through, and a choice of paths. Continue ahead to Feldmoos, from where another farm road steadily descends to Schwarzenbach.

## WALK 54: CAPANNA BASODINO (1856m: 6089ft)

| | |
|---|---|
| Valley base: | Valle Maggia |
| Start: | San Carlo (938m: 3077ft) |
| Distance: | 5km (3 miles) to the hut |
| Time: | 2½hrs |
| Total ascent: | 918m (3012ft) |
| Map: | LS 1271 'Basodino' 1:25,000 |

*Set on a hillside shelf at the very head of Val Bavona whose river drains the southern slopes of the Cristallina massif, Capanna Basodino enjoys a grandstand view of one of the most attractive of Lepontine mountains the graceful Basodino itself, whose broad yet shallow glacier acts as a great reflector of the sun, and whose summit is a noted viewpoint. Not surprisingly the hut is used by climbers making the ascent of that mountain, as well as providing access to routes on neighbouring peaks, and walkers' trails that explore this granite upland dotted with numerous tarns. Since the hydro engineers began using some of these tarns as a source of power, it has been possible to ride a cable-car from San Carlo to Lago di Robiei, thereby shortening the approach march to about 20 minutes. But unless you're heavily laden the traditional approach on foot is to be preferred.*

Val Bavona is arguably the finest valley in the Swiss canton of Ticino, with soaring granite slabs, chestnut woods and glorious little hamlets. There are hanging valleys and a seductive tributary

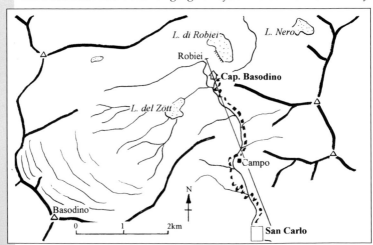

glen above Foroglio worth exploring, in addition to the challenge of the Cristallina massif. As for access, buses from Locarno reach Bignasco, and the ubiquitous Postbus continues to San Carlo, the valley's highest settlement.

*Capanna Basodino*

From San Carlo walk up the road towards the Robiei cableway station, but leave it on a narrow tarmac road which cuts off to the north. This soon becomes a track winding through forest. On coming to a concrete building above the Bavona stream, the track crosses to the west bank. When this ends follow the continuing footpath which climbs steeply and in 5mins reaches a trail junction. Turn right, still in forest, but when you finally emerge from the trees (about 45mins from San Carlo) the way crosses a rustic bridge with the alp hamlet of Campo seen ahead, backed by the rocky defile through which you will soon be wandering.

Passing to the left of Campo the path rises through pastures and enters the defile heading north. This leads to a short and narrow glen at the head of which the Basodino Hut is to be found. At first the way rises without undue effort, but this becomes much steeper towards the top where it snakes in switchbacks beneath the cableway, then crosses a stream just below the hut.

*Capanna Basodino can sleep 70 in its dormitories. Owned by the Locarno Section of the SAC, it is manned from mid-June to mid-October when meals are available (Tel: 091 753 2797).*

A highly recommended outing from here visits the Cristallina Hut – see Walk 55.

# WALK 55: CAPANNA CRISTALLINA (2349m: 7707ft)

| | |
|---|---|
| Valley base: | Valle Maggia |
| Start: | Cap. Basodino (1856m: 6089ft) |
| Distance: | 7km (4 miles) one way |
| Time: | 3½hrs |
| Total ascent: | 712m (2336ft) |
| Descent: | 219m (719ft) |
| Map: | LS 1251 'Val Bedretto' 1:25,000 |

*Located at the head of Val Torta on the northern side of the mountain after which it is named, the Cristallina is the largest, and no doubt the busiest, of all huts in the Lepontine Alps. With a bevy of accessible peaks, and a number of interesting walks from it, this popularity is easy to understand. There are several approach routes too, the shortest being a 1½hr walk from the Lago del Naret roadhead via Passo del Naret, and another (the standard approach) through Val Torta from Ossasca in Val Bedretto in 3–3¼hrs. The route suggested below, however, makes a southerly approach and is one of the best of all walks from the Basodino Hut. It skirts a trio of lakes and crosses a pass to the northwest of Cristallina, before descending to the hut.*

Out of the Basodino Hut briefly descend the path which goes down to San Carlo, then at a stream leave the main trail for one which climbs to the left via steep zigzags up a grass-covered spur. With superb views across to the glacial upper slopes of Basodino, cross an obvious saddle after about 25mins, and go down into a grassy basin. Pizzo Cristallina (2912m) rises ahead, while below to the left is a hydro works road.

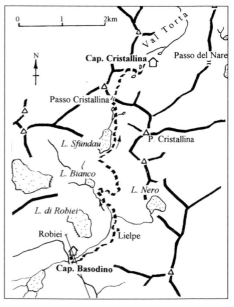

138

Follow the path through the basin to reach the small alp hut of Lielpe. Now wander northward alongside a stream, and gaining height come onto the road by a bridge. Bear right along it for about 5mins. Soon after drawing level with Lago Bianco, break away to the right on a path which climbs steeply – there's a signpost which gives 2hrs to the hut.

The way is both steep and rocky in places, and about 45mins from the road it reaches a path junction where you bear left. Climbing a little at first, the trail then makes an easy rising traverse to a rocky saddle above Lago Sfündau, which is seen below, lying in a deep and stony well. Descend among rocks a short distance, then traverse round the east flank of the well, but some way above the water's edge. Cables have been fitted for security in places, although under normal summer conditions these may seem surplus to requirements. However, a slip could have serious consequences.

*Lago Sfundau between the Basodino and Cristallina Huts*

Beyond the lake the path climbs a little higher, crosses a stream, then skirts to the right of a small tarn, or pool, and reaches Passo di Cristallina (2568m: 8425ft), marked by several lofty cairns. On the northern side, descend among rocks and boulders, then hugging the left-hand slope you'll see the hut below. This is gained about 30mins from the pass.

*Capanna Cristallina is a large and comfortable hut belonging to the Ticino Section of the SAC. With places for 160 it is manned between mid-June and mid-October, when a full meals service is available (Tel: 091 869 2330).*

## WALK 56: CAPANNA LEIT (2260m: 7415ft)

| | |
|---|---|
| Valley base: | Airolo, Valle Leventina |
| Start: | Dalpe (1192m: 3911ft) |
| Distance: | 6km (3½ miles) to the hut |
| Time: | 3½hrs |
| Total ascent: | 1068m (3504ft) |
| Map: | LS 1252 'Ambri-Piotta' 1:25,000 |

*In a secluded hanging valley remote and high above the busy Valle Leventina which funnels traffic bound for the Italian lakes from both the St Gotthard and Nufenen Passes, Capanna Leit offers overnight accommodation for walkers tackling multi-day journeys among the Lepontine mountains, as well as a base for ascents of such peaks as Campolunga and Prévat. There's a rich choice of passes nearby, and determined hillwalkers with experience of wild and in some cases, trackless, terrain, could conjure some exciting circuits in the neighbourhood of the Leit Hut.*

Take the Postbus to Dalpe *villagio* set upon a large hillside shelf southeast of Fiesso. The setting-down point for the Postbus is on the north side of the village, and from there you wander up a side street to the church, then bear right at a junction just beyond.

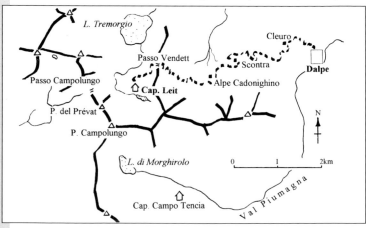

Follow this narrow road heading northwest, but on reaching a junction with three tracks facing, wander ahead on the central track which goes through trees then out to a group of buildings at Cleuro (1272m). Bear left along a further section of narrow road which degenerates to a dirt track through larchwoods. At another junction marked as Boscobello, bear right and continue winding through forest, gaining height easily until you come to a small open pasture with a hut (Scontra) on the left of the track. Just beyond this a signposted path takes you towards a gully on the right. The path crosses the gully and mounts a slope carpeted with bilberries and trees, then contours to join another track. Wandering along this, Passo Vendett can be seen high up on the right.

*Capanna Leit*

Shortly after joining the track leave it and go straight ahead up a waymarked path to gain the pastures of Alpe Cadonighino (1739m), although the alp huts are hidden from view. It will take another hour to gain Passo Vendett from here, via the small hut of Stuei. Passo Vendett (2138m) is reached about 3hrs from Dalpe; a saddle of grass and glaring white rock, with good long views.

Ignore the path which descends to the right and wander straight ahead on a signposted route to Capanna Leit. The way crosses rocky terrain as if making for Passo Campolungo, then swings left to climb the last few metres to the hut.

*Capanna Leit is not a Swiss Alpine Club hut, but is owned by the SAT and is open to all. There are places for 64 and the hut, though unmanned, is unlocked from June to mid-October. Self-catering facilities, but food must be carried in (Tel: 091 868 1920).*

A cross-country trek to Fusio in Val Lavizarra is possible in 3hrs via Passo Campolungo, or to Dalpe via the Morghirola Pass and Campo Tencia Hut in 2hrs.

## WALK 57: CAPANNA CADAGNO (1987m: 6519ft)

| | |
|---|---|
| Valley base: | Airolo, Valle Leventina |
| Start: | Lago Ritom (1852m: 6076ft) |
| Distance: | 6km (3½ miles) to the hut |
| Time: | 2hrs |
| Total ascent: | 248m (814ft) |
| Descent: | 113m (371ft) |
| Map: | LS 1252 'Ambri-Piotta' 1:25,000 |

*The pasturelands of Val Piora form a high cradle in the northern Lepontines between Valle Leventina and Valle Santa Maria. Bounded by accessible mountains of modest height, sparkling with tarns, and with a number of easy passes leading to neighbouring glens, the valley offers innumerable opportunities for the walker and lover of fine scenery. In this wonderland sits Capanna Cadagno, a comfortable and very popular hut at a junction of trails. There are several ways to it; some long and convoluted, others short and undemanding. The route offered here is relatively straightforward, but is one on which few other walkers are likely to be met – despite its many attractions.*

Lago Ritom, where the walk begins, is trapped more than 800m (2625ft) above the bed of Valle Leventina. A tortuous road snakes up the hillside above Piotta to a small dam at the southern end of the lake where there's limited parking and a restaurant. Walkers

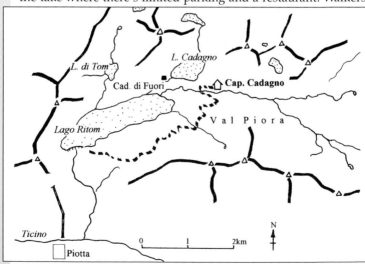

142

without transport, however, can ride Switzerland's steepest funicular which mounts the same hillside and deposits passengers onto the narrow road about 20mins from the dam. Cross to the east side on a track cutting below it. Just beyond the restaurant it curves to meet the top of the dam where a path heads up a long groove of hillside adorned with alpenrose, pine and bilberry. Although there are snatched-views onto the lake, a glorious panorama to south and west is revealed as you gain height. This

*Lago Ritom from the path to Capanna Cadagno*

is across Valle Leventina (unseen but hinted from here) to its opposite wall of peaks, and out to the west through Val Bedretto. After 40mins pass below a solitary hut, gain a little more height, then reach a path junction marked as Pinett (2070m).

Bear left on a well-made route paved with hundreds of cleverly inlaid steps. The paving winds up a grassy gully, then ends at a minor ridge with another tremendous panorama. Cross to the north side and descend with the lakes of Ritom and Cadagno, joined by a waterfall, seen ahead. The alp buildings of Cadagno di Fuori are tucked against the southwest shore of the Cadagno tarn. Continuing down you come to a small hut, then climb to a saddle with yet more fine views. Descending once more bear left when the path forks, cross the Murinascia stream and turn right along a track which takes you directly to the hut.

*Owned by the SAT Capanna Cadagno has 53 places and is manned between June and the end of October; full restaurant service (Tel: 091 868 1323).*

Of the many walking opportunities using this hut as a base, mention should be made of a circuit of Pizzo Colombe, ascent of Piz dell'Uomo, and a tour of the Cadlimo glen. Study the map and guidebook for details.

# WALK 58: CAPANNA BOVERINA (1870m: 6135ft)

| | |
|---|---|
| **Valley base:** | Campo Blenio |
| **Start:** | Campo Blenio (1216m: 3990ft) |
| **Distance:** | 6km (3½ miles) to the hut |
| **Time:** | 2¼hrs |
| **Total ascent:** | 654m (2146ft) |
| **Map:** | LS 1253 'Olivone' and 1233 'Greina' 1:25,000 |

*Edging the northeastern limit of the Lepontines, virtually on the border with the Adula Alps, Valle di Blenio flows south to join the Ticino at Biasca. Thanks to its sunny disposition it's known as the valle del sole (the Valley of the Sun). Below Olivone vines straggle along granite terraces, there are chestnuts, walnuts and mulberries, and as you travel south, so the vegetation becomes almost subtropical. But north of Olivone through a tight little gorge, the upper valley, called Val Camadra, is mostly pastoral and offers good walking prospects. The little village of Campo Blenio serves as an unpretentious base, located between two transverse glens that have been moulded from mountains to east and west, while tucked in the western of these two feeder glens is Capanna Boverina. It sits among ruffled hillocks, gazing across valley to the 3000m ridge of the Adula Alps daubed with tiny glaciers.*

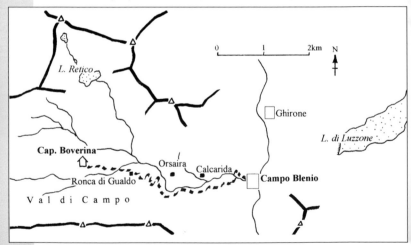

Leave Campo along a small road heading northwest beside a stream flowing from Val di Campo. When the road ends at a farm a track continues. A few paces later cross a footbridge over the stream, then bear right at the next path junction. The way now climbs steeply in woods, but you soon emerge along a grassy shelf with views east to Val Luzzone where a huge dam blocks the unseen Lago di Luzzone. Ahead small hamlets can be seen spaced along the flanks of Val di Campo. At another junction by a water trough, continue directly ahead past a barn, then slope down to a bridge crossing the stream to Calcarida. Ignore this and follow a track instead which rises into forest. This traces the river upstream and becomes a footpath once more.

About 1hr from Campo come to another path junction. Ignore that which breaks away to Orsaira and continue ahead among larch and juniper, then at a narrow road follow this uphill. When you

*Capanna Boverina*

see paths with white-red-white waymarks shortcutting the hairpins, follow these and come to a track leading to the alp hamlet of Ronca di Gualdo. Fork right by a house and walk along a path beside a wooden fence. Cross a stream by a water trough, and mount a grass slope among trees on a vague path (watch for waymarks). Gaining height steeply in woods the path grows more evident. At another path junction bear right and continue climbing, so to reach the group of alp buildings of Boverina. The waymarked path leads directly to the *capanna*.

*Capanna Boverina belongs to the UTOE, but is open to all. With 46 places, meals are sometimes available when a guardian is in residence, otherwise use self-catering facilities. The hut is usually open between June and October (Tel: 091 872 1529).*

Suggested outings from here visit Lago Retico, north of the hut, or cross Passo di Gana Negra to the Lukmania Pass.

## WALK 59: CHAMANNA TUOI (2250m: 7382ft)

| | |
|---|---|
| Valley base: | Guarda, Zernez or Scuol |
| Start: | Guarda (1653m: 5423ft) |
| Distance: | 7km (4 miles) |
| Time: | 2½hrs to the hut |
| Total ascent: | 597m (1959ft) |
| Map: | LS 1198 'Silvretta' 1:25,000 |

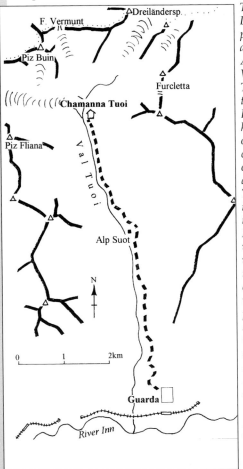

*The north slope of the Lower Engadine forms part of the Silvretta Alps, a range it shares with the Austrian provinces of Vorarlberg and Tirol. Though not the highest of the Silvretta Alps, Piz Buin (3312m) is the best-known and most popular of its mountains with climbers, and standing on the Austro-Swiss border at the head of Val Tuoi, it is this peak which is the dominant feature of the approach to the Tuoi Hut. It's a straightforward, undemanding walk, beginning in one of the most attractive and culturally interesting of villages in the Romansch part of Switzerland, and striking north through a valley rich in wild flowers in early summer. The hut is found near the head of the valley, on the east bank of the upper basin. From it the most popular outing is the ascent of Piz Buin, but there are many interesting walks to be had too.*

146

Huddled upon a natural hillside terrace nearly 300m (980ft) above the River Inn, Guarda is the quintessential Lower Engadine village. Consisting of sturdy, stone-walled houses with arched doorways leading to inner courtyards; tiny, deeply-set windows behind wrought-iron grilles; outer walls, doorways and windows decorated with traditional *sgraffito* ornamentation – all facing one another across narrow, cobbled alleys, or round a square with water gushing from a fountain. Geraniums dazzle against white-washed walls in summer, and one may be forgiven for thinking that time stands still... The village is served by Postbus. It also has a station on the St Moritz-Scuol branch line of the Rhaetian Railway, and there's a small amount of parking space in the village itself. Behind it to the north stretches the lovely Val Tuoi.

A signpost at the upper end of Guarda's main street indicates the start of the walk where a path climbs through meadows to join a track (which leaves from the eastern end of the village) marked to Alp Suot and Chamanna Tuoi. The track is motorable, but private vehicles are fortunately banned from using it. It soon leads into the

*Val Tuoi, leading to Chamanna Tuoi*

mouth of Val Tuoi, from which there's a pleasant view back into the Lower Engadine. At first there are patchy larchwoods, then open pastures as you progress deeper into the glen, always on the east bank of the stream. Piz Buin appears at the head of the valley to the left of the glacial Fuorcla Vermunt; the Dreiländerspitz is the high point east of the saddle. The track rises sharply then skirts to the east of Alp Suot (2018m) before easing towards the upper basin. A final sharp uphill stretch leads to the hut, an attractive building with Val Tuoi spread before it.

*Chamanna Tuoi belongs to the Engiadina bassa (Lower Engadine) Section of the SAC. Built in 1913 it was more recently enlarged and renovated in 1989. It can now sleep 95. Meals are provided when the guardian is in residence – usually from mid-July to October (Tel: 081 842 6391); self-catering facilities available at other times.*

## WALK 60: BLOCKHAUS CLUOZZA (1880m: 6168ft)

| | |
|---|---|
| Valley base: | Zernez |
| Start: | Zernez (1472m: 4829ft) |
| Distance: | 6km (3½ miles) one way |
| Time: | 3hrs to the hut |
| Total ascent: | 650m (2132ft) |
| Descent: | 320m (1050ft) |
| Map: | LS 1218 'Zernez' 1:25,000 |

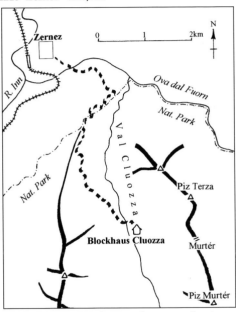

*Switzerland's only National Park is located in the Lower Engadine, on the east side of the River Inn. It's the oldest in Europe, and one of the 'purest' in terms of nature preservation, for although visitors are welcome there are strict regulations in force that protect virtually every aspect of the natural environment. This is one of those rare corners of Europe where Man's needs are subordinate to those of Nature, an Alpine sanctuary protected from human interference. As a consequence a very special atmosphere prevails.* Apart from Hotel Il Fuorn on the only road which cuts through the Park, there's just one place where overnight lodging may be had within the Park boundaries. This is at Blockhaus Cluozza, a rustic, inn-like building on the east bank of Val Cluozza, from which red deer can usually be studied grazing nearby in early morning and evening.

The walk begins on the Ofen Pass road about 1km from the National Parkhaus in Zernez. On the right-hand side of the road there's a covered wooden bridge and a National Park notice board. Cross the bridge and follow a track through meadows and into forest. Gaining height in long switchbacks, the track soon becomes a path which zigzags steeply up the rounded spur forming the western 'gateway' to Val Cluozza. The valley is densely forested with pine and larch that provide exquisite colouring in October. Red squirrels scamper in the branches and, if you walk quietly, you may well see red or roe deer.

*Blockhaus Cluozza*

About an hour or so after setting out you gain a viewpoint which reveals the deep cut of the valley stretching south, with bare mountains rising from it. Streams scour their flanks and minor tributary glens drain from the southwest into the main valley. The path continues along the west flank heading south. There are no alternatives to consider and the way is clear. In places there are scars where avalanches have swept through the trees, then the path sweeps downhill, passes what must once have been an alp, crosses the Ova da Cluozza by timber bridge, and climbs an easy slope to gain the rustic hut at a junction of trails.

*Blockhaus Cluozza belongs to the National Park authority. With room for about 50, it is open and manned between the end of June and the middle of October. Booking is essential for accommodation (Tel – hut: 081 856 1235; National Parkhaus: 081 856 1378). A full meals service is available.*

A return to Zernez by the same path will take about 2½hrs. Alternatively, a cross-country route via Fuorcla Val Sassa (2857m) to the Varüsch Hut is recommended for strong walkers (6hrs), or eastwards via Murtér (2545m) to Hotel Il Fuorn in 6½hrs.

# WALK 61: COAZ HUT (2610m: 8563ft)

| | |
|---|---|
| Valley base: | Pontresina |
| Start: | Pontresina (1805m: 5922ft) |
| Distance: | 13.5km (8 miles) one way |
| Time: | 4hrs to the hut, 3hrs back |
| Total ascent: | 805m (2641ft) |
| Map: | LS 1277 'Piz Bernina' 1:25,000 |

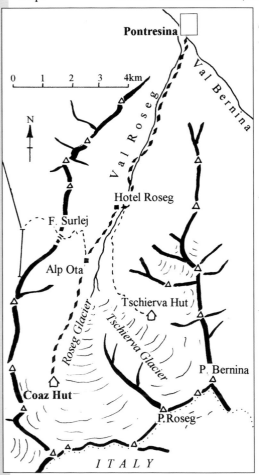

*With its opening directly opposite Pontresina, Val Roseg is the northernmost tributary of Val Bernina, which it reaches shortly before the latter valley spills into the Upper Engadine. It's a delightful glen with spacious larchwoods in its lower reaches, a grey glacial plain in its mid-region, and headed in the south and east by a series of cascading glaciers that converge below the Coaz Hut. The eastern glacier pours from Piz Bernina, Piz Scerscen and Piz Roseg, with the Tschierva Hut located on its northern lateral moraine at 2573m. The southern glacial stream, however, comes from the wave-like Sella peaks across whose summit ridge runs the Swiss-Italian border, and it is on the*

*edge of this glacier that the Coaz Hut has been built. It's a handsome hut in a remarkable situation, and with a very pleasant approach walk.*

There are two non-glacial approaches to the Coaz Hut. The first comes from the middle station of the Corvatsch cable-car which rises from Surlej near Silvaplana in the

*Val Roseg, the route to the Coaz and Tschierva Huts*

Engadine Valley, crosses the 2755m Fuorcla Surlej and descends the west flank of Val Roseg. When the path forks a short way below the saddle, it is the right branch which leads to the Coaz Hut. (About 3½hrs from the middle station.) The second route is the gentle valley walk from Pontresina, described as follows.

Cross Val Bernina from Pontresina, and take the obvious track which leads into Val Roseg among larchwoods. Motor vehicles are not allowed, other than those which service a hotel built halfway to the hut, but horse-drawn carriages act as taxis to ferry visitors preferring not to walk. A footpath alternative strikes through the woods on the east side of the Roseg stream, and joins the track shortly before it emerges to the glacial plain. It's a charming walk, although views are restricted until just before the woods end. When you come to the open plain the track curves right towards Hotel Roseg, while the path to the **Tschierva Hut** continues directly ahead on the left-hand side of the valley. (Allow 3½hrs from Pontresina – 100 places, wardened from June to October, meals provided: Tel: 081 842 6391).

For the Coaz Hut remain on the track as far as the hotel, then on a marked path which remains in the bed of the valley until rising to the buildings of Alp Ota (2257m). The way continues along the hillside with dramatic views ahead and across the valley where Bernina, Scerscen and Roseg rise caked in billowing folds of ice, passes the site of the former Coaz Hut (2385m), joins a second path and contours at last to the present hut.

*The Coaz Hut stands on a rock perch known as Plattas. It's a 16-sided building opened in 1964 by the SAC. With places for 80 there's usually a guardian from the end of June to late-September, when meals are provided (Tel: 081 842 6278).*

# WALK 62: BOVAL HUT (2495m: 8186ft)

| | |
|---|---|
| Valley base: | Pontresina |
| Start: | Pontresina (1805m: 5922ft) |
| Distance: | 10.5km (6½ miles) |
| Time: | 3½hrs one way |
| Total ascent: | 690m (2264ft) |
| Map: | LS 1277 'Piz Bernina' 1:25,000 |

*With tremendous glacier views up, down, and across the valley, the Boval Hut is one of the busiest in the Swiss Alps. Used as a base by climbers tackling the major peaks of the Bernina Group, it is also immensely popular with day visitors, for whom the approach from Morteratsch Station (on the St Moritz-Poschiavo-Tirano branch of the Rhaetian Railway) makes a spectacular walk of just 2hrs. The Morteratsch Glacier is one of the dominant features of this walk. Beginning on the Bellavista crest at more than 3800m, this glacier descends in a seemingly motionless cascade, and pushes its way north towards*

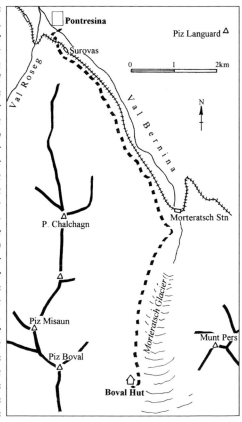

*the Val Bernina. However, like all Alpine icefields, the Morteratsch Glacier is rapidly receding, and marker posts indicate the speed and extent of its retreat in recent years. The Boval Hut is sited on the left-hand lateral moraine, at the foot of Piz Boval.*

Whilst it is perfectly feasible to ride the train from Pontresina to Morteratsch Station, it is recommended to walk all the way. After all, it only requires another 1½hrs, and there are undoubted pleasures to be gained by taking the woodland path along the edge of Val Bernina.

*Piz Bernina from the Boval Hut*

Begin by crossing the valley from Pontresina towards the mouth of Val Roseg, where a path will be found heading left to Surovas, a railway halt. For a while the walk goes alongside the railway line, a woodland path of some charm which, as you progress, strays to the right and gains height in order to avoid an unnecessary detour to Morteratsch Station. Coming to the mouth of the Morteratsch Valley, join the main path and veer right to be confronted by a glorious panorama of snow- and ice-capped mountains forming a huge wall in the south. As the path progresses, so the view broadens: the triple buttressed Piz Palü is at the far left, then the creamy waves of Bellavista rising to Piz Zupò, followed by the Crast' Agüzza and finally, from select places only, Piz Bernina itself. Left of the path the snout of the Morteratsch Glacier spews out its torrent like a flood of cold coffee, among the dirty terminal moraines.

The path is well-defined and will, no doubt, be shared with plenty of other walkers and climbers, all with the same destination. It leads without difficulty directly to the hut, from whose terrace you should be able to pick out ropes of climbers on neighbourhood peaks, or descending the glaciers.

*The Boval Hut belongs to the Pontresina-based Bernina Section of the SAC. With 100 places it has a guardian on duty usually from mid-March to October, during which period meals are provided (Tel: 081 842 6403). In the summer a local guide often leads walkers across the glacier from the Boval Hut to Diavolezza.*

# WALK 63: ALBIGNA HUT (2336m: 7664ft)

| | |
|---|---|
| Valley base: | Maloja or Vicosoprano |
| Start: | Pranzaira (1195m: 3921ft) |
| Distance: | 7km (4 miles) |
| Time: | 3½hrs to the hut |
| Total ascent: | 1141m (3743ft) |
| Map: | LS 1296 'Sciora' 1:25,000 |

*As you descend the hairpins below the Maloja Pass into Val Bregaglia, high up to the south a forbidding concrete wall appears to block the entrance to a hinted tributary glen. This is the Val Albigna. The dam holds back an icy lake which is fed from the melt of the Albigna Glacier (Vadrec da l'Albigna), while the granite peaks which contain it to south, east and west, have an undoubted appeal to rock climbers. The east wall borders Val del Forno, the south carries the Italian frontier, while the western crest is marked by the saw-tooth Scioras at the head of Val Bondasca; a savage land. The hut overlooks the lake from its east shore and is more easily gained in about 40mins from the cableway which serves the dam. The walk suggested here, however, is a pleasant one,* climbing through patches of forest on a route used long before a plan was conceived to dam the valley's entrance.

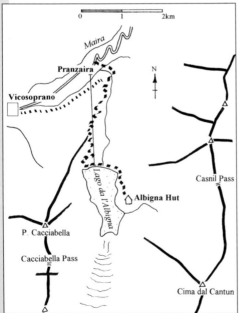

About 2km upvalley from Vicosoprano the Albigna cableway rises from Pranzaira, where there's car parking spaces and a Postbus stop. Walk up the road towards the Maloja Pass, and after about 300m a broad track will be seen cutting off to the right. Follow this through woods, and you'll soon be led across the Albigna torrent by footbridge. Beyond this the track continues, winding in long switchbacks among the trees before narrowing to path dimensions. Shortly after this it meets another path coming from Vicosoprano (add 30mins if walking from there). Heading roughly south and gaining height a red and white waymark indicates the point at which you leave the main path to climb more steeply to the right.

The way now maintains a severe gradient, twisting in zigzags up the western edge of the Albigna ravine, using a rib which angles down from the Cacciabella crest, and with the cableway swinging effortlessly overhead.

*The Albigna Hut*

The path leads directly to the base of the dam wall, and from there you cross to the eastern side, then climb to the head of the wall. This is reached about 3hrs from Pranzaira. The continuing path to the hut strikes away from the water's edge to work a way over rough boulder slopes, gaining the hut about 35mins from the dam wall.

*The Albigna Hut (Capanna da l'Albigna) is owned by the SAC. It has accommodation for 90 and a guardian in residence from about mid-June to mid-September. During this time meals are usually available Tel: 081 822 1405).*

Cross-country routes from here include one across the 2975m Pass da Casnil to the Forno Hut, and another by way of the 2897m Cacciabella Pass to the Sciora Hut.

# WALK 64: SASC-FURÄ HUT (1904m: 6247ft)

| | |
|---|---|
| Valley base: | Promontogno or Vicosoprano |
| Start: | Promontogno (821m: 2694ft) |
| Distance: | 6km (3½ miles) one way |
| Time: | 3½hrs to the hut |
| Total ascent: | 1083m (3553ft) |
| Map: | LS 1296 'Sciora' 1:25,000 |

*Gazing out across the depths of Val Bregaglia towards Soglio, the Sasc-Furä Hut enjoys a stunning location. Behind it soaring walls of granite form the Trubinasca cirque, with the bold north ridge of Piz Badile capturing one's attention. Approached by a steeply climbing path, Sasc-Furä is like an eyrie from which to keep a lookout over Val Bondasca. Very much a climber's hut, it does however offer an interesting route for experienced mountain walkers by which to approach the Sciora Hut which sits at the very head of the glen. This route is described as Walk 65. Meanwhile, the following walk is noted for the severity of the path, and for its sheer variety. It rises out of luxurious, almost rampant vegetation, to the base of stupendous rock slabs and towering mountain peaks seemingly devoid of life, and there one gazes across the treetops to a contrast of green alps warmed by the sunlight of Lombardy.*

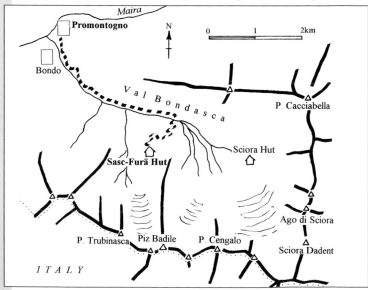

From the main road in Promontogno take the narrow cobbled street which cuts back to the south towards Bondo. Just before reaching the stone bridge leading into Bondo, find a path on the left which climbs among trees and eventually spills onto a dirt road. This pushes into Val Bondasca and is often used by climbers, for by driving along it one can save about an hour's walking time from Bondo. Ahead rise the jagged Sciora aiguilles. (Should you have your own transport, there are parking spaces at the roadhead.)

*The Sasc-Furä Hut*

At the end of the road/track a footpath heads upvalley, but this eventually divides with the trail to the Sciora Hut continuing ahead. We, however, fork right and cross the Bondasca torrent – there is a footbridge. Now on the south side of the river a narrow trail leads across a rough meadow and then plunges into dense vegetation before starting to climb. Waymarked with paint flashes and occasional cairns, the trail grows more prominent as height is gained. But it is a steep and abrupt route, and on my visit footholds had been cut into the trunks of living trees to facilitate the ascent.

For much of the way the path remains among trees, and there is only one short stretch where the gradient eases sufficiently for a brief traverse to be made to the right. Cross a stream, then turn the edge of a spur and resume the climb, but very soon you'll emerge from the trees and discover the hut just ahead, with Piz Badile's impressive north ridge rising behind it, and with Piz Trubinasca to the right of that.

*The Sasc-Furä Hut (Capanna Sasc-Furä) is owned by the Bregaglia Section of the SAC. With places for just 45 it is often without a guardian – there are self-catering facilities, but take your own food. (Tel: 081 822 1252). In the event of it being locked, ask for the key in Promontogno (Tel: 081 822 1221).*

## WALK 65: SCIORA HUT (2118m: 6949ft)

| | |
|---|---|
| Valley base: | Promontogno or Vicosoprano |
| Start: | Sasc-Furä Hut (1904m: 6247ft) |
| Distance: | 4km (2½ miles) |
| Time: | 3½hrs hut to hut |
| Total ascent: | 296m (971ft) |
| Descent: | 82m (269ft) |
| Map: | LS 1296 'Sciora' 1:25,000 |

*"Piz Badile is situated in the most enchanting cirque of mountains that one could imagine." (Gaston Rébuffet) In the midst of this enchanting cirque the Sciora Hut is backed by slender peaks like granite fenceposts, although it is positioned so close to them that the stiletto-sharp aiguilles are seriously foreshortened. These, and Badile itself, are better viewed from the cross-country route linking the Sasc-Furä and Sciora huts via the 2200m Colle Vial. A route for experienced mountain walkers only, it should not be attempted in unsettled conditions.*

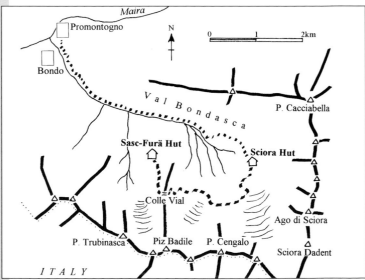

The standard approach to the Sciora Hut from Promontogno takes about 4hrs, leading all the way through the magical Val Bondasca from its entrance at Bondo. There's a fair amount of height-gain, and the way is steep in places, but with ragged mountains as the lure. The hut is located on a shelf of rock among moraines at the foot of the Bondasca Glacier, with a view over the length of the valley to the distant south-facing slopes of Val Bregaglia, dotted with haybarns and small stone-built villages.

*The Sciora Hut*

Our route, however, begins at the Sasc-Furä Hut whose approach is described as Walk 64. Immediately behind it the way leads up smooth slabs, guided by paint flashes, then on a vague trail of waymarks heading in a southerly direction towards the north ridge of Piz Badile. When the few trees and shrubs have been left behind, the trail, where it exists, takes you up rough granite boulders, trending to the right of the spur coming from Badile's ridge. After about 30mins cairns direct the route slightly leftwards, towards the crest, and eventually you come to the notch of Colle Vial, marked by a cairn and several paint flashes. The view down the east side is sobering, for it falls steeply via a series of ledges to moraines of the Cengalo Glacier. The Sciora Hut may be seen as little more than a red blob on another moraine to the east.

A narrow gritty path leads down to an exposed 'ladder' of ledges. Descend these with care to the foot of the wall where more cairns and paint flashes guide the way through a boulder-field and up to a moraine cone. Beyond this cross a number of glacial slabs, followed by another boulder wilderness, more moraines, streams and a short stretch of stone-littered glacier. Although marked throughout, in mist the route could be difficult to follow. It finally crosses one last moraine to reach the hut.

*The SAC-owned Sciora Hut has places for 42. Occasionally wardened, otherwise self-catering only (Tel: 081 822 1138). Reservations and enquiries to Bruno Hofmeister in Bondo (Tel: 081 822 1164).*

Descend by the well-marked valley path, allowing 2–2½hrs to reach Promontogno.

# THE ITALIAN ALPS

Italy's Alps hug the northern rim of the country, beginning by the Mediterranean where they share the Maritime Alps with France, and curving in a great arc round to the Julian Alps which run into Slovenia northeast of Venice. The mountains can be divided into two main types. In the northwest, from the Gran Paradiso through the Pennines to the Italian Bregaglia, Ortler, Adamello and Presanella groups, snowpeaks and glaciers adorn the high places with characteristic Alpine features, while the Dolomites of South Tirol, and the Julians just to the east, are wildly impressive with stark limestone peaks bursting from the pastures.

## GRAN PARADISO

The Gran Paradiso National Park, located south of Mont Blanc across Valle d'Aosta, boasts no less than 57 glaciers and dozens of summits in excess of 3000m, while the mountain after which the Park is named, is the highest entirely in Italy at 4061m (13,323ft). The Gran Paradiso group, in fact, forms the major part of the eastern Graian Alps, and provides a wealth of walking opportunities of assorted lengths and degrees of difficulty. There are some very fine huts, but prospective visitors are warned that these can be extremely busy at the height of the season.

Guidebooks: *Walking in Italy's Gran Paradiso* by Gillian Price (Cicerone Press), *Long Distance Walks in the Gran Paradiso* by J W Akitt (Cicerone Press), *Walking the Alpine Parks of France and Northwest Italy* by Marcia R Lieberman (Cordee/The Mountaineers).

## THE BREGAGLIA AND BERNINA ALPS

The Italian Bregaglia region is one of narrow shafted valleys and steep granite walls. It's a magical place in summer and early autumn, the tree-lined streams swilling through meadow and woodland, while high above the ragged mid-height slopes challenge with airy paths safeguarded here and there with fixed cables. To reach any of the huts usually entails a stiff uphill walk, but there are plenty of rewards for those who tackle them. The neighbouring Bernina Alps are by contrast wide open, with alp farms nestling among remote pastures with views to Monte della Disgrazia across Val Malenco. This southern face of the Bernina Alps is very different to the Swiss side, but the walking is every bit as grand.

Guidebook: *Walking & Climbing in the Alps* by Stefano Ardito (Swan Hill Press) describes a 10-day traverse from Novate Mezzola to Poschiavo.

## ORTLER AND ADAMELLO ALPS

The Adamello-Presanella Group lies southeast of the Bernina Alps, and is separated from the Ortler Alps by the Val di Sole. Both ranges have a coating of ice and snow, with a central block of mountains from which tributary glens splay out like the spokes of a wheel. It is from these tributary glens that some of the finest walks begin, and as height is gained so each neighbouring group comes into distant view. Both Ortler and Adamello are fairly compact and self-contained, and are typically Alpine in appearance, yet only a short walk away across Valle Rendena east of the Adamello Alps, the Brenta Dolomites announce their limestone presence in startling fashion.

Guidebook: *Walking in the Central Italian Alps* by Gillian Price (Cicerone Press).

## THE DOLOMITES

Many individual mountain groups make up the Dolomites, the most bizarre, colourful and eccentric collection of peaks one could imagine. By Alpine standards they are not especially high, and only 50 or so exceed 3000m, but the extravagant manner by which they burst out of pasture and forest in a sudden upthrust of glaring limestone makes a startling impact on the first-time visitor. Then there are the trails. Some are gentle belvederes winding across screes at the foot of soaring rock faces; others (the famed vie *ferratae*) are led by iron rungs, vertical ladders and fixed ropes into situations that elsewhere would be the sole preserve of the gymnastic rock climber. There's no such thing as a dull Dolomite path, while the majority of huts are set in idyllic locations, and are exceedingly popular.

Guidebooks: *Walking in the Dolomites* by Gillian Price, *Via Ferrata: Scrambles in the Dolomites* by Höfler/Werner and translated by Cecil Davies, *Alta Via: High Level Walks in the Dolomites* by Martin Collins – all published by Cicerone Press. *Huts & Hikes in the Dolomites* by Ruth Rudner (Sierra Club).

*Tre Cime di Lavaredo*

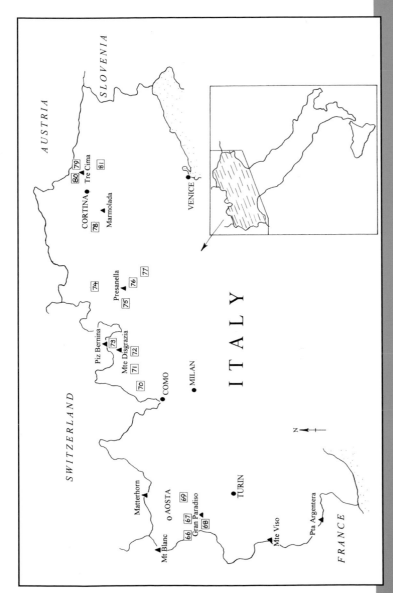

163

## WALK 66: RIFUGIO BENEVOLO (2285m: 7497ft)

| | |
|---|---|
| Valley base: | Val di Rhêmes |
| Start: | Thumel (1879m: 6165ft) |
| Distance: | 4km (2½ miles) to the hut |
| Time: | 1½–2hrs up, 1hr down |
| Total ascent: | 406m (1332ft) |
| Map: | FMB 'Gran Paradiso' 1:50,000 |

*Val di Rhêmes is the most westerly of the valleys contained within the boundaries of the Gran Paradiso National Park, with accommodation to be found in both Rhêmes-St-Georges and Rhêmes-Notre-Dame. South of the latter village a road continues to a large parking area on the outskirts of the hamlet of Thumel. This is the limit of public access by vehicle, although a dirt road projects beyond this as far as Rifugio Benevolo. Walkers are not restricted to this road, however, for a good path winds up through pastures to gain memorable views of the sheer-walled Granta Parei that dominates the upper valley. Above the hut the Franco-Italian border is carried by a series of peaklets that rise above sweeping glaciers.*

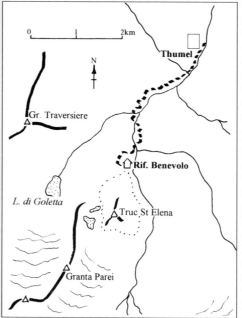

From the Thumel parking area walk south along the road until it curves sharply to the right, at which point a footpath continues slightly left ahead, rising steadily. It climbs above a minor gorge to enter an upper valley region where, high above to the right, can be seen some alp hutments visited by the continuing dirt road. Although the Granta Parei is unseen from here, as the walk progresses so it gradually reveals itself.

The valley narrows as the path climbs alongside a fine waterfall, then ahead over a boggy area. The route remains on the right-hand side of the stream, the Dora Rhêmes, weaving among shrubs and wild flowers, and about 1¼hrs after setting out, climbs to join

*Rifugio Benevolo*

the dirt road. Rifugio Benevolo can just be seen above, peeking over a bluff. The dirt road crosses a bridge over the Dora Rhêmes, immediately beyond which you leave it for a path with yellow waymarks climbing steeply to the right. This brings you beside the road a little higher, then resumes the climb until you are forced onto the road once more where it crosses a side stream on another bridge. The easy way to the hut now remains on the dirt road, but a waymarked path cutting up by some stone alp buildings offers an alternative route. This is quite a steep section, with a bit of easy scrambling involved up some smooth, worn rocks, before emerging by the hut.

*Rifugio Benevolo has 62 beds and is manned from July to mid-September, with a full meals service on offer (Tel: 0165 936 143). The hut is owned by the Italian Alpine Club (CAI); it is used as an overnight stage on the Grand Traverse of the Gran Paradiso, and is also very popular with day visitors.*

Experienced walkers could make an interesting 2½–3hr circuit of the Truc Santa Elena which rises south of the hut. Good visibility will be necessary for the 'path' is neither waymarked nor cairned, and is non-existent in places. But it's a splendid outing for all that, with terrific views – not only of the glaciers that block the head of the valley, but a close view too of the great walls of Granta Parei. Study the map for an outline.

## WALK 67: RIFUGIO F. CHABOD (2750m: 9022ft)

| | |
|---|---|
| **Valley base:** | **Valsavarenche or Aosta** |
| **Start:** | **Val Savarenche (1890m: 6200ft)** |
| **Distance:** | **4km (2½ miles) to the hut** |
| **Time:** | **2½hrs** |
| **Total ascent:** | **860m (2822ft)** |
| **Map:** | **FMB 'Gran Paradiso' 1:50,000** |

*Val Savarenche projects into the heart of the Gran Paradiso National Park, and provides the best access to Gran Paradiso itself and to its shapely immediate neighbours, among which one of the finest is the Herbetet. Below the glaciers of this lovely peak sits Rifugio Chabod, named after Federico Chabod, first president of the autonomous Valle d'Aosta, who was himself a climber. The hut is both comfortable and well-appointed, while the uphill walk to it is a true gem of an outing.*

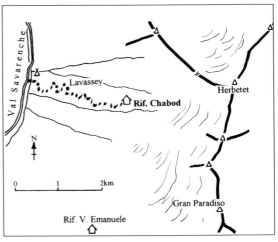

About 18km (11 miles) south of Villeneuve, the village in Valle d'Aosta which marks the entrance to Val Savarenche, the valley road crosses to the west bank of the Savara river by Camping Gran Paradiso. Just beyond this crossing there's an obvious parking area next to a substantial footbridge, with a signpost indicating the route to Rifugio Chabod. Cross the bridge and veer right on a path waymarked with a yellow "5". The path is well-made, and it climbs through larchwoods at a comfortable gradient for a little over an hour, until you come to the alp building of Lavassey (2190m). Here the trail divides. Take the right-hand option, a winding route still in woods, although these are now thinning as more height is gained.

Above the treeline the path maintains its generous zigzags, and climbs into an upper corrie, or hanging valley, backed by the Herbetet-Gran Paradiso wall dazzling its snowfields and glaciers – an impressive sight. As the way progresses, so the corrie becomes more stony, with scattered boulders and glacial slabs providing clear evidence of the smoothing work of past glaciers.

At an altitude of about 2265m pass a footbridge on your right – this takes a linking trail to Rifugio Vittorio Emanuele – see Walk 68 – and continue on the main path as it climbs on for another 15–20mins to gain the Chabod Hut.

*The Herbetet-Paradiso ridge overlooks Rifugio Chabod*

*Rifugio F. Chabod is owned by the Society of Valsavarenche Guides, has 100 beds and offers a full meals service when manned – this is usually from July to mid-September (Tel: 0165 95 574).*

A return to the valley by the same path will take about 1½–2hrs, but there are two further options to consider. The first continues above the hut on a route which crosses Colle Gran Neyron on a ridge-spur below the Herbetet, then works its way northward to join the long distance Via Alta 2 across Col Lauson to Rif. Vittoria Sella. This is a challenging route for experienced Alpine walkers, while the second option makes a traverse heading southwest below Gran Paradiso and goes to the Vittorio Emanuele Hut, from where a steep descent can be made to the valley. This is given as Walk 68.

## WALK 68: RIFUGIO VITTORIO EMANUELE (2730m: 8957ft)

| | |
|---|---|
| Valley base: | Valsavarenche or Aosta |
| Start: | Rif. F. Chabod (2750m: 9022ft) |
| Distance: | 6km (3½ miles) to the hut |
| Time: | 2½–3hrs |
| Total ascent: | c.300m (984ft) |
| Map: | FMB 'Gran Paradiso' 1:50,000 |

*Named after the hunter king who turned the Gran Paradiso area into a royal hunting reserve, this hut is a very popular base for climbs on the Paradiso and its neighbours. There are, in fact, two rifugios here, facing west across the valley, the older of the two described by R.L.G. Irving before the last war as being "perfectly situated at the upper end of the pastures, above the Moncorvé Glacier." Thanks to global warming, however, this glacier now lies some way above the level of the hut. Irving went on: "Here the chuckling of hens and the tinkling of cow-bells remind one pleasantly of food which has never been inside a rucksack." The standard approach route leaves the head of Val Savarenche at Pont, and takes about 2½ hours. The following walk is a very fine one, and quite different to the usual approach, albeit somewhat rough underfoot,*

and it makes an obvious extension of the walk to Rifugio Chabod.

Leaving the Chabod Hut descend to a footbridge trail junction about 10mins below, and cross to a path marked "1a". Heading roughly south, then southwest, it works its way over streams and below moraines and glacier-smoothed slabs on an undulating traverse of the

*The Paradiso massif above Rifugio V. Emanuele*

mid-height mountainside. Though foreshortened, the upper battlements of the mountain are impressive with bullying ridges, crags and the gleaming snouts of glaciers, while the valley at times appears a long way below. The route is well-marked, not only with yellow paint flashes but also with cairns – the latter especially useful where there's little evidence of a path as such among boulders and slabs.

Whilst never descending below about 2450m (8038ft) the trail makes a regular switchback to avoid natural obstacles as it works over the various folds of mountainside high above the valley. Eventually you turn a spur and enter another rock-strewn, desolate corrie topped by the shapely La Tresenta, and gain a brief glimpse of the hut ahead.

Shortly after crossing a boulder-tip come to an unmarked path junction and veer left. The alternative trail is used on the descent to Pont. Now the way crosses a more open countryside, and about 25–30mins from the junction, reaches the huts.

*Rifugio Vittorio Emanuele; both huts owned by the CAI with a total of 160 places. Meals are only provided in the new hut (Tel: 0165 95 920). Manned from Easter to mid-September, beds are at a premium in July and August – booking advised.*

The descent to Pont at the roadhead will take about 1¾–2hrs and is by an obvious path on which it's impossible to lose the way. It's a remarkable trail, paved in places as befits a mule track built for a king!

## WALK 69: RIFUGIO VITTORIO SELLA (2584m: 8478ft)

| | |
|---|---|
| Valley base: | Cogne or Valnontey |
| Start: | Valnontey (1666m: 5466ft) |
| Distance: | 4km (2½ miles) to the hut |
| Time: | 2½hrs |
| Total ascent: | 918m (3012ft) |
| Map: | FMB 'Gran Paradiso' 1:50,000 |

*The Valnontey is a beautiful tributary glen feeding into the long Valle di Cogne a little southwest of Cogne itself – the only true resort within the Gran Paradiso region. At its head it is blocked by an impressive cirque of glaciated mountains, of which the Gran Paradiso forms the southwest cornerstone, while dramatic icefalls hang suspended from the high walling ridge. The road serving this glen from Cogne ends at a small village which takes its name from the valley. Above to the west of Valnontey village a green scoop of hillside is home to a vast herd of ibex (numbering about 300), and visitors to the Sella Hut have an excellent chance to observe these once-endangered animals in their natural habitat.*

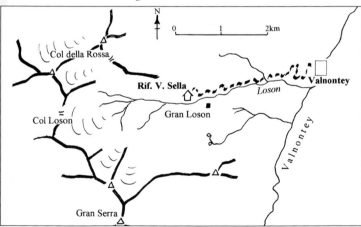

At the entrance to Valnontey village cross the bridge spanning the river (also named Valnontey) to the west bank where there's a signpost directing the way to the hut. Walk up a minor road to a car park entrance where you'll find a footpath on the left, way-marked with a number "18". This rises above a meadow, beyond which you go alongside the boundary fence of an alpine garden which, with some 1500 plant species on show, is worth a visit on another occasion. Before long you enter spacious larchwoods on a well-made and much-used path adopted by the Via Alta long distance traverse route (the waymark number "2" within a triangle denotes this route). It switchbacks steadily up the hillside, bordering a fine cascade that was clearly seen from the village.

Above the treeline the long windings continue, working a way up to a hidden area of grassland. On the opposite side of the Loson

*Rifugio Vittorio Sella*

stream the light-coloured buildings of the Gran Loson alp (Alpe Lauson) are evident, and a breakaway path cuts across to them. Ignore this and continue uphill, now with the trail split into numerous braidings where shortcuts have been created. Then you come over the lip of a basin, pass a national park house (a one-time hunting lodge), and just below this come to the complex of buildings that comprise Rifugio Vittorio Sella.

*Rifugio Vittorio Sella is named after the distinguished mountain explorer, photographer and founder of the Italian Alpine Club. It has places for 160, a full restaurant service, and is manned from Easter until late-September (Tel: 0165 74310).*

The best place to view ibex is in the high meadows behind the hut, although individuals are often found grazing all along the hillside. Recommended walks from Rifugio Sella include Col della Rossa (to the northwest), Col Loson to the west, or a first-rate traverse of hillside to the south (some exposure) to the L'Herbetet viewpoint.

# WALK 70: RIFUGIO LUIGI BRASCA (1304m: 4278ft)

| | |
|---|---|
| Valley base: | Novate Mezzola |
| Start: | Novate Mezzola (212m: 696ft) |
| Distance: | 10km (6 miles) to the hut |
| Time: | 4–4½hrs |
| Total ascent: | 1137m (3730ft) |
| Map: | Kompass 92 'Chiavenna Val Bregaglia' 1:50,000 |

*Novate Mezzola is an insignificant village on the east side of the Chiavenna-Como road near the northern end of Lago di Mezzola. Behind it Val Codera cuts into a shaft of granite mountains that form the western limits of the Bregaglia Alps – a rocky outlier of the snow-bound Bernina Alps. Val Codera is a truly wonderful glen. Untouched by any road, an ancient mule-trail gives access to a romantic, permanently-inhabited village (Codera), half a dozen hamlets and, near its head, the Luigi Brasca Hut backed by pinewoods and overlooked by ragged granite peaks. This hut walk is quite tough, but there's a special atmosphere that pervades the whole valley and will help to make this a memorable outing.*

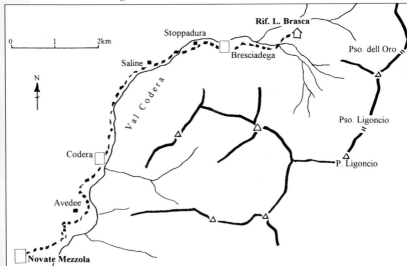

From the main road walk up through the village by a maze of narrow streets, until you reach the highest point, marked as Mezzolpiano on the map. Here you'll find an open parking area with a signposted footpath to the left of its entrance. From the start this tackles a flight of stone steps, with occasional views out to Lago di Mezzola. Where the gradient slackens, steps give way to ancient paving, and before long lead through sweet-chestnut woods. After passing a wayside shrine the woods are a mixture of chestnut and birch, with heather and bracken lining the path. At about 750m come to a few stone buildings, shortly after which you pass below the hamlet of Avedee and gain a first view into Val Codera proper, with Codera village almost engulfed by dense chestnut woods ahead.

The mule-trail descends to a pair of galleries built against the steep mountainside to protect the route from avalanche, then rises to enter Codera (825m: 2707ft) in about 2hrs. Waymarks direct the route up narrow alleys and path-

*Codera, in the wild Val Codera*

ways, and about 20mins beyond the village the path forks. Keep on the left side of the river as the valley curves eastward, and reach the hamlet of Saline (3hrs). Now the valley grows wilder, and at 1145m (3757ft) a footbridge takes you across to the south bank. Another tiny hamlet (Stoppadura) is passed, then you come to flat open meadows and the renovated houses of Bresciadega (3½hrs). A broad track now eases towards the head of the valley through forest and open glades as neat as an English park. It crosses two tributary streams draining a high hanging valley, then curves to the right with the hut just ahead.

*Rifugio Luigi Brasca is owned by the Milan Section of the Italian Alpine Club. It has about 30 places and is manned in July and August when meals are provided.*

Allow 3–3½hrs to return by the same route to Novate Mezzola. Experienced walkers could cross the eastern mountains by a choice of passes to gain Rif. Omio (4½hrs) or Rif. Gianetti (5½hrs), above the Valle del Bagni. But these are tough routes.

# WALK 71: RIFUGIO A. OMIO (2100m: 6890ft)

| | |
|---|---|
| Valley base: | San Martino |
| Start: | Bagni del Masino (1172m: 3845ft) |
| Distance: | 6km (3½ miles) round trip |
| Time: | 2½hrs up, 1½hrs down |
| Total ascent: | 928m (3045ft) |
| Map: | Kompass 92 'Chiavenna Val Bregaglia' 1:50,000 |

*Facing east from a rough, untamed hillside overlooking Valle del Bagni, Rifugio Omio has a view of Monte della Disgrazia, as well as a host of jagged granite peaks and hanging valleys of the Italian Bregaglia – a rock climber's playground, whose popularity in recent years has rocketed. The Omio Hut, however, is not so much a climber's hut as one which gives access to pass crossings that lead into Val Codera. In addition it may be used as one of the stages on the classic, but strenuous, Sentiero Roma – a demanding high-level route that hiccups along the north wall of the Valles del Bagni and Mallo before crossing a ridge projecting from Disgrazia and descending to the Ponti Hut and, eventually, to Val Masino. The approach to the Omio Hut described here is steep for much of the way, but is varied throughout.*

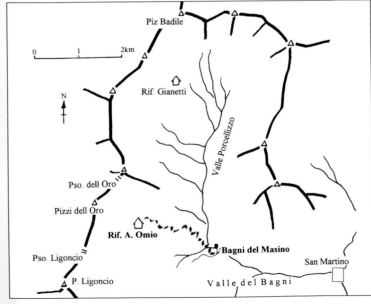

The narrow Valle del Bagni road ends at the Bagni del Masino spa, and is served by bus from San Martino in summer. There's also a small parking area just short of the roadhead where walkers with their own transport should leave their vehicles. From this point walk past the big, barrack-like spa building, through woods and out to a meadow where the path forks. The path which continues straight ahead goes to the Ginetti Hut (Rifugio Badile) in 3½hrs, while the Omio route is the left-hand option. It crosses a stream, then veers right through another rough meadow between two streams. (Note: if you cross a second bridge here, an open meadowland has picnic tables and a tremendous view upvalley to towering cirque walls streaked with waterfalls.)

*Rifugio Omio*

Across the meadow enter mixed woods where the path begins its steep ascent. Waymarks are plentiful, and although the trail has many braidings, it's impossible to lose the way. After about an hour you leave the woods and come to a small pasture in which there's a single stone building. Off to the right you can see the Porcellizzo glen, and you may be able to spot the Gianetti Hut, with Piz Badile – which appears less impressive than from the Swiss side – above that.

The path returns to woods and climbs steeply once more until emerging against a big granite slab. Now the way eases leftwards and enters a high, sloping shelf of pasture leading to crags that form the dividing ridge between the Bagni glen and Val Codera. At about 1865m pass a small stone building off to your left, and climb steeply to another – this is on the right, but is not seen until you reach it. From here the Omio Hut will be visible about 200m above. The final stage cuts directly up the hillside, using exposed granite slabs waymarked with red paint flashes.

*Rifugio A. Omio belongs to the Milan Section of the Club Alpino Italiano. With about 40 places, it is manned during July and August, when meals are available.*

# WALK 72: RIFUGIO C. PONTI (2559m: 8396ft)

| | |
|---|---|
| Valley base: | San Martino |
| Start: | Sasso Bisolo Valley (1175m: 3855ft) |
| Distance: | 16km (10 miles) round trip |
| Time: | 4hrs up, 3hrs down |
| Total ascent: | 1384m (4541ft) |
| Map: | Kompass 92 'Chiavenna Val Bregaglia' & 93 'Bernina-Sondrio' 1:50,000 |

*This truly delightful hut walk leads through one of the loveliest valleys in the Italian Alps. It begins on the Valle di Sasso Bisolo road which was cut by an immense rockfall in the 'seventies, about 3.5km above Cataeggio, the village at its entrance in Val Martina. But above the rockfall there's a wonderland of forest, high meadows, streams and waterfalls, all overlooked by the handsome Monte della Disgrazia. As long ago as 1911 the way was described thus: "I remember no more beautiful hut walk... I spare you descriptions of the lonely loveliness both of the woods and the green open space which ought to be lake and is not, just before the last great step of the valley. The Disgrazia alone would make the walk memorable." (Peaks and Pleasant Pastures by Claud Schuster) Those sentiments are just as true today.*

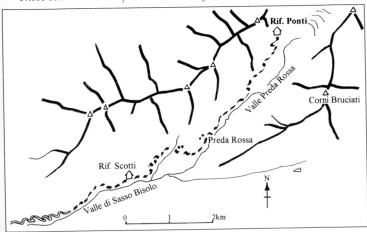

From the present roadhead follow an obvious track which skirts the rockfall site and rises to rejoin the original road some way beyond the chaos of rocks and boulders. Walk up the road through forest interrupted here and there by open meadows, and after about an hour you'll reach Rifugio Scotti. About 10mins later leave the road for a path on the left climbing steeply through forest – the first of a series of footpath sections to shortcut the road. Waymarks guide the onward route. On reaching the alp buildings

of Cascina Zecca, the path veers to the right, climbing still, and then rejoins the road for the last 100m to the roadhead at Preda Rossa (1955m – about 2¼hrs).

Follow a track which continues from the roadhead, keeping left of a lovely mountain stream. When the track veers right to cross the stream walk ahead through the centre of a large flat meadowland (Piano di Preda Rossa) through which the

*Piano di Preda Rosso and Monte della Disgrazia*

stream meanders in lazy oxbows. Disgrazia looms ahead. On the far side of the meadows the path rises up the left-hand side of the stream to enter an upper level among low-growing larches, and with alpenrose and juniper growing among the rocks. This is the Valle Preda Rossa. Keep to the left-hand edge of the valley, then make a steepish ascent of the hillside, crossing a small boulder tip, then zigzagging up grass slopes littered with more rocks and boulders, making towards a big scree tip coming from Monte della Disgrazia. Abundant waymarks lead the path directly to the hut.

*Rifugio Cesare Ponti has Disgrazia as a backdrop. Owned by the CAI, the hut can sleep about 50, and is manned in summer when meals are generally available.*

The hut is on the route of the Sentiero Roma, but there's another challenging cross-country route for experienced walkers to tackle from here too. It crosses Passo di Corna Rossa (2836m), south of Disgrazia, to Rifugio Desio in 1¼hrs, and continues from there down to Chiesa in Val Malenco, thereby linking with the Bernina Alps.

# WALK 73: RIFUGIO LONGONI (2450m: 8038ft)

| | |
|---|---|
| Valley base: | Chiareggio or Chiesa |
| Start: | Chiareggio (1612m: 5289ft) |
| Distance: | 5km (3 miles) to the hut |
| Time: | 2½hrs |
| Total ascent: | 843m (2766ft) |
| Map: | Kompass 93 'Bernina-Sondrio' 1:50,000 |

*Val Malenco cuts a deep swathe through the mountains southwest of the Bernina massif, and drains the glaciers of both Bernina and Disgrazia. Truly Alpine at its head, the lower end of the valley spills out to vineyards and orchards of the sunny Valtellina. Situated halfway up the valley on its west flank, Chiesa is the main township, while Chiareggio at the roadhead serves as a good, if simple, base for a walking holiday. One of the best outings on offer here is the walk to Rifugio Longoni, tucked under rocks that support the lower Scerscen Glacier. From the hut, as from many outstanding viewpoints along the way, Monte della Disgrazia manages to hold your attention.*

The walk begins at the eastern end of Chiareggio where there's layby parking on the right-hand side of the approach road. A

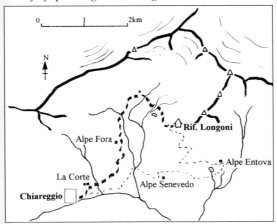

signpost marks the start of the route which initially takes a walled track rising to the few houses of La Corte. When the track curves sharply to the right, walk ahead up grass slopes waymarked with yellow/red paint flashes.

The way cuts into a gully and over a stream, then rises into forest with a brief view to the Disgrazia glaciers and several cirque glaciers tucked in the frontier ridge at the western end of the valley.

Leaving the forest the path continues to rise into Val Forasco, the way a little boggy in places, then veers left and passes well to the right of the buildings of Alpe Fora. Above the alp top a projecting grass spur, beyond which the path climbs steeply to another spur. Shortly after this cross a stream on stepping stones, then climb again to enter a marshy upper basin topped by crags that form the Italian/Swiss frontier.

Coming to a small alp hut at 2302m, pass this to your left and cross several minor streams. The way now curves right with waterfalls showering down cliffs. If you stray from the path, about 150m to the right you'll find a small tarn unmarked on the Kompass map, from which you gain a magnificent view of Disgrazia. Cross the stream emanating from the waterfalls, then rise over a series of slabs to gain a high point of about 2455m. Moments before reaching this a path descends to the right offering an alternative return

*Monte della Disgrazia from Alpe Fora*

to Chiareggio. Ignore this and 5mins later you'll come to the hut.

*Rifugio Longoni belongs to the Seregno Alpine Club, has 30 beds and is manned in summer. Simple meals available. From the terrace there's a fine view southeast down the valley, across the mountainside to Lago Palü, and south to Monte della Disgrazia.*

Allow 2–2½hrs to return to Chiareggio via the alps of Entova and Senevedo. This is a fine walk, but so is a return by the outward path, which would need 1½–2hrs.

## WALK 74: RIFUGIO LARCHER (2608m: 8556ft)

| | |
|---|---|
| Valley base: | Cogolo or Péjo |
| Start: | Malga Mare (1983m: 6506ft) |
| Distance: | 10km (6 miles) round trip |
| Time: | 1¾hrs to hut, 3hrs back |
| Total ascent: | 737m (2418ft) |
| Map: | Kompass 72 'Ortler/Ortles Cevedale' 1:50,000 |

*The largest of Italy's national parks extends east and south of the Stelvio Pass, and includes much spectacular mountain scenery, not least the glaciated Ortler Alps. On the south side of these Valle di Péjo drains into the Val di Sole, the valley which effectively divides the Ortler from the Adamello-Presanella Groups. The upper Valle di Péjo north of Cogolo is known as Val de la Mare, and it is from a roadhead hydro plant that this walk makes its way towards the very head of the glen where Rifugio Larcher (or Rif. Cevedale as it is also known) is well-positioned for climbers tackling a variety of peaks. It's a short walk to the hut, but a return is suggested via several tarns and steep hillsides – a first-class introduction to the area.*

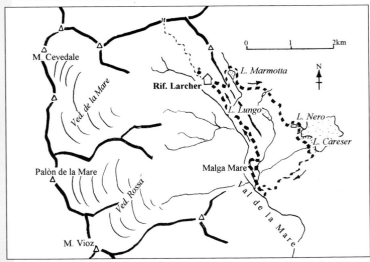

From the roadhead car park a broad, well-made path strikes across pastures, rising to the former alp buildings of Malga Mare, now converted to a restaurant. Above these the path narrows and climbs on to provide western views to Monte Vioz, Palon de la

Mare and the attractive Vedretta Rossa glacier. A traverse to the right leads onto a grassy shelf adorned with alpenroses and a few small larch trees. Over this the way swings left and, rising, enters the lower end of Val Venezia, a little corrie topped by snow mountains, glaciers and bare moraine walls. Pass a small hut at the midway point of the hut's material lift and, ignoring an alternative path breaking off to the right, continue upvalley along the right flank with Rifugio Larcher in view. The gradient steepens

*Rifugio Larcher*

towards the head of the valley and brings you to another path junction, barely a minute from the hut. The right-hand option is taken on the return to Malga Mare.

*Rifugio Larcher al Cevedale belongs to the SAT (Società Alpinisti Tridentina) – a branch of the CAI. It has 80 places, and a full meals service is on offer when it is manned – between mid-June and mid-September (Tel: 0463 751770).*

The hut looks directly across to the Vedretta de la Mare and a gleaming snow and ice crest from which the glacier is suspended. Just beyond the hut there's a small chapel, and a path continues upvalley, climbing to the col of La Forcola (3032m 1½hrs) for a magnificent view of glaciers, snowfields and a sea of mountains.

To return to Malga Mare go to the path junction just one minute from the hut, and take the upper branch leading to Lago Marmotta. Bear left along the ridge crest, then slant down to make a clockwise circuit of the tarn. At its southeastern end follow the outlet stream to a sluice where you bear left (east) on another path which contours round to Lago Nero – a jade-green tarn at 2622m. Beyond this descend to the larger Lago Càreser, cross below the barrage and on the south side of the dam bear left on a signposted descent path leading down to Malga Mare.

## WALK 75: RIFUGIO MANDRONE (2450m: 8038ft)

| | |
|---|---|
| Valley base: | Carisolo or Mad. di Campiglio |
| Start: | Malga Bédole (1584m: 5197ft) |
| Distance: | 4.5km (3 miles) to the hut |
| Time: | 2½hrs up, 1½hrs down |
| Total ascent: | 866m (2841ft) |
| Map: | Kompass 070 'Adamello-Brenta' 1:40,000 |

*Val Genova has been described as "the Alps' ultimate paradise", and although this is an extravagant claim, there can be no denying its beauty. Scoured by long-withdrawn glaciers, it's a green and fertile glen with mixed forests, open pastures and a series of spectacular waterfalls which drain eastwards to join the Sarca, whose valley divides the Adamello-Presanella Groups from that of the Brenta Dolomites. Carisolo, a modest little township, sits at the mouth of the valley a dozen kilometres below Madonna di Campiglio. A narrow road projects from it, and private vehicles are allowed as far as Rifugio Adamello Collini 'Al Bédole'. In the peak summer period a bus journeys from Carisolo to Malga Bédole, a short distance below the Bédole Hut, where the approach to Rifugio Mandrone begins. (Note that only the first two services of the day begin in Carisolo, the rest shuttle between Ponte Verde and Malga Bédole.) Both the hut's situation, and this walk to it, are worthy of the valley's reputation.*

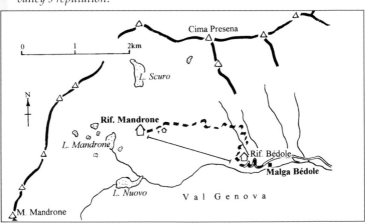

Walk up the road from Malga Bédole to the Bédole Hut, and take a signposted path into forest on the right. As you gain height, so the trees thin to allow grand views both up and down valley, and when you rise above the forest glaciers become more evident, as does the work of past glaciations in creating the lovely U-shaped valley itself.

*One of the many tarns below Rifugio Mandrone*

In a little over an hour from Rifugio Bédole pass a large slab on which the letters B-M and ½ Via have been painted to indicate that this is the halfway point between the two huts. It is also a fine viewpoint. Just beyond this the path skirts a steep rockface where it is safeguarded with a short length of fixed cable. Rising ever higher, sometimes quite steeply and with numerous zig-zags, more jagged crests appear above, while the Presanella glacier can be seen to the east. At about 2250m there's a trail junction and a sign giving an optimistic 30mins to the Mandrone Hut.

The Julius Payer study centre appears ahead. This is a modest stone building standing beside the path, in which there are displays detailing the extent of glacial retreat. Outside is a small alpine garden, beyond and below which a line of 14 headstones mark the graves of soldiers who perished there in 1916. The path continues and soon reaches a chapel and the hut's material lift. Rifugio Mandrone stands just beyond.

*Rifugio Mandrone – or Rif. Città di Trento al Mandrone to give its full title – is a large building owned by the SAT. It can sleep 100, and a full meals service is on offer between mid-June and mid-September when manned (Tel: 0465 501193).*

Below the hut numerous tarns and pools are worth exploring. Views are simply magnificent. Allow 1½–2hrs for the return to Malga Bédole by the same path.

## WALK 76: RIFUGIO TUCKETT (2272m: 7454ft)

| | |
|---|---|
| Valley base: | Madonna di Campiglio |
| Start: | Rif. Vallesinella (1514m: 4967ft) |
| Distance: | 3.5km (2 miles) one way |
| Time: | 2¼hrs up, 1½hrs down |
| Total ascent: | 758m (2489ft) |
| Map: | Kompass 73 'Gruppo di Brenta' 1:50,000 |

*With its forest of bold, soaring towers, the Brenta is an awe-inspiring district for the mountain walker, scrambler and experienced climber. There are routes for all tastes, and a number of large huts have been built in idyllic locations to accommodate visitors. But in the peak summer season these huts, and many of the trails leading to them, can be notoriously busy. If possible, visit midweek in September when it's possible to enjoy a degree of peace and solitude. The following walk is one of the best-known of all Brenta approach routes, while the Tuckett Hut, and the neighbouring Rifugio Sella, have been popular with activists throughout the 20th century – the Sella being built in 1900, the Tuckett Hut six years later.*

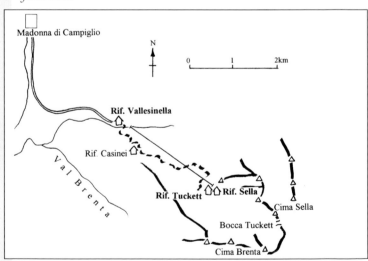

The privately-owned Rifugio Vallesinella stands at the head of a narrow dirt road southeast of Madonna, from which it is served by mini-bus taxi. Walkers and climbers with their own transport, however, use a huge car park by the hut, while those who choose to walk all the way from Madonna should allow an hour.

Leaving the car park go through the archway of a barn-like building and descend in forest to a rustic footbridge over a stream. Across this the way begins to climb and shortly comes to crosstracks where you continue ahead. The path now has many braidings, but by the time you reach **Rifugio Casinei** (1825m 60 beds) after about 45mins, they will have reunited as a single trail. The Casinei Hut, like the Vallesinella, is also privately-owned, and sits at the edge of forest on a sloping meadow with its back to the Brenta towers. The way passes to the left of the hut, then forks. The upper trail goes to Rifugios Brentei and Tosa, the lower option is signposted to Rif. Tuckett.

Shortly after this leave the forest and gain the first real Brenta view of the walk, with the Castellatto inferior soaring above the larches ahead. Although the forest has been left behind, there are still plenty of trees – mostly larch, with alpenrose and bilberry growing between them. At almost the upper extent of the trees the way cuts beneath the hut's material cable lift, and views grow wilder and more impressive. As you gain height, vegetation becomes more scarce and you pass a large patch of limestone pavement. About one minute before reaching the hut, another path breaks off to the right and is the one to take for Rifugio Brentei as described in Walk 77.

*Rifugio Tuckett*

*Rifugio Tuckett, named after British climber, Francis Fox Tuckett, is owned by the CAI, Trento Section, as is Rifugio Sella next door. About 120 bed spaces and meals provided when manned – between mid-June and mid-September (Tel: 0465 441226).*

The classic Brenta *via ferrata*, the Sentiero delle Bocchette, begins nearby.

## WALK 77: RIFUGIO BRENTEI (2182m: 7159ft)

| | |
|---|---|
| Valley base: | Madonna di Campiglio |
| Start: | Rifugio Tuckett (2272m: 7454ft) |
| Distance: | 3km (2 miles) hut to hut |
| Time: | 1½hrs |
| Total ascent: | 145m (476ft) |
| Descent: | 235m (771ft) |
| Map: | Kompass 73 'Gruppo di Brenta' 1:50,000 |

*An obvious extension to Walk 76 follows a trail heading west then south from the Tuckett Hut, and provides astonishing views of the Crozzon di Brenta, Val Brenta Alta and the Bocca di Brenta – a landscape of jutting towers, pinnacles and gritty ridges like sharks' teeth, and with huge walls of cream, pink or orange hues that rise either from forested valleys or from a turmoil of scree and boulder-slope. One would be forgiven for thinking that such a land is the sole preserve of rock gymnasts, but well-engineered trails have been created to enable mountain walkers to penetrate to the very heart of the range, and to tour from hut to hut unencumbered with ropes and ironmongery. This short walk is a magnificent example.*

Descend briefly from the Tuckett Hut and a minute later bear left at a junction. The trail (no:322) descends to a chaos of white rocks and blocks and is guided through by red-white waymarks. Beyond this turmoil the path meanders down grass slopes among tufts of alpenrose and juniper, to a minor saddle where the hillside is cloathed in dwarf pine. Wandering through the Sella del Freddolin, cross an exposed rib of

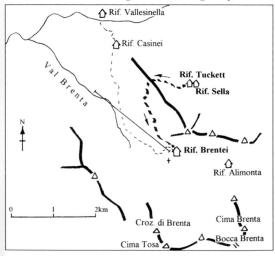

186

limestone which requires a little care, and moments later come to a path junction at about 2040m (35mins). The right-hand trail here descends to the Casinei Hut and Vallesinella, but we bear left, now on path no:318, the Sentiero Bogani.

The trail ma-
kes a gentle
rising traverse
and suddenly
turns a corner
round a rocky
bluff to be con-
fronted by the
i n c r e d -
ible tower of
Crozzon di
B r e n t a
d o m i n a t i n g
the way ahead.
H e a d i n g
south-south-
east above the

*Rifugio Brentei*

deep Val Brenta the way follows an undemanding contour, in places cut into rock walls and safeguarded by fixed cable handrails. At one point the path squeezes through a very narrow cleft with a small Madonna in it, then swings left to pass through a short tunnel. On emerging from this you catch sight of a chapel just beyond the Brentei Hut. As the way progresses more and more peaks, spires and turrets crowd your field of vision. Just before reaching the hut a path cuts into a small glen on the left and climbs to Rif. Alimonta; another descends right to a water supply, while a third path breaks away to the right by the shed housing the Brentei Hut's material lift, and offers a recommended return to Vallesinella through the Val Brenta.

*Rifugio Maria e Alberto ai Brentei was built in 1932 for the Italian Alpine Club. It has places for 90 and meals are provided when wardened, usually from mid-June to mid-September (Tel: 0465 441244). The setting is truly impressive.*

Opportunities abound for extending the walk further, or return to Vallesinella by way of the Sentiero Violi and Val Brenta Alta in another 2–2½hrs.

# WALK 78: RIFUGIO VIEL DEL PAN (2432m: 7979ft)

| | |
|---|---|
| Valley base: | Canazei |
| Start: | Passo Pordoi (2242m: 7356ft) |
| Distance: | 13km (8 miles) round trip |
| Time: | 4–4½hrs (1¼hrs to hut) |
| Total ascent: | 323m (1060ft) |
| Map: | Kompass 55 'Cortina d'Ampezzo' 1:50,000 |

*This circular walk follows part of the historic, and exceedingly popular, 'Viel del Pan' which was used from medieval times as the only route of communication between Val Gardena and the Cordevole. The trail is a gently undulating one, and for much of the way there are tremendous views south to the snowy block of the Marmolada, which here looks less like a Dolomitic peak, than something transported from the Western Alps. The hut has limited accommodation, but in the peak season it is exceedingly busy during the day by walkers stopping for refreshment.*

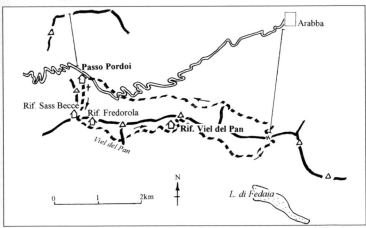

Passo Pordoi is a broad pastoral saddle at the southern foot of the Sella Dolomites, a busy place served by bus from Canazei, Arabba and the Sella Pass. The walk begins behind Albergo Savoia on a major path (no:601) heading south as far as a small chapel. Thereafter the trail narrows as it rises to an obvious col adorned with ski machinery. At the col bear left to pass below **Rif. Sass Beccé** and come to **Rif. Baita Fredarola**, after which the path forks. Bear right and cut along the south side of the ridge with the Marmolada now in full view. The continuing path has its ups and downs, but the traverse more or less maintains the 2400m contour. Well-made and undemanding, it leads easily across steep grass slopes, then comes to a high point from which the dammed Lago di Fedaia can be seen ahead and some 400m below. About 1hr 15mins from the Pordoi Pass you arrive at Rifugio Viel del Pan set on a small projecting spur.

*The Marmolada from Rifugio Viel del Pan*

*Rifugio Viel del Pan is privately owned, with just 14 beds. Open from June to September, with full restaurant service (Tel: 0462 601720).*

While the continuing path slopes down a little beyond the hut, another trail rises behind it and gains a narrow gash in the ridge from which a very fine view is to be had of the Sella Group above the Passo Pordoi, and the Langkofel trinity way to the left. From this viewpoint a path slants down to rejoin the Viel del Pan route, while an alternative cuts west along the ridge crest (Alta Via del Creste) as far as Rif. Fredarola, then down to the Pordoi Pass.

Continue along the Viel del Pan, and about 45mins from the hut the way forks. Path 601 descends to Fedaia in about 30mins, but our route rises to turn a spur with a short exposed step where caution is advised. After this it's a straightforward path that leads up to the Porta Vescovo, dominated by the cableway station linked with Arabba. Pass below the building on a track, but leave this at a right-hand hairpin where a narrow path (no:680) descends a steep slope of loose soil, then crosses rough stones and rocks before easing on scant pastureland. Waymarks and faint signs of a path lead on to the Pordoi Pass which is seen for some way before you reach it.

## WALK 79: RIFUGIO PIAN DI CENGIA (2547m: 8356ft)

| | |
|---|---|
| Valley base: | Cortina d'Ampezzo |
| Start: | Rif. Auronzo (2320m: 7612ft) |
| Distance: | 5km (3 miles) to the hut |
| Time: | 2hrs |
| Total ascent: | 425m (1394ft) |
| Map: | Kompass 55 'Cortina d'Ampezzo' 1:50,000 |

*The tiny Pian di Cengia Hut offers a direct contrast to many of the inn-like rifugios found elsewhere in the Dolomites. Otherwise known as the Büllelejochhütte, it occupies a secluded, rocky ledge on a ridge to the east of the Paternkofel (Monte Paterno) with wild peaks filling every horizon. This approach, like so many others in the district, follows mule-trails dating from the First World War, and passes remnants of battles fought in seemingly impossible situations. The first hour of the walk is bound to be busy, but the crowds will inevitably become much more sparse thereafter.*

The way begins at the head of an expensive toll road above Misurina where there's a large terraced car park and the hotel-like Rifugio Auronzo, served by bus from Cortina. If you have your own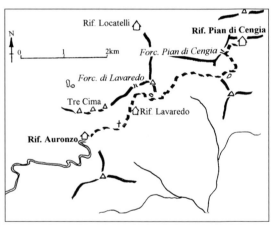

transport and object to the toll charged for the final 7.5km of road, an alternative track/path will take about 2hrs to negotiate on foot from the toll booth. From Rif. Auronzo walk east along a broad jeep track which cuts along the base of the famous Tre Cima di Lavaredo, with the bristling Cadini pinnacles off to the right standing like a collection of huge stone spears. In 15mins come to a chapel, beyond which the track veers left and in another 5mins brings you to **Rifugio Lavaredo** (2344m). Remain on the track as it heads into a lunar-like landscape. Croda Passaporta stands to the north, Cima Piccolissima to the west, with the obvious saddle of the Forcella di Lavaredo linking the two. About 10mins beyond the Lavaredo Hut an alternative path (no:104) breaks off to the right near a ruined building. This is the path to take, although it would be worth continuing up to the Lavaredo saddle first to enjoy a spectacular view of the Tre Cima seen in profile, and the distant Locatelli Hut set against a background of Gothic mountains. (See Walk 80.)

At the junction take path no:104 which passes a tarn, descends through a cleft, then veers left below screes and crags. After losing about 200m, the way rises again beyond a corrie on the left. Ignore two paths descending to the Valle di Cengia and zigzag up against orange- and grey-coloured crags to enter a hanging valley in which you'll find Lago di Cengia. The way switchbacks up the far

*Rifugio Pian di Cengia*

side of the valley, then divides. (Right to the Toni bivouac hut.) Continue ahead past wartime fortifications, go through a desolate region, then onto the Forcella Pian di Cengia (2522m). Bear right along the ridge crest with amazing views in all directions, then veer right along a ledge supported by timber struts to gain the hut.

*Rifugio Pian di Cengia is privately owned with places for just 11. Meals provided during the high season (Tel: 0474 70258).*

Either return by the same path in 1½hrs, or follow Walk 80 via Rif. Locatelli.

# WALK 80: RIFUGIO LOCATELLI (2405m: 7890ft)

| | |
|---|---|
| Valley base: | Cortina d'Ampezzo |
| Start: | Rif. Pian di Cengia (2547m: 8356ft) |
| Distance: | 7km (4½ miles) in all |
| Time: | 3–3½hrs to car park (1hr to hut) |
| Total ascent: | c.150m (492ft) |
| Map: | Kompass 55 'Cortina d'Ampezzo' 1:50,000 |

*Rifugio Locatelli is also known as the Drei Zinnen or Tre Cima Hut. A large stone building with a magnificent view of the north face of the Tre Cima di Lavaredo, it is perhaps the busiest of all mountain huts in the Dolomites – as opposed to rifugios directly accessible by road. The Tre Cima being virtually the symbol of the Dolomites, and the hut being reached by a broad and easy path, this is hardly surprising. The majority of the summer crowds approach from the roadhead at Rif. Auronzo, skirt the southern base of the mountains, then cross Forcella di Lavaredo to gain the hut after about 1½hrs. The walk described below, however, approaches by the 'back door' as it were, and is an extension of Walk 79. It also continues to the Auronzo roadhead car park by way of Forcella Col di Mezzo, thus completing a full circle of these incredible mountains.*

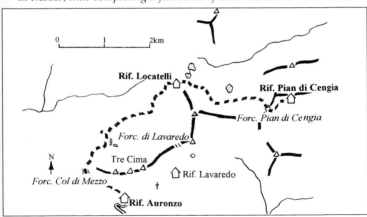

On leaving Pian di Cengia bear right and retrace the path back to the Forcella Pian di Cengia, which is yet another impressive viewpoint. Descend northwestward into a steep, rocky valley on path no:101, passing tangles of old barbed wire dating from the 1914–18 war, then swing left above a hauntingly blue tarn. The way crosses a huge scree slope, then weaves a course over undulating ground among white boulders before easing up to the saddle on which the Locatelli Hut is located – on the way passing two more small tarns.

*Forcella di Lavaredo, Sexten Dolomites*

*Rifugio Locatelli is a large building that can sleep about 180. Owned by the Padua Section of the CAI, it is staffed in summer and offers a full restaurant service (Tel: 0474 72002). Sunset views can be magnificent here and, should you plan to stay, you'll find plenty of ways to fill a few hours. Try, for example, the novel tunnel route and via ferrata on the Paternkofel to the southeast, or wander any of the surrounding trails which explore a variety of surreal landscapes.*

The route back to the car park begins by the hut where you take path no:105 northwest for about 1min, then bear left when it forks. Descend to a second junction below the main path and at this and subsequent junctions, take the 105 route option. (The initial diversion was in order to gain additional views of the Paternkofel pinnacles.) The way goes steeply down into a grassy basin, passes another trail junction then slants up the hillside ahead left, reaching a spur bright with dwarf pine and with the Tre Cima soaring directly overhead. Passing to the left of a shepherd's hut the path climbs again to a saddle at the western end of the Tre Cima. One final scree slope remains to be crossed before gaining the Forcella Col di Mezzo (2315m) where yet another panorama unfolds. The way now cuts round the southwest flank of the mountains and brings you to the roadhead car park.

## WALK 81: RIFUGIO VANDELLI (1928m: 6325ft)

| | |
|---|---|
| Valley base: | Cortina d'Ampezzo |
| Start: | Passo di Tre Croci (1809m: 5935ft) |
| Distance: | 15km (9 miles) in all |
| Time: | 6–6½hrs (2hrs to hut) |
| Total ascent: | 569m (1867ft) |
| Map: | Kompass 55 'Cortina d'Ampezzo' 1:50,000 |

*The Tre Croci Pass lies a short distance to the northeast of Cortina, and is served by bus in summer. To the north stands the Cristallo Group, while to the south the Sorapiss massif is like an enormous chair whose arms curve round a deep cirque above which hang three small glaciers. In the mouth of this cirque stands the Vandelli Hut, reached by a pretty woodland walk in about 2hrs. The walk on offer here, however, extends that approach into a full circuit. The tremendous range of scenery which gradually unfolds makes this a true classic, while the route itself has immense variety, is challenging in places, and will reward all who enjoy wild landscapes.*

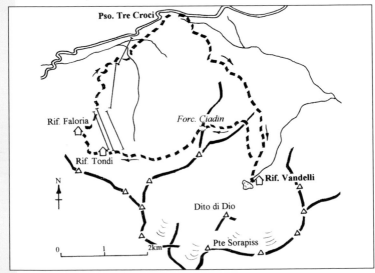

From Hotel Tre Croci on the pass, walk down the road heading east (direction Misurina) for a short distance until you see path no:215 breaking off to the right across an open meadow. On the far side of this enter woodland. The path veers left and soon narrows as it descends a little and crosses the mouth of a minor tributary valley with views north to the unmistakable Tre Cima. Shortly after crossing a rocky stretch safeguarded with a wire

*Rifugio Vandelli*

handrail, the path climbs, leading to three metal ladders from which views not only include the Tre Cima, but also the lake of Misurina and its forest-clad valley. There are more fixed cable sections as the way continues to climb, working into the cirque which gives the massif its distinctive appearance. The Vandelli Hut can be glimpsed several minutes before it is reached, but before doing so, note path no:216 cutting to the right. This will be used on the walk after leaving the hut.

*Rifugio A. Vandelli is a neat, 3-storey building owned by the Venice Section of the CAI. It has 60 places and a full meals service on offer when manned in summer (Tel: 0436 39015).*

Return along the approach path to the junction with path no:216, and bear left. The path rises steeply as it fights a way among dwarf pine and alpenroses. Near the upper tree limit it digs across patches of scree before gaining a high point on a shoulder of Cima di Laudo from which wonderful views are to be had of Monte Cristallo, the Misurina valley, Tre Cima and the Cadini Group. Over this high point descend by rocky ledges (one extensive shelf has fixed cable handrail) and come to the edge of a broad scree slope where the path divides. Follow the upper trail with cairns guiding across the screes, then climb to the Forcella Ciadin (more fixed cable) to be greeted by a huge panorama. Descend leftwards to more screes. Stay high when the path forks and cross a series of steep scree slopes, and eventually gain Forcella Faloria. Bear right and soon descend to Rif. Tondi. Continue to nearby Rif. Faloria and follow a dirt road down to the Tre Croci Pass.

# THE AUSTRIAN ALPS

Perhaps even more so than Switzerland, Austria promotes a culture of mountain activity. All year round locals of all ages head up into their mountains to walk, climb or ski – or simply to enjoy the ambience of a mountain hut. Of these there are more than a thousand in the Austrian Alps alone, many of them inn-like and comfortable – among the best huts to be found anywhere in the Alps. Roughly half are owned by member clubs of the Austrian or German Alpine Clubs (the *Alpenverein*), the remainder are privately-owned, or belong to other clubs or organisations. As for the mountains themselves, these are separated into numerous Alpine Groups, mostly named after the major valley or town of the region – such as the Zillertal Alps and Radstädter Tauern – but more conveniently gathered into just two major regions: the *Hochgebirge* and *Mittelgebirge*. The first is the southern chain of mostly snowpeaks, many of which exceed 3000m; the second comprises the Northern Limestone Alps which form the Austro-German border – of these only one, the Parseierspitze, reaches the 3000m mark.

## SILVRETTA, ÖTZTAL AND STUBAI ALPS

Describing from west to east, these three groups carry the borders of Switzerland and Italy, and neatly fold one against another. As part of the so-called *Hochgebirge* their summits are mostly crowned with snow and ice, glaciers flow down to the northern valleys and, apart from their comparatively modest height, they give every appearance of being an extension of the Western Alps. For a first Alpine climbing season, they make a near-perfect location, and a number of snow and ice climbing courses take place here. There are also some wonderful hut to hut tours to be made by experienced mountain walkers, and no end of shorter day walks leading from valley resort to mountain hut.

Guidebooks: *Silvretta Alps* and *Stubai Alps & South Tirol* by Jeff Williams (West Col). *Mountain Walking in Austria* by Cecil Davies (Cicerone Press), *Walking Austria's Alps, Hut to Hut* by Jonathan Hurdle (Cordee/The Mountaineers), *Hut to Hut in the Stubai Alps* by Allan Hartley (Cicerone Press), *Hut Hopping in the Austrian Alps* by William E Reifsnyder (Sierra Club).

## KAISERGEBIRGE

The compact Kaisergebirge is just one section of the Northern

Limestone Alps. Rising north of Kitzbühel, and with access from Kufstein, Söll, Scheffau, Ellmau and St Johann, the Kaisergebirge is divided into the Zahmer ('Tame') and Wilder ('Wild') Kaiser, the latter being the impressive wall which displays itself to the south. Although the crags swarm with climbing activity, interesting trails entice out of the valleys and up to the foot of the walls, while others skirt the base of the mountains to create a long traverse. A handful of huts have been built here, and although only one approach walk is described in this selection, it provides perhaps the best possible introduction to an area that will no doubt demand further exploration.

Guidebook: *Mountain Walking in Austria* by Cecil Davies, and *Klettersteig: Scrambles in the Northern Limestone Alps* by Paul Werner – both published by Cicerone Press.

**THE KITZBÜHELER ALPS AND SALZBURGER SCHIEFER ALPS**
Spreading mostly south of Kitzbühel, midway between Innsbruck and Salzburg, these mountains are neither snow-capped nor steep-walled, but green and rolling, attractive overgrown hills that provide some of the best medium-grade walks in all Austria. Of the two, the Salzburger Schiefer Alps are by far the smaller, rising east of Zell am See as a near neighbour to the eastern Kitzbüheler Alps. In winter a number of resorts cater for skiers, but relatively few of the heights have been drastically adapted for downhill skiing, so the summer walker may still enjoy a vast arena of exercise without facing bulldozed pistes and naked tows. From their grass-bound crests a number of mountain groups of the Northern Limestone Alps will be seen in one direction, and the glacier-clad heights of the Hohe Tauern in the other. Mountain huts representing these groups in this book are likely to be less crowded than those of the main Alpine regions.

Guidebooks: *Kitzbüheler Alps & Wild Emperor Mountains*, and *Glemm Valley, Europa Sport Region & Gastein Valley* – both by Kev Reynolds (Inghams).

**GLOCKNER AND GRANATSPITZ GROUPS**
The Hohe Tauern is a large block of glaciated mountains lying south of the Salzach river. Among its highest groups are those of the Venediger and Glockner, with the more compact Granatspitz wedged in between. The Glockner Group is named after Austria's highest mountain, the 3798m Grossglockner, but it also includes

many other fine peaks. One of the best-known of these is the Kitzsteinhorn, a shapely mountain overlooking the Kapruner Tal and Zell am See. Summer skiing is practised on the north-facing glaciers, and at its feet lie two huts, both of which are worth visiting. The Granatspitz Group, on the other hand, is not so icy. Forming a north-south block between the Tauerntal on the west and Dorfertal on the east, the high ridges make splendid viewpoints.

Guidebook: *Mountain Walking in Austria* by Cecil Davies (Cicerone Press).

## CARNIC ALPS AND TÜRNITZER ALPS

Not only are these two groups situated far apart, they are very different in nature and appeal. The first marks the southern wall of the Gailtal, and rubs against the Austro-Italian border southwest of Villach. Modest limestone peaks spring from rough pastureland, and from some of their summits the rugged Julian Alps of Slovenia can be seen. The Türnitzer Alps, on the other hand, all but mark the eastern extremity of the Alps southwest of Vienna and south of St Polten. These are green, wooded hills in which one may wander for days at a time in high summer and meet only woodcutters and lonely farmers. Peaceful hills, attractive hills, with pleasant valleys at their feet.

Guidebooks: None in English.

*Wilder Freiger in the Stubai Alps*

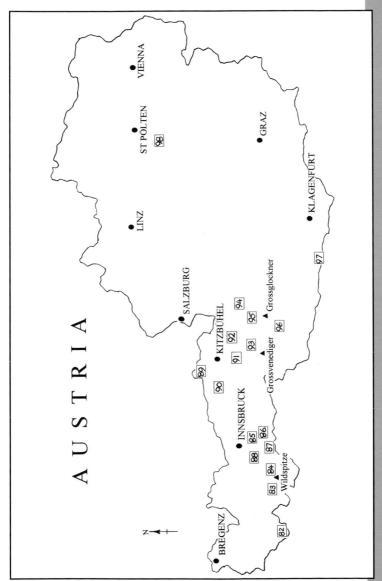

AUSTRIA

VIENNA

ST PÖLTEN
98

GRAZ

KLAGENFURT
97

LINZ

SALZBURG

Grossglockner
94
95
96

KITZBÜHEL
92
93
91

Grossvenediger
89
90

INNSBRUCK
85 86
87
88
84
83 Wildspitze
82

BREGENZ

N

199

# WALK 82: WIESBADENER HUT (2443m: 8015ft)

| | |
|---|---|
| Valley base: | Schruns or Galtür |
| Start: | Bielerhöhe (2036m 6680ft) |
| Distance: | 13km (8 miles) round trip |
| Time: | 2hrs there, 3½hrs back |
| Total ascent: | 616m (2021ft) |
| Map: | Kompass Wanderkarte 41 'Silvretta Verwallgruppe' 1:50,000 |

*With a veritable sea of glaciers spread before it, the Wiesbadener Hut enjoys a privileged position south of the Bielerhöhe road pass. Piz Buin, at 3312m (10,866ft) the highest Silvretta summit on the Austro/Swiss border, rises nearby, as do the Dreiländerspitze and Silvrettahorn that continue the border to east and west. Thanks to ease of access, the hut is very popular with day-trippers as well as climbers staying overnight prior to tackling neighbourhood peaks, and from the outset views are*

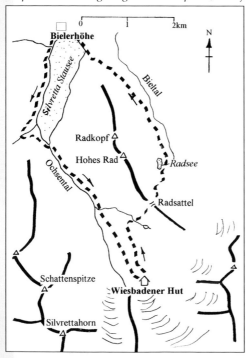

memorable. At first there is the milky blue Silvretta Stausee reservoir backed by a high crest carrying snow and ice. Then there are numerous 3000m mountains spilling their glaciers valleywards, while the return from the hut crosses a stony pass, with nearby tarns and a mass of distant mountains to gaze upon.

From the Bielerhöhe cross the dam wall at the northwestern end of the Silvretta Stausee and wander down the western side of the lake. When the path divides take the left branch to cross a stream and continue to the lake's end where you join a broad trail from the east bank. Bear right and walk through the narrows of the Ochsental, a valley which opens to glacier views and a blocking wall consisting of Dreilanderspitze, Piz Buin, Signalhorn and Silvrettahorn. The path continues without difficulty and leads directly to the hut, settled above the moraines of the Vermunt and Ochsental glaciers.

*The Wiesbadener Hut was built in 1898, but it has since been enlarged and improved three times. It can now sleep 200, and is staffed from the end of June to the beginning of October, when a full restaurant service is in operation (Tel: 05558 4233). It is owned by the Wiesbaden Section of the DAV. Other huts accessible from it: Tuoi, Jamtal, and Saarbrucker.*

*The Radsattel above the Wiesbadener Hut*

A return to the Bielerhöhe by the same route should only be contemplated in the event of bad weather, for a longer but more interesting walk makes a circuit of the Radkopf-Hohes Rad massif, with a fresh perspective being presented of both the Silvretta and neighbouring Ferwall mountain groups.

Just beyond the hut bear left on the Edmund Lorenz Weg, a narrow path which climbs to the Radsattel, a 2652m (8700ft) col on the southeast ridge of the Hohes Rad which rises north of the hut. Guided by cairns and waymarks the trail climbs over a high, stone-littered hillside, continues over pastures sliced with streams and pools, then makes a steep pull onto the col. Over this drop steeply over rocks, then head northeast in tight zigzags to reach the floor of the Bieltal shortly after passing the Radsee tarn. The trail strikes through the glen, and at its northern end, curves left to the Bielerhöhe.

## WALK 83: TASCHACH HAUS (2434m: 7986ft)

| | |
|---|---|
| Valley base: | Mittelberg or Plangeross |
| Start: | Gepatschhaus (1928m: 6325ft) |
| Distance: | 18km (11 miles) |
| Time: | 6½–7hrs to the hut, 3hrs down |
| Total ascent: | 1167m (3829ft) |
| Descent: | 1361m (4465ft) |
| Map: | Kompass Wanderkarte 43 'Ötztaler Alpen' 1:50,000 |

*This walk makes a crossing of the high ridge that divides the Kaunertal from the Pitztal in the western Ötztal Alps, and links two huts – the rustic Gepatsch Haus, and the mountaineering centre of the Taschach Haus. The first is set among pine trees at the southern end of the Gepatsch reservoir, the second has a cascading icefall as its close neighbour – an icefall tumbling from the Wildspitze, at 3772m the highest of the Ötztal peaks. It's a challenging, butscenically spectacular, route with a high point of 3095m (10,154ft) at the Ölgruben Joch, but with the option of climbing another 200m to the summit of the neighbouring Hinterer Ölgrubenspitze, for those with the necessary time and energy.*

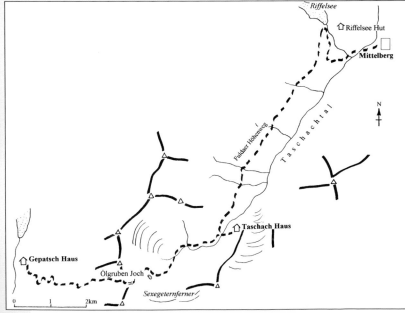

The Gepatsch Haus is reached by bus from Landeck railway station via Prutz. It is open from mid-June to mid-September, has places for 86, and meals are available (Tel: 05442 3814). The path to the Ölgruben Joch begins about 200m south of the hut, indicated by a sign on the left of the road. Climb a vegetated hillside, cross a bluff topped by an ornate crucifix, then resume uphill with numerous switchbacks. After about 1½hrs there's a trail junction, but the Ölgruben path continues up the hillside and soon passes alongside a boulder field. As grass gives way to rocks and a few snow patches, so the slopes ahead become more barren, and the final haul to the pass is over scree and, at times, more snow, but there is a vague trail.

*On the descent from the Olgruben Joch to the Täschach Haus*

The broad saddle of the Ölgruben Joch is gained in about 3½–4hrs. Suddenly a stunning view is gained of the Wildspitze ahead, and an arctic world of glaciers and snowfields stretching in a huge arc. Above to the right is the Hinterer Ölgrubenspitze, whose summit may be reached by an hour's diversion. Descend with caution on a cairned trail that edges above a steep cliff, then goes down glacial slabs and grit-covered shelves to a snowfield. Across this waymarks lead the path down the left-hand side of the Sexegertenbach stream, then over a bridge to the right bank followed by a short uphill stretch to the hut.

*The Taschach Haus was built in 1899 by the Frankfurt-am-Main Section of the DAV next to the Taschach Hut (1874) – the latter still in use as a winter room. It has since been enlarged and refurbished, and now has places for 125. Staffed from the end of June to end of September; meals available (Tel: 05413 8239). It is invariably busy.*

The most scenic descent to Mittelberg entails recrossing the bridge, then heading to the right along the Fuldaer Höhenweg, a splendid path protected in places by fixed wire ropes where it climbs over and round rocky bluffs, always with magnificent views. It leads to the Riffelsee tarn, then descends more gently to the road at Mittelberg.

# WALK 84: BRAUNSCHWEIGER HUT (2759m: 9052ft)

| | |
|---|---|
| Valley base: | Mittelberg, Plangeross or Sölden |
| Start: | Mittelberg (1730m: 5676ft) |
| Distance: | 14km (8½ miles) in all |
| Time: | 6½hrs (3hrs to hut) |
| Total ascent: | 1265m (4150ft) |
| Descent: | 1628m (5341ft) |
| Map: | Kompass Wanderkarte 43 'Ötztaler Alpen' 1:50,000 |

*Set on the edge of a sea of ice northwest of the Wildspitze, the Braunschweiger Hut is mostly used by mountaineers, but the route suggested here is a two-day crossing for experienced mountain walkers which leads from the head of the Pitztal to the main Ötztal resort of Sölden. The hut approach, though straightforward, is quite a demanding one, while the continuing route takes you up to a high ridge where ibex can often be spied, then crossing through the 2995m Pitztaler Jöchl, followed by descent (often on snow) to the Rettenbachtal which drains down to Sölden. This is a fine two-day route, but it should not be attempted by anyone suffering from vertigo.*

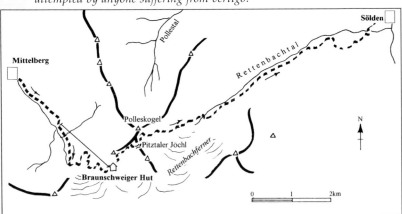

Mittelberg sits at a confluence of valleys, at the head of the stem of the Pitztal's inverted Y. The longer of the two upper arms is that of the Taschachtal, but the route to the Braunschweiger Hut leads into the shorter, southeastern branch which is blocked by a barrier of cliffs down which an impressive waterfall sprays the melt of the glaciers. Just beyond the Gletscherstübele café the track ends by the Braunschweiger Hut's material lift. (It's possible to arrange for rucksacks to be carried to the hut by this lift.)

The path works a way up the rock wall just to the left of the waterfall, weaving back and forth and often being dashed by the spray.

Above the cliffs you come to a splendid view of the lower reaches of the Mittelbergferner, beyond which the way steepens considerably. The path tackles another rocky section, then heads along an uphill ramp among alpenroses and yellow anemones,

*The Braunschweiger Hut sits on the edge of glaciers*

and rocky staircases with consistently fine views onto the glacier. The way switchbacks to and fro in a series of tight zigzags, then the hut comes into view where a seat has been placed to exploit the panorama. The final haul remains a steep one, but the hut is at last reached with some relief.

*Owned by the Braunschweig Section of the DAV, the Braunschweiger Hut has room for 125 plus 25 emergency beds. There's a guardian on duty from mid-June until the end of September, when meals are available (Tel: 05413 82360).*

Above the hut the route to the Pitztaler Jöchl is clear, and rises without difficulty to a sharp ridge from which there's a direct view to the Riffelsee above Mittelberg. Working a way along the ridge a few natural ledges on the right-hand side direct you to the col, which is little more than a brief gap in a shattered ridge (45mins from the hut). On the northern side descend with care at first, then more easily to a car park used by skiers on the Rettenbergferner. A series of linking footpaths continues the route through the Rettenbachtal, then down steeply through forest to Sölden, where it's possible to catch a bus further downvalley.

# WALK 85: INNSBRUCKER HUT (2369m: 7772ft)

| | |
|---|---|
| Valley base: | Neustift, Fulpmes or Neder |
| Start: | Neder (970m: 3182ft) |
| Distance: | 10km (6 miles) |
| Time: | 4–5hrs |
| Total ascent: | 1399m (4590ft) |
| Map: | Kompass Wanderkarte 83 'Stubaier Alpen Serleskamm' 1:50,000 |

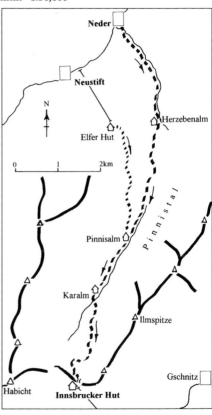

*Within an hour's journey of Innsbruck by public transport it's possible to be at the foot of the Stubai Alps, one of Austria's most popular mountain playgrounds. Ideal for climber, scrambler, walker and hut to hut trekker, the Stubai has a number of well-ordered huts, the Innsbrucker being one of the largest and busiest – especially on summer weekends. The popularity of the Innsbrucker is easy to understand, for not only is it a comfortable lodging with excellent views to the Tribulaun peaks, but the normal route on the 3277m Habicht starts virtually from its door, it's ideally situated for 'climbing path' enthusiasts tackling the Ilmspitze Klettersteig, and it forms the first stage of the multi-day Stubai High Route hut tour.*

From the bus stop in Neder near the bridge over the Ruetzbach follow a road south towards the entrance to the Pinnistal. A jeep track continues into the valley and this is followed to its head. It's a beautiful valley with impressive rock walls soaring from meadows lined with forest, and with the Pinnisbach stream for occasional company. Refreshments are available at several alms along the way. Although it is the mountains that form the east wall of the

*The Innsbrucker Hut*

valley which hold one's attention, on the approach to Pinnisalm the north-east flank of the Habicht comes into view ahead, just to the right of the obvious saddle of the Pinnisjoch, on the far side of which sits the Innsbrucker Hut.

An alternative start to this approach can be made by taking the Elfer chairlift from Neustift, and then following a good clear path along the upper western slopes of the Pinnistal before sloping easily down to Pinnisalm where you join the jeep track used by the main route.

The jeep road ends at Karalm, a short distance beyond Pinnisalm, and from there a clear path strikes across the stream and climbs another 600m (1969ft) to the Pinnisjoch. There's nothing difficult about the way, and it comes as a surprise to emerge at the saddle to find the hut just beyond.

*The Innsbrucker Hut was built by the Touristenklub of Innsbruck in 1884 and was rebuilt in 1982/83. It has 40 beds and 120 dormitory places, and a restaurant service when the guardian is in residence – from end of June to the end of September (Tel: 05276 295).*

From here the Habicht may be climbed in about 3hrs; a return to Neder by the same route of approach takes 3hrs, while the Gschnitztal can be reached in about 1½–2hrs. See Walk 86 for the next stage of the classic Stubia hut to hut tour.

## WALK 86: BREMER HUT (2413m: 7917ft)

| | |
|---|---|
| Valley base: | Neustift or Gschnitz |
| Start: | Innsbrucker Hut (2369m: 7772ft) |
| Distance: | 10km (6 miles) |
| Time: | 6–7hrs |
| Total ascent: | c.695m (2280ft) |
| Descent: | c.600m (1969ft) |
| Map: | Kompass Wanderkarte 83 'Stubaier Alpen Serleskamm' 1:50,000 |

*The Stubai High Route referred to in the previous walk makes a magnificent hut to hut tour of from six to eight days. Avoiding all but one brief glacier crossing, the route creates a circuit along the mid-height flank of the main Stubai range. It crosses a succession of ridges, visits tarns, waterfalls and high pastures, avoids roads and villages, and day after day enjoys an unfolding series of exquisite landscapes. But it needs saying that there are many exposed fixed rope sections that could be troublesome for walkers who suffer vertigo. A number of these are to be found on the stage which links the Innsbrucker and Bremer huts. This is described below, and is included in this selection of hut walks as an illustration of the delights to be had when journeying from hut to hut in Austria. Should you be interested in tackling the full tour, Allan Hartley's guidebook* Hut to Hut in the Stubai Alps *(Cicerone Press) is recommended. In it he refers to this tour as the Stubai Rucksack Route.*

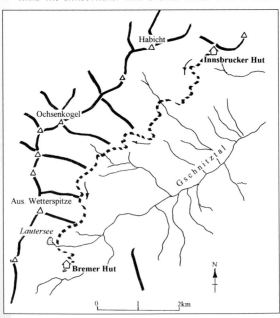

The Bremer Hut is located at the head of the Gschnitztal, and the trail to it makes a convoluted traverse of that valley's north wall, crossing one spur after another. The first comes shortly after leaving the Innsbrucker Hut where an obvious col at about 2559m carries the trail over a spur of the Alfeirkamm. This is followed by a long undulating contour with occasional fixed ropes, leading eventually into a brief corrie cut by streams. Here a steepish climb leads to a second col a little west of the Pramarnspitze outcrop; a narrow crossing, followed by a steep descent aided by more fixed ropes heading west and working a way into the pastures of Beilgrube. These lead to more rocky slopes of a spur projecting from the Ochsenkogel, then heading west and southwest once more to the Plattental.

*Walkers en route to the Bremer Hut*

Ahead, the east ridge of the Aussere Wetterspitze (3070m) appears to block the onward route, although a 2590m col offers a way over. The climb to this is often hampered by late-lying snow, even in mid-summer, and in such conditions caution is required to avoid breaking through into deep, leg-wrenching holes. The crossing of this col is the last on this particular stage, and about 20mins below it you round a bluff and catch sight of the Bremer Hut on the far side of the Simminger Alm. Continuing down into a grassy basin you come to a large cairn at a junction of paths. Bear right and pass below the Lautersee tarn to the foot of a band of rocks spilling east from the Innere Wetterspitze. The trail picks a route up these, with a few scrambling sections aided by fixed ropes, and leads directly to the Bremer Hut beside its tiny tarn.

*The atmospheric shingle-walled Bremer Hut is owned by the Bremen Section of the DAV; 25 beds and 30 dormitory places, meals available when the guardian is in residence; from end of June to end of September (Tel: 0663 57545).*

## WALK 87: FRANZ SENN HUT (2147m: 7044ft)

| | |
|---|---|
| Valley base: | Neustift or Milders |
| Start: | Oberiss (1742m: 5715ft) |
| Distance: | 3km (2 miles) one way |
| Time: | 1hr to the hut |
| Total ascent: | 405m (1329ft) |
| Map: | Kompass Wanderkarte 83 'Stubaier Alpen Serleskamm' 1:50,000 |

*This large and extremely busy hut is located near the head of the Oberbergtal, which feeds into the main Stubaital at Milders, a short distance upstream from Neustift. It was named in honour of the well-known local priest who did much to promote tourism in the Stubai Alps during the 19th century, and who originally suggested the construction of a hut here in the Alpeinertal (the upper reaches of the Oberbergtal). The hut is used not only as a base for walkers and climbers, but has plenty of patronage from day visitors, which is not surprising when one considers its ease of access and the range of opportunities available for extending any walk from it. Suggestions will be made at the end of the route description.*

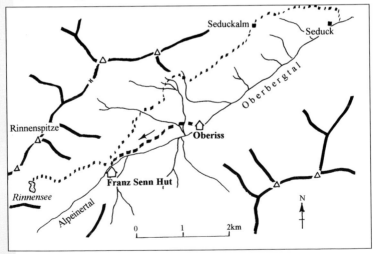

The surfaced road through the Oberbergtal ends about 9km (5½ miles) upstream of Milders at a parking area for the Oberiss Hut. (There are several other parking areas before this.) From here the Senn Hut path, which dates from 1907, strikes west across meadows and after about 10mins or so it divides. Both branches lead to the Senn Hut and come together some way before it. The preferred path is the right-hand option which climbs the steepening hillside in a series of zigzags, and provides views of snowfields, glaciers and waterfalls in the amphitheatre of mountains ahead. The hut soon comes into view and, after being joined by the alternative trail, the path goes along the right-hand side of a stream, rises again, this time over slabs, then crosses the stream by a bridge to gain the hut.

*The Franz Senn Hut*

*The Franz Senn Hut was first built in 1885, but the original two-storey building was enlarged in 1909, and again in 1932–33. Further extensions and adaptations have been made since, and the present four-storey building can accommodate 84 in bedrooms, and 176 in dormitories. Owned by the Austrian Alpine Club a full restaurant service is in operation from mid-February to mid-May, and from mid-June to the beginning of October (Tel: 05226 2218).*

One of the most popular excursions from the hut leads to the beautiful Rinnensee (2650m), a small tarn situated on the hillside west of the hut and below the Rinnenspitze. From the tarn magnificent reflected views of the Ruderhofspitze and Seespitze underline its popularity. (Reached by a marked path in 1½hrs.) An alternative walk suggestion heads directly through the valley behind the hut, following the Alpeiner Bach upstream towards the glacier at its head.

To return to the Oberbergtal a longer option than retracing the upward path is to follow the interesting Franz Senn Weg northeast to Seduckalm, and descend from there to Seduck in the valley. (Allow 3–3½hrs from the hut.) See also Walk 88.

## WALK 88: STARKENBURGER HUT (2237m: 7339ft)

| | |
|---|---|
| Valley base: | Neustift |
| Start: | Franz Senn Hut (2147m: 7044ft) |
| Distance: | 14km (8½ miles) |
| Time: | 6–6½hrs (hut to hut) |
| Total ascent: | c.500m (1640ft) |
| Descent: | c.400m (1312ft) |
| Map: | Kompass Wanderkarte 83 'Stubaier Alpen Serleskamm' 1:50,000 |

*Set upon a spur below the Hoher Burgstall, some 1200m (4000ft) above Neustift, the Starkenburger Hut commands an impressive panorama that includes much of the route followed by the Stubai hut to hut tour which ends here. To the south the north face of Habicht looks very fine, while the view southwest and west shows a glaciated horizon of peaks. There are several ways by which to approach the hut, but the walk suggested here is one of the longest. A full day's pleasuring should be had, for not only is the trail itself both varied and interesting, but the quality of the scenery is first class. And it makes an obvious extension to Walk 87.*

Crossing the bridge over the Alpeiner Bach by the Franz Senn Hut the path heads northeast, ignoring another trail which cuts

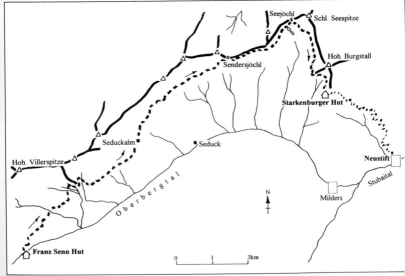

left (for the Rinnensee) and, soon after, a second path which heads up to the Horntaler Joch. Route 117, the Franz Senn Weg, contours easily for a while along the left flank of the valley, but then it

*The Starkenburger Hut*

climbs over small rocky promontories, and in places crosses patches of erosion with a small chance of stonefall, although this is short-lived. Mostly the way is clear and untroubled.

After about 2hrs you will reach the building of Seduckalm (2249m) where there's an opportunity for simple refreshment. An alternative path breaks off down to the valley, while ours slants up the hillside, angling across the upper slopes of the Hohe Schöne in order to gain the ridge at the 2477m Sendersjöchl, which gives a sudden view north into the shallow but broad Senderstal. To the northeast a first hint of the Dolomitic-looking Kalkkogel comes as a complete surprise, for there's nothing remotely like these savage peaks to be seen anywhere near the Franz Senn Hut.

Instead of crossing the Sendersjöchl the path continues along the ridge among masses of alpine flowers before cutting round the boulder-strewn slopes of the Steinkogel above a pair of small tarns with an uninterrupted view of the Schlicker Seespitze and its great fan of screes. The way goes to the Seejöchl (2518m) where there's a junction of trails, then breaks off to the right (southeast) across the screes at the foot of the Schlicker Seespitze whose organ-pipe formations tower overhead, then round the base of the Hoher Burgstall to a grassy saddle which acts as a grandstand from which to study the length of the Oberbergtal and the distant speck of the Franz Senn Hut. A short descent leads directly to the Starkenburger Hut.

*The Starkenburger Hut is DAV owned, and with places for 56 in bedrooms and dormitories. Wardened, with meals provided, from early June to early October (Tel: 05226 2867). Descent from here to Neustift takes about 1½–2hrs.*

## WALK 89: GRUTTEN HUT (1620m: 5315ft)

| | |
|---|---|
| Valley base: | Ellmau, Söll or Scheffau |
| Start: | Scheffau (744m: 2441ft) |
| Distance: | 15km (9 miles) in all |
| Time: | 6½hrs (4hrs to the hut) |
| Total ascent: | 876m (2874ft) |
| Descent: | 818m (2684ft) |
| Map: | Mayr Wanderkarte 51 'Wilder Kaiser' 1:25,000 |

*Stretching along Austria's frontier with Bavaria, the Northern Limestone Alps are broken into a whole series of mountain groups. The Kaisergebirge is a compact group accessible from Kufstein in the west, and a whole string of attractive resorts to the south. Several huts are dotted along the flanks of both the Zahmer ('Tame') Kaiser and the Wilder ('Wild') Kaiser to answer the needs of both walkers and climbers, for whom there's tremendous scope on the soaring crags. This approach to the Grutten Hut follows a section of the so-called Wilder-Kaiser-Steig, a route that makes a complete traverse of the Wilder Kaiser's south face. The walk begins in Scheffau and ends in Ellmau, the two villages being linked by bus.*

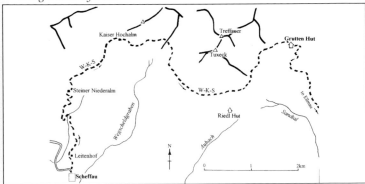

From Scheffau church walk uphill to where the main street makes a sharp left-hand bend. A footpath rises directly ahead and leads to a service road at Leitenhof. Follow this to the right until it curves towards a farm, then break away on a path signposted to Kaiser Hochalm. On reaching another narrow road bear left, and 1min later turn right on a track. When this reaches a house, turn right on a second track which you follow as far as the Steiner Niederalm (1087m). A narrow path continues ahead, picking a way steeply up the hillside to a crossing path, the Wilder-Kaiser-Steig – although there's no indication at first that this is the WKS.

Bear right through beechwoods, then out to a wild mountain scene. Kaiser Hochalm (1417m) is reached in a little under 2½hrs from Scheffau. Pass the alm buildings up a slope to a high point, beyond which you descend a short but steep pitch on hewn-out steps, then wander towards a fan of screes. (Watch for chamois here.) Passing through more woodland the WKS path rounds the south flank of Tuxeck, then confronts a vast scree slope with a magnificent view south to the Kitzbüheler Alps. On the far side of the screes, enter yet more woodland where there are two or three path junctions. Keep ahead on the main path, and when at last you

*The Grutten Hut*

leave the woods, the Grutten Hut appears on a jutting spur ahead. The way rises directly to it, hugging the lower crags of Ellmauer Halt (2344m), highest of all Kaisergebirge mountains, on the way.

*The Grutten Hut is a large building with accommodation for 170. First built in 1899, it is owned by the German Alpine Club (DAV) and is manned from early June to mid-October (Tel: 05358 2242). The warden provides a full restaurant service.*

There are several descent routes to choose from, the easiest being a good path which continues east for a short distance, then breaks off to the right, sloping down across screes to reach a roadhead at Wochenbrunner Alm. From there a combination of road, track and footpath leads to Ellmau.

## WALK 90: BRECHHORNHAUS (1660m: 5446ft)

| | |
|---|---|
| Valley base: | Westendorf or Brixen im Thale |
| Start: | Talkaser (1766m: 5794ft) |
| Distance: | 15km (9 miles) in all |
| Time: | 6hrs round trip (1hr to hut) |
| Total ascent: | 297m (974ft) |
| Descent: | 1207m (3960ft) |
| Map: | Mayr Wanderkarte 56 'Brixental' 1:25,000 |

*The little resort of Westendorf lies to the west of Kitzbühel among mostly grass-covered mountains that attract walkers of modest ambition. Chairlifts and gondolas give access to the upper slopes of some of these mountains, from which countless trails provide almost unlimited opportunities for both short and easy, and long days of activity. The following walk visits a privately-owned hut from the top station of the Alpenrose gondola lift, then climbs to the summit of the 1957m Gampenkogel before descending through a 'back-of-beyond' valley for a devious return to Westendorf.*

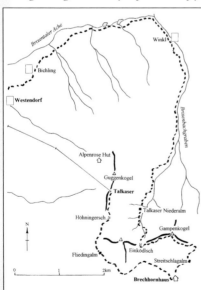

The Alpenrose gondola ferries walkers and paragliding enthusiasts to the upper slopes of the Nachsollberg, on whose northwest flank sits the DAV-owned Alpenrosehütte. The upper station of this lift is known as Talkaser, and it stands on a broad ridge below the summit of the Guggenkögel (1886m). A diversion to the summit is recommended, if you have time. But for the main walk, take the track which slopes southward from Talkaser down to the Höhningerscharte saddle and a junction of trails. One of these makes a pleasant short-cut to the Brechhornhaus. However, on this occasion it is preferable to stay on the track as it curves round the hillside and soon reaches Jausenstation Fleidingalm. Just beyond this the track forks. Take the upper

216

branch, rising in a gentle curve, and at the next fork continue on the main track which leads directly to Berggasthaus Brechhornhaus.

*Berggasthaus Brechhornhaus serves as a restaurant by day, but has 30 beds and 20 dormitory places. Open from mid-December to the end of October (Tel: 0663 59342).*

*Talkaser Niederalm*

Continue on the track beyond the tall shingle-walled building until you reach a grass-covered saddle at Streitschlagalm. Take a path left of the alm buildings and soon enter trees. Just before the trail leaves these, head left on another path to climb a steep slope among alpenrose, juniper and bilberry, so to gain the summit of the Gampenkogel which is marked by a tall wooden cross. Descend the western slopes with care, and on coming to the Einködlscharte saddle bear right, cross a fence and continue down a narrow trail to the upper pastures of the Brixenbachgraben valley.

Make your way to the farm buildings of Talkaser Niederalm at 1462m. A track begins here, crossing to the right-hand side of the valley. Instead of taking this, however, it is better to take instead a waymarked path on the left flank. Though thin in places, it eventually brings you onto the same track much lower down. Stay with this for about 1½hrs, keeping close to the Brixenbach stream for much of the way until just before reaching Brixen railway station. Bear left on a minor road and follow signs to Westendorf alongside streams and through meadows.

# WALK 91: BOCHUMER HUT (1432m: 4698ft)

| | |
|---|---|
| Valley base: | Kitzbühel |
| Start: | Hechenmoos (820m: 2690ft) |
| Distance: | 11km (6½ miles) to the hut |
| Time: | 5hrs |
| Total ascent: | 1275m (4183ft) |
| Map: | Mayr Wanderkarte 55 'Kitzbühel' 1:25,000 |

*South of Kitzbühel the mountains are little more than big green hills, with occasional upthrusting peaks of bare rock jutting from them. Cattle graze their ridges, and clusters of small tarns lie on gentle saddles amid bogs of cotton-grass. There are neither glaciers nor permanent snowfields, but footpaths are plentiful and the hillwalker can spend weeks exploring – almost always with snowy Alps rimming the horizon. This walk makes a devious approach to the Bochumer Hut (it could be reached in 1½hrs from Hechenmoos) by way of remote working alms, two cols and a rocky summit. On a clear summer's day there are vast panoramas to enjoy.*

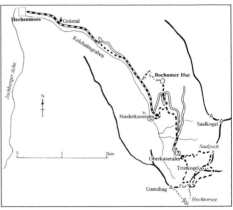

About 6km south of Kitzbühel on the Jochberg/Pass Thurn road, the small village of Hechenmoos is served by bus. From here wander into the Kelchalmgraben glen whose road starts beside Gasthof Hechenmoos. When this forks take the right branch. After passing the tiny Grüntal chapel the road is unpaved and the valley uninhabited, except during the summer months when farmers occupy the upper alms. Using footpath options as and when they occur, continue towards the head of the valley until the service road cuts left at Niederkaseralm. Now take a path which rises behind the farm, then curves left to give distant views of the Kaisergebirge. Briefly rejoin the road, but almost immediately break off to the right on the continuing path. Again you rejoin the road, then when it forks keep ahead through a gate, and as you approach another farm (Oberkaseralm) take a path cutting up the slope to it, and continue from there to the obvious col known as Tor (1933m) which lies between the rocky summits of Tristkogel (left) and Gamshag. Big views ahead show the Glemmtal and a great mass of hills and far-off mountains. (A 15min diversion to the right leads to the attractive Hochtorsee where another option is to climb the Gamshag in an hour's round trip.)

*The Bochumer Hut*

Bear left and very soon the path forks. Either take the lower option across the east flank of the Tristkogel, or use the alternative path which climbs steeply in 20mins to the summit. Descent to the northeast should only be attempted by experienced hillwalkers with a good head for heights, otherwise return by the same path and join the east flank route. The two paths rejoin on the grassy northeast ridge of the mountain, then slope down to the Saaljoch where you bear left. A thin path now crosses open pastures (more big views) and meanders down to Oberkaseralm. Reverse your upward route, but when the path brings you onto the road a little above Niederkaseralm, bear right, then left on a path leading directly to the Bochumer Hut.

*The Bochumer Hut is owned by the DAV and has 70 places. It's permanently open, and has a restaurant service (Tel: 0663 56521). Allow 45mins to descend to Hechenmoos.*

# WALK 92: SCHÖNLEITEN HUT (1804m: 5919ft)

| | |
|---|---|
| Valley base: | Saalbach |
| Start: | Saalbach (1002m: 3287ft) |
| Distance: | 12km (7½ miles) to the hut |
| Time: | 4½hrs |
| Total ascent: | 908m (2979ft) |
| Map: | Mayr Wanderkarte 72 'Saalbach Hinterglemm' 1:25,000 |

*The Glemmtal flows roughly eastward a little north of Zell am See. That its two main resorts, Saalbach and Hinterglemm, have become extemely popular among walkers, is easy to understand, for the valley is walled by friendly green hills that invite rather than challenge, that have numerous well-marked footpaths and trackways winding across them, while from their ridge crests groups of more demanding mountains crowd every horizon. The walk suggested here is part of the Saalachtaler Höhenweg, a ridge-walk of considerable charm, and one to enjoy for its full variety.*

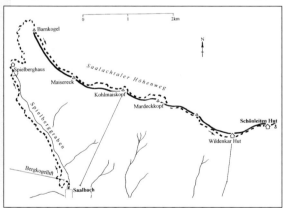

The first place to aim for is the Spielberghaus northwest of Saalbach. Walk up the service road left of the Bernkogellift, and when it forks by some houses take the right branch and continue up the road until it makes a left-hand bend. Go through a gate on the right, cross a meadow and then follow the Pascherweg trail through forest and among clumps of bilberry. Eventually this path spills onto a jeep road which you follow to the Spielberghaus (1319m). Immediately past this turn right on a narrow trail climbing to a track. Turn right as far as the farm buildings of Wirtsalm. Take the left-hand track which rises steadily, but before long break off on a signposted path climbing to the right. This leads to the viewpoint of Barnkogel (1709m) and the start of the Saalachtaler Höhenweg. (With sufficient time and energy, the ascent of nearby 2044m Spielberghorn is highly recommended – allow 2½hrs to get there and back.)

The Saalachtaler Höhenweg heads southeast on an undulating course, at first among trees with hinted views, then with more open aspects as you near the Kohlmaiskopf. The path avoids this summit and its gondola lift by skirting the north flank, then comes onto a saddle just to the east. The way continues along the left-hand side of the ridge with fine views to the Leoganger Steinberge range. On coming to a path junction bear left round the north side of the Mardeckkopf and regain the ridge near an emergency

*The Saalachtaler Höhenweg above the Schönleiten Hut*

shelter. Beyond this the trail runs along the narrowing crest with a panorama that includes Hohe Tauern snowpeaks and the limestone wall of the Steinernes Meer. Pass beyond the curious, half-circular Wildenkar Hut and keep on the grassy crest as it slopes down to a saddle to reach Hotel Seidlalm and the Schönleiten Hut.

*The Schönleiten Hut is privately owned with 80 places in bedrooms and dormitories, and a full meals service. Open from late June to mid-October (Tel: 06541 7229).*

A quick return to Saalbach next day is possible by retracing the ridge as far as the Kohlmaiskopf (1hr) and riding the gondola lift down. Alternatively, continue along the ridge, crossing the Geierkogel, Haiderbergkogel and Sausteige, then descend to the Jahn Hut where a clear track continues down to Viehhofen in the valley – allow 4–5hrs.

# WALK 93: BÜRGL HUT (1699m: 5574ft)

| | |
|---|---|
| Valley base: | Zell am See |
| Start: | Schmittenhöhe (1965m: 6447ft) |
| Distance: | 32km (20 miles) in all |
| Time: | 11–12hrs in all (8–8½hrs to hut) |
| Total ascent: | c750m (2461ft) |
| Descent: | c1900m (6235ft) |
| Map: | Freytag & Berndt 382 'Zell am See, Kaprun, Saalbach' 1:50,000 |

*There are two main destinations on the Pinzgauer Spaziergang – a sce-nic high-level traverse of the long ridge system stretching west from Zell am See. The shorter and more popular of the two breaks away from the ridge near the Hochkogel and heads north to the Schattberg and Saalbach. The longer version continues beyond the Hochkogel – almost as far again as the distance from Schmittenhöhe – before descending the south side to Mittersill in the upper Salzach Valley via the Bürgl Hut. It's a challenging walk, and a very rewarding one, while an overnight at the simple dairy farm-cum-mountain hut will surely be a unique and memorable experience.*

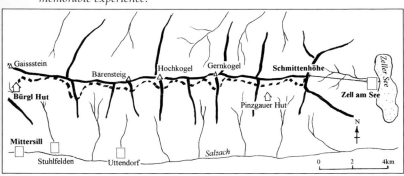

Take the cable-car from Zell am See to the Schmittenhöhe, then go down a wide track to the left with views south to the Hohe Tauern mountains. At a major junction of tracks turn right and descend to a grassy saddle by a small ski hut. Ascend the slope opposite, but near the top veer left on a narrow path among shrubs. In an hour or so from the Schmittenhöhe pass above the Hochsonnberg Alm and continue across open pastures. The way sweeps round a large basin, briefly visits the Rohrertörl, then crosses a spur projecting from the Gernkogel. There's a junction of paths and a turnstile. Through this maintain direction round another large basin and pass a small emergency shelter – useful in a storm, but without any facilities.

*Walkers on the Pinzgauer Spaziergang en route to the Bürgl Hut*

About 3hrs along the Spaziergang you will come to a major trail junction southeast of the Hochkogel, and another emergency shelter. The right-hand path breaks off to Saalbach in the Glemmtal (a splendid walk in its own right), while we continue ahead on the Uttendorf path. This contours round the steep slopes of Hochkogel, curves round yet another pastoral basin, then forks at a marshy area. Keep right and climb round the southern slopes of the Bärensteig (the left-hand trail descends to Uttendorf). Cross a spur by an electricity pylon and continue over more pool-dotted pastures.

The way now follows the ridge crest and descends to the Sommertor saddle. Continue along the ridge for a further 10mins and at the next junction bear right to climb steeply. Rounding the Marnitz Kogel cross a pastureland, and pass above the solitary Hoch Alm building beyond which you catch sight of the Bürgl Hut below.

*The privately-owned Bürgl Hut is in fact a dairy farm with dormitory and simple bedroom facilities for about 35. Open from June to mid-October with meals provision (Tel: 06522 4526).*

On leaving, simply follow the farm track/road down to either Mittersill or Stuhlfelden for transport (train or bus) back to Zell am See.

## WALK 94: STATZERHAUS (2117m: 6946ft)

| | |
|---|---|
| Valley base: | Zell am See |
| Start: | Thumersbach (756m: 2480ft) |
| Distance: | 21km (13 miles) round trip |
| Time: | 9hrs in all (4½–5hrs to hut) |
| Total ascent: | 1361m (4465ft) |
| Map: | Kompass Wanderkarte 030 'Zell am See-Kaprun' 1:30,000 |

*Zell am See is one of Austria's most popular 'lakes and mountains' resorts. At the northern end of its valley stands the limestone wall of the Steinernes Meer, to the south the graceful snow peaks of the Hohe Tauern, while to east and west grass-covered mountains make attractive neighbours. On the summit of the Hundstein across the Zeller lake, the Statzerhaus is a simple mountain hut with a 360° panorama of great variety and beauty. The normal way of approach is from the north via Maria Alm, but the following route begins in Thumersbach on the east shore of the Zeller See, and traces the complete Hundstein horseshoe – a fine, two-day outing.*

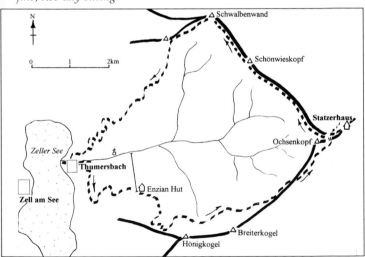

From the jetty at Thumersbach walk up to the village and cross directly ahead into Talstrasse. Take the first road on the right, Erlberg Weg, and follow this for about 1.5km. At the first hairpin bend after passing Jausenstation Schönblick bear left on a footpath to the Enzian Hut. Continue along a track beyond the hut, winding through forest with occasional views to the Kitzsteinhorn. Whenever there are alternative tracks or paths the way to the Hundstein is obvious. Eventually forest gives way to high slopes of pasture, with the track cutting along the right-hand side of a ridge. Then, just below the Ochsenkopf, the track turns down towards an isolated farm. At this point take a path ahead leading to a junction of trails at 1931m. The ridge facing rises to the Hundstein summit. One trail climbs this ridge (steep but not difficult), while another skirts the left flank, passes below the summit, then cuts back along a track to reach the Statzerhaus.

*The Statzerhaus, or Hundstein Hut, is owned by the Austrian Touring Club (ÖTK) and is manned from Easter until mid-October. Simple meals provision, and places for 33 (Tel: 06542 4438).*

Leaving the summit go back down the ridge to the trail junction between Hundstein and Ochsenkopf, and take the right-hand option towards

*Evening view from the Statzerhaus*

the Schwalbenwand. This soon leads to a grassy saddle and another junction. Ignore the descending path and take that which climbs the ridge crest. About 1½hrs from the Statzerhaus gain the cross-marked summit of Schönwieskopf (1994m), then continue along the ridge to the Schwalbenkopf (2011m) whose 'summit' cross is not on the actual summit, but a few metres beyond. Turn sharp left and follow marker posts, then waymarks, down a broad grassy ridge to another large cross at 1895m. Descend open pastureland to a major path heading roughly south. Easing along the left side of the ridge, pass through forest and follow waymarks to a forest road, and there turn right. At Mitterberghof bear left on a metalled road, then take another waymarked path that eventually leads to Thumersbach.

# WALK 95: SALZBURGER HUT (1867m: 6125ft)

| | |
|---|---|
| Valley base: | Kaprun or Zell am See |
| Start: | Maiskogel (1540m: 5052ft) |
| Distance: | 9km (5½ miles) one way |
| Time: | 4½–5hrs to the hut |
| Total ascent: | 894m (2933ft) |
| Descent: | 473m (1552ft) |
| Map: | Kompass 030 'Zell am See, Europa Sport Region' 1:30,000 |

*Overlooking the valley of the Salzach River on the northern edge of the Hohe Tauern, the shapely Kitzsteinhorn (3203m) attracts skiers in summer as well as winter.*

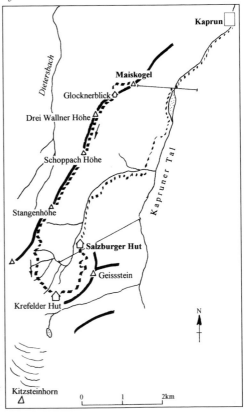

Below the glaciers that support summer skiing stands the Krefelder Hut, while below that, nestling in a quiet basin of pastureland, is the little rustic Salzburger Hut. The approach suggested here makes a long ridge-walk south from the Maiskogel (cable-car from Kaprun), with big snow- and ice-capped peaks in view most of the way. It leads first to the Krefelder Hut, then descends steeply to the Salzburger Hut, with a superb continuing route down to the valley next day.

From the southern outskirts of Kaprun, take the

cable-car to the summit of the Maiskogel. If you prefer to walk all the way, allow 2hrs for this from Kaprun. From Maiskogel take a broad track winding round the forested hillside and rising to Alpengasthof Glocknerblick, where a path strikes uphill among trees and, 3mins later, forks. Take the left branch and continue to rise through pastures, then alpenroses, to gain the cross-marked crown of the Drei Wallner Höhe (1861m). The path now descends to a saddle before climbing to another high point on the ridge with Hohe Tauern snowpeaks dazzling ahead. The Schoppach Höhe (2069m) is also marked by a cross, and as you continue along the ridge you can gaze down into the Grubbach glen, near the head of which will be found the Salzburger Hut.

The path, the Alexander-Enzinger-Weg, avoids the next few tops by cutting along the left (east) flank, more or less following the 2070m contour, before sloping down to another saddle at 2055m. From this point the path climbs to the highest part of the ridge (Stangenhöhe: 2212m) which is not so much a summit as a narrow section of ridge safe-guarded by a length of

*The Salzburger Hut*

fixed cable. At the end of this section the trail deserts the ridge, slants down the grassy left flank and comes to a large cairn marking a junction of paths. The left-hand option makes a short-cut down to the Salzburger Hut, but we continue ahead, over a rucked hillside, to reach the **Krefelder Hut** (80 places, open July to end-September, meals provided; Tel: 06547 7780). Take path 711 directly below the hut towards the shark's fin of the Geissstein (lovely views), then twist down its left-hand slope and zigzag below a cable-car station to reach the Salzburger Hut.

*The Salzburger Hut has only 5 dormitory places. Owned by the ÖTK it is open from mid-June to end-September. Meals provided (Tel: 06549 349).*

Descent to the valley is by a steep and narrow, but glorious, path directly below the hut. Among alpenrose and bilberry, following streams and dodging in and out of forest, it's an ever-varied walk. Allow 3hrs to reach Kaprun.

## WALK 96: KALS-MATREIER-TÖRLHAUS (2207m: 7241ft)

| | |
|---|---|
| Valley base: | Matrei-in-Osttirol |
| Start: | Goldried (2100m: 6890ft) |
| Distance: | 8km (5 miles) in all |
| Time: | 2½–3hrs in all |
| Total ascent: | 110m (361ft) |
| Descent: | 885m (2904ft) |
| Map: | Kompass Wanderkarte 48 'Kals am Grossglockner' 1:50,000 |

*The Granatspitz Group of mountains forms a long ridge-like block extending in a north–south direction and linking the Venediger and Glockner Groups in the Hohe Tauern National Park. Towards the south-ernmost extent of this ridge the Kals-Matreier-Törlhaus occupies a saddle overlooking the Tauerntal to the west and the Dorfertal to the east. Since it is easily accessible by chairlifts from both valleys, and the walk which links the two is the noted Europa Panoramaweg, the hut receives lots of patronage from day visitors. But once the chairlifts have stopped running it settles to a more peaceful ambience. A variety of walks are pos-sible from the hut, some of which are mentioned below, while the route described is the short but classic traverse of the Panoramaweg, from*

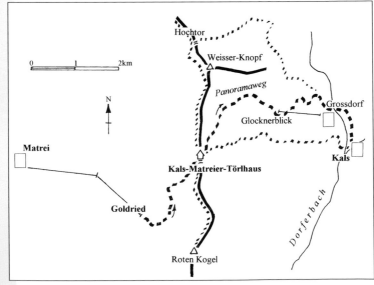

*which it is claimed that no less than sixty 3000 metre mountains are visible. In July the trail is bordered by a mass of alpine flowers.*

Thanks to a series of jeep tracks that switchback up the mountain-side above Matrei, there is little point in walking the first part of the ascent. Instead you are advised to ride the two-section Goldried chairlift which gives exhilarating views, and effectively reduces the hut approach to no more than an hour. (If it is your intention to return to Matrei at the end of the walk, it is worth buying a combined ticket which is valid for both the chairlift and the Postbus from Kals back to Matrei.) From the chairlift top station bear right onto a broad and easily-graded track which soon curves northeast round the hillside and leads directly to the saddle and the hut, and a junction of paths.

*Kals-Matreier-Törlhaus*

*The Kals-Matreier-Törlhaus is privately owned. Open from the beginning of July to the end of September (check at the tourist office in Matrei for bookings), the hut has places for 14 in bedrooms and 9 dormitory spaces. Meals are provided when open.*

Whilst the Europa Panoramaweg continues on the eastern side of the ridge by heading northeast, there are several other walks on offer from the Törlhaus. The shortest heads south along the ridge to the 2762m viewpoint of the Roten Kogel. Another strikes off to the north along the Sudetendeutsch Höhenweg. This impressive route has several fixed rope safeguards between the Kals-Matreier-Törlhaus and the Sudetendeutsch Hut (3–3½hrs), but it also provides an alternative route down to the Dorfertal from the Hochtor saddle. A final option from the Törlhaus cuts steeply down the eastern hillside below the Panoramaweg as a direct descent to Kals-am-Grossglockner.

Resuming the Europa Panoramaweg the trail angles easily across the hillside with ever-expanding views and signs at all junctions. On gaining the Glocknerblick chairlift (1970m) where most walkers call a halt, the continuing path descends below it and twists down to Grossdorf, a short distance from Kals.

## WALK 97: NASSFELDHAUS (1513m: 4964ft)

| | |
|---|---|
| Valley base: | Hermagor |
| Start: | Nassfeld Pass (1530m. 5020ft) |
| Distance: | 12km (7½ miles) in all |
| Time: | 5–5½hrs round trip |
| Total ascent: | 516m (1693ft) |
| Map: | Kompass Wanderkarte 'Gailtaler Alpen, Karnische Alpen'   1:50,000 |

*Carrying the Austro-Italian border east of the Dolomites, the Carnic Alps are ragged limestone peaks of modest stature, but considerable charm. For the most part they create a southern wall to the gentle Gailtal, and the classic walk here is the multi-day high route known as the Karnischer Höhenweg which frequently dodges from one side of the international frontier to the other. One of the huts used as a staging post on this walk is the Nassfeldhaus built in 1970 near the Nassfeld road pass southwest of Hermagor, a hut as popular with skiers in winter as it is with walkers in summer. The route suggested below is a circular one* using the Nassfeldhaus as a base. It follows part of the Karnischer Höhenweg along the frontier ridge, but also explores the lovely rolling pastures from which the mountains spring.

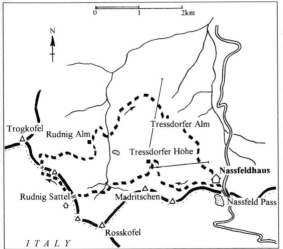

About 100m north of the pass, a footpath heads west marked to Rossalm, Rosskofel and Trogkofel. Crossing high pastures it soon curves roughly northwest, then north towards Tressdorfer Höhe where a large building services the ski industry. At trail junctions the route to take is that marked for Rosskofel and Trogkofel. On a saddle just short of Tressdorfer Höhe, join the Karnische

Höhenweg and descend southwest to more pastures with shrubs, trees and clear streams, then climb into increasingly stony country towards the Rudnig Sattel. Weaving among rocks and boulders, then up a final slope, the trail brings you to the Rudnig Sattel (1945m) on the Austro-Italian frontier. Bare mountain peaks rise to right and left, while just below on the Italian slope there's a small, orange-coloured bivouac hut.

*Rudnig Alm near the Nassfeldhaus*

Bear right (northwest) here and keep along the frontier crest. The path soon strays onto the Italian flank, then regains the ridge once more at another saddle immediately below the southeast face of the Trogkofel. Cross back into Austria and descend a waymarked trail in tight zigzags, then into a boulder tip where it forks. Take the right branch which leads over a hillside spur, then descends to a stream and a track. Bear left to the dairy farm at Rudnig Alm (refreshments available).

Descend in front of the alm to a crossing path, and turn right. In a few paces the path divides. Continue ahead on the upper trail, soon among trees where you cross the Rudnig Bach. On the eastern side of the stream the way progresses as a pleasant forest walk with signs leading the way to Tressdorfer Alm and Sonnenalpe Nassfeld where you'll find the hut.

*The Nassfeldhaus is owned by the Hermagor Section of the ÖAV. It has places for 18 in bedrooms and 100 in dormitories. Open from mid-June to the end of September, meals provided (Tel: 04285 8276).*

## WALK 98: JULIUS-SEITNER HUT (1185m: 3898ft)

| | |
|---|---|
| Valley base: | Türnitz |
| Start: | Türnitz (466m: 1529ft) |
| Distance: | 13km (8 miles) round trip |
| Time: | 2½hrs up, 2hrs down |
| Total ascent: | 725m (2379ft) |
| Map: | 'Wanderkarte Türnitz' 1:25,000 |

*South of St Pölten in Lower Austria, the Traisen valley pushes into a region of modest but charming wooded mountains. The valley and its feeder glens are drained by clear trout streams, and a branch line of the Federal railway system serves a string of small towns and villages along the main valley. Türnitz lies at the end of an offshoot of this line; a trim, peaceful little town with a variety of walks radiating from it. Some lead into tributary glens. Others climb to mountain ridges and entice from one easy summit to the next, while the Traisental Rundwanderweg is promoted locally as a multi-day tour of the valley. Northwest of Türnitz the Julius-Seitner Hut perches on the summit of the Eisenstein with panoramic views over a green maze of forested valleys and hills that fold against each other. This circular walk visits the hut and serves as the best possible introduction to the district.*

About 150m southwest of Türnitz church turn north off the main street, cross the bypass road and wander into the Sulzachgraben valley on a lane which soon becomes a track. When it forks take the right-hand option, direction Hochgraser and Eisenstein. The valley narrows, is heavily wooded and noted for two former 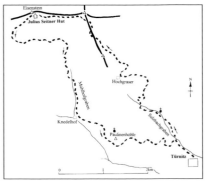 watermills and a tiny chapel. The track forks again. This time take the left branch, soon emerging to open meadows and a farm. Here you go between farm buildings, and continue into a narrow wooded cleave where the track winds uphill. The way narrows as the gradient steepens, and you come to a wooded ridge to join the route of the Traisental Rundwanderweg. Five minutes later by a small shrine at a junction of tracks, bear left and cross an open pasture to reach the Hochgraser farm buildings. Just beyond these turn sharp right and re-enter the forest, but at a major crossing track bear left. The way narrows again on a steady contour before rising to a ridge where the trail strays from one side of the crest to another. Eventually reach a high sloping meadow where a faint path leads to the hut on the Eisenstein summit.

*The Julius-Seitner Hut*

*The shingle-walled Julius-Seitner Hut was built in 1910, and is owned by the Austrian Alpine Club. It has 40 places and is normally staffed throughout July and August, but at weekends only from May to the end of June, and from September to November. Meals are generally available when the guardian is present (Tel: 0222 422657).*

Leaving the hut head southwest, descending across open pastures to the edge of a wood. Bear left and continue downhill, joining a farm track until it enters forest. At this point take a minor track cutting below on the left. The way continues down into the Mühlgraben valley which you follow to the Knedelhof farm, then over meadows to Fohrabauer (another farm). Linking paths and tracks thereafter lead to a farm road that slopes downhill into Türnitz.

# THE JULIAN ALPS OF SLOVENIA

Once part of the Austro-Hungarian empire, then a republic within Tito's Yugoslavia, Slovenia at last gained independence in the political upheavals of the early 1990s. The Slovenes are passionate about their mountains, and show a determination to resist commercial pressures that would devalue the natural beauty of the Julian Alps – especially within the 84,000 hectares (208,000 acres) of the Triglav National Park which was established in 1981. Cablecars and chairlifts that lace many other Alpine groups are missing here, but footpaths are plentiful and within the Park's boundaries there are more than 35 mountain huts – known in the Slovene language as Planinska Koca.

The Julian Alps lie in the northwestern corner of the country where they butt against the Italian border, while Austria's border is marked by the Karawanken range on the northern side of the Sava Dolinika's valley. The Julians are limestone mountains. Though of relatively modest altitude (Triglav is the highest at just 2864m) the valleys are low, thus the difference in altitude between valley bed and mountain summit is, in a number of instances, as great as that of the higher Western Alps.

The valleys are lush with flower-rich pastures and broad-leaved forests. Crystal rivers hasten through them, fed by countless tributary streams and waterfalls. Farmers scythe the June meadows and drape the grass over wooden frames to dry, their alp farms displaying a unique architectural style, their villages oozing a romantic tradition of hospitality.

Within the mountains one gains an impression of untamed wilderness, despite the trails and huts and, on some of the higher peaks, the ironwork of *vie ferratae*. Chamois and marmots are plentiful and, thanks to the limestone, the flora can be breathtaking.

A number of UK travel companies organise all-inclusive holidays to such places as Kranjska Gora, Bled and Bohinj, while independent travellers have a choice of flight or rail to Ljubljana, with onward bus routes (or car hire) into the Julians. Because the mountains are fairly compact and with a fair selection of huts, a two-week holiday could usefully be spent exploring a good part of the Julians on a hut to hut tour.

Guidebooks: *Walking in the Julian Alps* by Simon Brown (Cicerone Press), *Julian Alps* by Robin G Collomb (West Col), and *How to Climb Triglav* by Stanko Klinar (Planinska Zalozba Slovenije, Ljubljana).

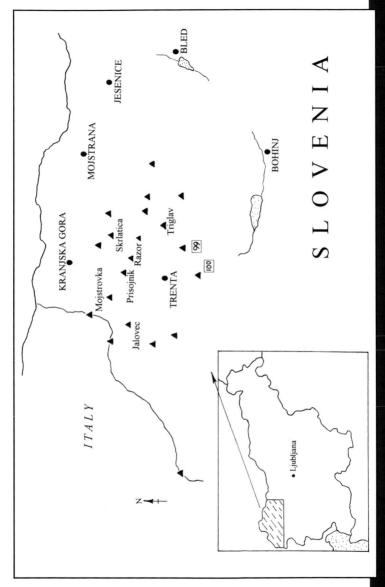

BLED

JESENICE

MOJSTRANA

KRANJSKA GORA

Mojstrovka

Prisojnik

Razor

Skrlatica

Triglav

99

100

TRENTA

Jalovec

ITALY

BOHINJ

S L O V E N I A

N

Ljubljana

235

# WALK 99: TRIGLAV LAKES HUT (1683m: 5522ft)

| | |
|---|---|
| Valley base: | Bohinj |
| Start: | Savici Hut (653m: 2142ft) |
| Distance: | 6km (3½ miles) one way |
| Time: | 3½hrs up, 2–2½hrs down |
| Total ascent: | 1030m (3379ft) |
| Map: | Geodetski zavod Slovenije 'Julijske Alpe' 1:50,000 |

*Situated in the delectable Seven Lakes Valley (Dolina Triglavskih Jezer) southwest of Slovenia's highest mountain, the true name of this refuge is Koca pri Triglavskih Jezerih, but it's better known among English-speaking visitors as the Triglav Lakes Hut. The setting is idyllic, but this approach walk is a tough one with some very steep uphill sections and rough mountain paths. Although it is a popular route for the ascent of Triglav, that particular mountain is not visible from it. However, a string of tarns, larches and alpenroses, and the long limestone wall that contains the valley which lies at the centre of the Triglav National Park, more than compensate.*

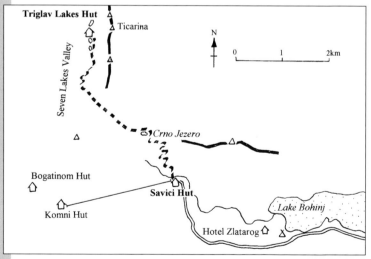

At the western end of Lake Bohinj a dirt road extends beyond a shoreline campsite near Hotel Zlatarog, and leads to Kóca pri Savíci, a hut/restaurant at the roadhead. This is served by public bus from Bohinj, and the restaurant is well-patronised in summer. The path begins between buildings at a bridge over the Savica river where an optimistic sign suggests 2¾hrs for the walk. Having crossed the bridge a broad path enters beechwoods, but after about 200m you break away from this on a rising path to the left – waymarks have a white spot surrounded by a red circle. Gaining height, the altitude is marked every few hundred metres in red paint. The gradient steepens, and in places the path is aided by fixed cable, or with metal rings or pegs hammered into the rock. All this is in forest, the beechwoods of the initial route giving way to conifers. At the top of the steep climb a fine view is gained over Lake Bohinj nearly 700m below.

Easing now the path slips through a wooded cleft and comes to the 'Black Lake' (Crno Jezero, 1294m), so-called because it's trapped some-what gloomily among boulders and the dark conifer woods. Go round the north,

*Dvojno Jezero, one of the Triglav Lakes*

or right-hand, shore and at the far end be careful not to stray too far left on an alternative path which bears the same waymarks as those for our route. The path for the Triglav Lakes Hut goes north-west through a narrow, rocky cleft of a valley, and as it tucks under a steep white cliff, trees begin to thin out. Shortly after passing this cliff the way swings sharply to the right and resumes its steep climb with numerous zigzags in order to gain the upper valley. The way leads to the beautiful larch-studded Komna Plateau and keeps due north, passing to the right of a small tarn and a second soon after, and so gains the hut.

*The Triglav Lakes Hut is a three-storey, shingle and stone building with places for 200, staffed from June to October and with a restaurant service.*

More lakes lie to the north amid wild scenery. The summit of Triglav is about 5hrs from the hut, but in just 1hr Ticarica (2091m) to the east makes a good viewpoint. A recommended alternative return to the valley goes via the Bogatinom and Komni Huts.

# WALK 100: BOGATINOM HUT (1513m: 4964ft)

| | |
|---|---|
| Valley base: | Bohinj |
| Start: | Triglav Lakes Hut (1683m: 5522ft) |
| Distance: | 10km (6 miles) in all |
| Time: | 2½hrs to hut, + 2hrs to roadhead |
| Total descent: | 1030m (3379ft) |
| Map: | Geodetski zavod Slovenije 'Julijske Alpe' 1:50,000 |

*This walk is offered as an alternative return from the Triglav Lakes Hut, and continues from the Bogatinom Hut down to the valley by way of a third hut, the busy Komni. The Bogatinom Hut lies in a sheltered grassy bowl at a junction of cross-country routes, no more than 15mins walk from the Komni which, because of its accessibility, attracts the lion's share of business in the mountains west of Lake Bohinj. This walk passes through a range of different landscapes, mostly vegetated, but with ribs of limestone projecting here and there. There's a good chance of seeing chamois or deer, and bird activity is lively among the trees and shrubs.*

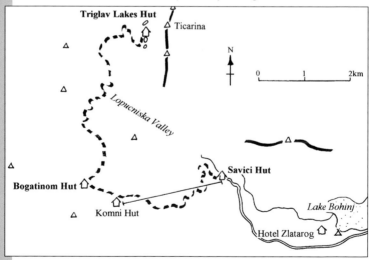

A signpost at the Triglav Lakes gives 2½hrs to the Komni Hut, but fails to mention the Bogatinom, although for the most part the same path is used for both huts. On setting out return to the nearest tarn and take the path which skirts the western (right-hand) side. This soon rises into woodland, initially with a few insignificant ups and downs along the upper rim of the Lopucniska

Valley, before descending to its head. This is richly vegetated with trees and shrubs, but there are also several little open glades, some with modest pools lying in them. After about 30mins come to a path junction with the right-hand trail making for Planina Za

Skalo from where descent is possible to the lovely Trenta Valley. Our route, however, continues ahead, marked to Komni.

Now the way rises up the south flank of the valley, but when it forks after about 5mins, take the upper trail – this is not very clear at first,

*The Bogatinom Hut*

although it is waymarked. After a few more undulations the trail contours round the head of the valley among lush vegetation, and when trees allow, the long line of crags above the Triglav Lakes Hut can be seen to the northeast. Gaining a little plateau where ribs of limestone project among shrubs and dwarf pine, the trail weaves across it, then rises once more to a national park notice board at 1645m. As the route continues note a series of metal direction arrows, some fitted to tall posts – green arrows bear the letter 'K' for the Komni Hut, while red arrows with '7J' indicate the Lakes Hut path. Weaving round numerous hollows filled with shrubs, you suddenly see the large Komni Hut ahead, backed by wild-looking peaklets draped with screes. At another trail junction bear right to gain a high point from which you look down onto the Bogatinom Hut.

*Kóca Pod Bogatinom enjoys a secluded location, but no real views. It can sleep 56 and meals are provided when manned – usually June to October, and January to May.*

To continue down to the Savici roadhead follow a broad path to the *Komni Hut* where an obvious woodland trail descends through beechwoods and passes close to the well-known Slap Savica waterfall.

## APPENDIX A

USEFUL ADDRESSES

**Alpine and Mountaineering Organisations with Reciprocal Rights in Huts:**

Alpine Club
55 Charlotte Road
London EC2A 3QT

Austrian Alpine Club (UK Branch)
PO Box 43
Welwyn Garden City
Herts. AL8 6PQ

British Mountaineering
Council
177–179 Burton Road
Manchester M20 2BB

### Guidebook Publishers:

Cicerone Press
2 Police Square
Milnthorpe
Cumbria LA7 7PY

Inghams
10–18 Putney Hill
London SW15 6AX

Cordee
3a De Montfort Street
Leicester LE1 7HD

West Col Productions
Goring
Reading
Berks. RG8 9AA

### Map Suppliers:

Cordee
3a De Montfort Street
Leicester LE1 7HD

The Map Shop
15 High Street
Upton-Upon-Severn
Worcs. WR8 0HJ

Edward Stanford Ltd.
12–14 Long Acre
London WC2E 9LP

World Leisure Marketing
11 Newmarket Court
Newmarket Drive
Derby DE 24 8NW

### Tourist Information:

Austrian National Tourist Office
14 Cork Street
London W1X 1PF

Italian State Tourist Office
1 Princes Street
London W1R 8AY

Swiss National Tourist Office
Swiss Court
London W1V 8EE

French Government Tourist
Office
178 Piccadilly
London W1V 0AL

Slovenian Tourist Board
Center za Promocijo Turizma
Slovenije
Dunajska 156
1000 Ljubljana
Slovenia

# APPENDIX B

SUGGESTED EQUIPMENT LIST

Experienced hill walkers will no doubt have their own equipment preferences, but for first-time visitors to the Alps the following may help.

**Clothing:**
* Walking boots – must be comfortable, well-fitting, with ankle support and plenty of grip in the soles
* Wind- and waterproof anorak/cagoule and overtrousers
* Woollen hat and sunhat
* Gloves/mittens
* Gaiters (optional, but useful in snow or long wet grass)
* Fleece or woollen sweater
* Shirts – 2–3 for fortnight's holiday
* Warm long trousers/breeches (not jeans which when wet become very cold)
* Shorts (optional)
* Tracksuit or similar for evenings in huts
* Long woollen socks
* Underwear
* Trainers or similar for hut wear

**Miscellaneous:**
* Rucksack – with waterproof liner and/or cover
* Sheet sleeping bag (for overnights in huts)
* Bivouac bag (polythene) – in case of emergencies
* Trekking pole(s) (very useful on steep descents, scree, snow, stream crossings)
* Headtorch + spare batteries & bulbs
* Water bottle
* Sunglasses, suncream/sunblock & lip salve
* Washing kit and small towel (not supplied in huts)
* First aid
* Map(s) and compass
* Whistle
* Watch
* Guidebook(s)
* Alpine Club (or similar) membership card for discount rates in huts
* Emergency repair kit
* Handkerchiefs
* Toilet paper
* Penknife
* Camera & binoculars (optional)

*Food:*
* Lunch supplies
* Emergency reserves (sweets, chocolate, dried fruit, glucose tablets, or biscuits Teabags, coffee, sugar, powdered m i l k , m u e s l i , packet soups etc (hot water can be bought at most huts)

# APPENDIX C
## GLOSSARY

| English | French | German | Italian |
| --- | --- | --- | --- |
| alp (high past./farm) | alp | alp/alm | alpe |
| bakery | boulangerie | bäckerei | panetteria |
| bread | pain | bröt | pane |
| breakfast | petit déjeuner | frühstück | prima colazione |
| bridge | pont | brücke | ponte |
| cableway | télépherique | seilbahn | teleferica/funivia |
| cairn | cairn | steinmann | mucchio di pietre |
| campsite | le camping | zeltplatz | campeggio |
| chairlift | télésiège | sesselbahn | seggovia |
| closed | fermé | geschlossen | chiuso |
| cold | froid | kält | freddo |
| crest (ridge) | crête | kamn | cresta |
| danger | danger | gefahr | pericolo |
| dinner | diner | abendessen | pranzo/cena |
| dormitory | dortoir | matratzenlager | dormitorio |
| bunk beds | couchettes | – | cuccetta |
| east | est | ost | est |
| exchange (currency) | change | geldwechsel | cambio |
| footpath/trail | sentier/chemin | wanderweg/bergweg | sentiero |
| free | libre | frei | libero |
| full (accommodation) | complet | besetzt | completo |
| full-board | pension complète | vollpension | pensione completa |
| glacier | glacier | gletscher | ghiaccaio/verdretta |
| gorge/ravine | gorge/ravin | schlucht | burrone |
| half-board | demi-pension | halbpension | mezza pensione |
| help | aide/secours | hilfe | soccorsa |
| high route | haute route | höhenweg | alta via |
| hotel | hôtel/auberge | hotel/gasthof | albergo |
| hour | heure | stunde | ora |
| hut | refuge | hütte | capanna/rifugio |
| keeper | gardien | – | custode |
| lake | lac | see | lago |
| left (direction) | gauche | links | sinistra |
| lightning | éclair/foudre | blitz | lampo/fulmine |
| lunch | déjeuner | mitagessen | pranzo |
| map | carte | karte/wanderkarte | carta geografica |
| minute | minute | minute | minuto |
| mountain | montagne | berg | montagna |
| mountain pass | col | pass | passo/forcella |

| English | French | German | Italian |
|---|---|---|---|
| mountain stream | torrent | bach/wildbach | torrente |
| north | nord | nord | nord |
| open | ouvert | offen | aperto |
| peak | pic/sommet | gipfel | cima |
| rain | pluie | regen | pioggia |
| reservoir | réservoir | stausee | serbatoio |
| ridge | aréte | grat | cresta |
| right (direction) | droit | recht | destra |
| river | ruisseau | bach | fiume |
| rockfall | chute de pierres | steinschlag | caduta sassi |
| room | chambre | zimmer | camera |
| rucksack | sac à dos | rucksack | zaino |
| scree | éboulis | geröllhalde | frana/ghiaione |
| snow | neige | schnee | neve |
| south | sud | sud | sud |
| spring (water source) | fontaine/source | quelle | sorgente |
| storm | tempête/orage | sturm/gewitter | tempesta |
| thunder | tonnere | donner | tuono |
| tourist office | office du tourisme | verkehsverein | azienda di soggiorno é turismo |
| valley | val/vallée | tal | valle |
| village | village | dorf | villaggio |
| water | eau | wasser | acqua |
| water (non drinking) | eau non potable | kein trinkwasser | acqua non potable |
| weather forecast | météo | wettervoraussage | previsione del tempo |
| west | ouest | west | ovest |
| wind | vent | wind | vento |

# BIBLIOGRAPHY

The Alpine library is vast, therefore the following list of books is of necessity a very selective one. I've included several classic Victorian titles, for the tales of the Alpine pioneers often make entertaining reading, and it's interesting to compare the Alps as they are today, with descriptions from a hundred years or so ago. Titles long out of print may be obtainable on special order from public libraries, although there are a number of specialist mountain book dealers who may have just what you need. Check outdoor press for names and addresses.

Ardito, Stefano: *Walking & Climbing in the Alps* (Swan Hill Press, 1995) Lots of ideas for multi-day routes. Splendid photographs, but poor text translated from the Italian original.

Conway, W.M.: *The Alps from End to End* (Constable, 1895 – many subsequent editions, the latest by Cape, 1933) The famous account of a high-level traverse in 1894, from Monte Viso to the Grossglockner.

Gilbert, Josiah & Churchill, George: *The Dolomite Mountains* (Longmans, 1864) A classic of Alpine travel, arising from journeys in the Eastern Alps in 1861, '62 and '63.

Irving, R.L.G.: *The Alps* (Batsford, 1939) A book for travellers, it describes most of the Alpine range, with asides on walks and low-key climbs.

Kugy, Julius: *Alpine Pilgrimage* (Murray, 1934) One of the most fascinating and readable of all Alpine books. Kugy was the authority on the Julian Alps.

Lieberman, Marcia R.: *The Outdoor Traveler's Guide: The Alps* (Stewart, Tabori & Chang, New York, 1991) Much of the Alpine range is covered in this book, with descriptions of selected regions, and magnificent colour photos by Tim Thompson.

Merrick, Hugh: *Rambles in the Alps* (Country Life, 1951) A selection of walks, mostly in the Bernese Alps. A large-format book with black and white illustrations.

Moore, A.A.: *The Alps in 1864* (Most recent edition, Blackwell, 1939) Moore was with Whymper and Horace Walker on their Alpine campaign of 1864, and this volume provides good descriptions of their climbs and journeys.

Reynolds, Kev: *Walking in the Alps* (Cicerone Press, 1998) This book covers virtually the whole Alpine range and gives ideas for day walks, multi-day routes, hut information etc.
*Classic Walks in the Alps* (Oxford Illustrated Press, 1991) Thirty walks, mostly multi-day, are described and illustrated.
*The Mountains of Europe* (Oxford Illustrated Press, 1990) The major Alpine regions are described by a variety of authors.

Smith, Janet Adam: *Mountain Holidays* (Dent, 1946/The Ernest Press, 1997) This is a charming account of pre-war holidays in Scotland and the Alps which remains as fresh as when it was first published.

Tuckett, F.F.: *A Pioneer in the High Alps* (Arnold, 1920) From this published collection of Tuckett's diaries, the modern wanderer can learn much about assorted Alpine groups. Tuckett's energy and experience were amazing.

Walker, J. Hubert: *Walking in the Alps* (Oliver & Boyd, 1951) An inspirational volume which describes high-level routes and ascents in eight selected areas.

Whymper, Edward: *Scrambles Amongst the Alps* (Murray, 1871 – numerous more recent editions, including Webb & Bower, 1986 with colour photos by John Cleare) Perhaps the best-known of all mountaineering books, of interest to walkers and climbers and all who love the Alps.

Will, Alfred: *Wandering Among the High Alps* (Bentley, 1856, but most recent edition by Blackwell, 1937) Another classic account of Victorian wandering and mountaineering, by an early President of the Alpine Club.

## CICERONE GUIDES
## WALKING AND TREKKING IN THE ALPS

**WALKING IN THE ALPS** *Kev Reynolds* The popular author of many of our Alpine guidebooks now draws on his vast experience to produce an outstanding comprehensive volume. Every area covered. Not for over half a century has there been anything remotely comparable. Fully illustrated. *ISBN 1 85284 261 X  Large format  Case bound  496pp*
**CHAMONIX TO ZERMATT - The Walker's Haute Route** *Kev Reynolds* The classic walk in the shadow of great peaks from Mont Blanc to the Matterhorn. In 14 stages, this is one of the most beautiful LD paths in Europe. *ISBN 1 85284 215 6  176pp*
**THE GRAND TOUR OF MONTE ROSA** *C.J. Wright*
**Vol 1: - MARTIGNY TO VALLE DELLA SESIA (via the Italian valleys)** *ISBN 1 85284 177 X 216pp*
**Vol 2: - VALLE DELLA SESIA TO MARTIGNY (via the Swiss valleys)** *ISBN 1 85284 178 8 182pp* The ultimate alpine LD walk which encircles most of the Pennine Alps.
**TOUR OF MONT BLANC** *Andrew Harper* One of the world's best walks - the circumnavigation of the Mont Blanc massif. 120 miles of pure magic, split into 11 sections.  Reprinted and updated. *ISBN 1 85284 240 7  144pp  PVC cover*

## FRANCE, BELGIUM AND LUXEMBOURG
**WALKING IN THE ARDENNES** *Alan Castle*  53 circular walks in this attractive area of gorges and deep cut wooded valleys, caves, castles and hundreds of walking trails.  Easily accessible from the channel. *ISBN 1 85284 213 X 312pp*
**SELECTED ROCK CLIMBS IN BELGIUM AND LUXEMBOURG** *Chris Craggs* Perfect rock, good protection and not too hot to climb in summer. *ISBN 1 85284 155 9  188p  A5*
**THE BRITTANY COASTAL PATH** *Alan Castle* The GR34, 360 miles, takes a month to walk. Easy access from UK means it can be split into several holidays. *ISBN 1 85284 185 0 296pp*
**CHAMONIX - MONT BLANC - A Walking Guide** *Martin Collins*  In the dominating presence of Europe's highest mountain, the scenery is exceptional.  A comprehensive guide to the area. *ISBN 1 85284 009 9  192pp  PVC cover*
**THE CORSICAN HIGH LEVEL ROUTE - Walking the GR20** *Alan Castle* The most challenging of the French LD paths - across the rocky spine of Corsica. *ISBN 1 85284 100 1  TOP  New edition expected autumn 2000*
**WALKING THE FRENCH ALPS: GR5** *Martin Collins* The popular trail from Lake Geneva to Nice. Split into stages, each of which could form the basis of a good holiday. *ISBN 1 85284 051 X 160pp*
**WALKING THE FRENCH GORGES** *Alan Castle* 320 miles through Provence and Ardèche, includes the famous gorges of the Verdon. *ISBN 1 85284 114 1  224pp*
**FRENCH ROCK** *Bill Birkett* THE guide to many exciting French crags! Masses of photo topos, with selected hit-routes in detail. *ISBN 1 85284 113 3.  332pp  A5 size*
**WALKING IN THE HAUTE SAVOIE** *Janette Norton* 61 walks in the pre-Alps of Chablais, to majestic peaks in the Faucigny, Haut Giffre and Lake Annecy regions. *ISBN 1 85284  196 6 312pp*
**TOUR OF THE OISANS: GR54** *Andrew Harper* This popular walk around the Dauphiné massif and Écrins national park is similar in quality to the celebrated Tour of Mont Blanc.  A two week suggested itinerary covers the 270km route. *ISBN 1 85284 157 5  120pp  PVC cover*
**TOUR OF MONT BLANC** *see Walking and Trekking in the Alps, above*
**WALKING IN PROVENCE** *Janette Norton* 42 walks through the great variety of Provence - remote plateaux, leafy gorges, ancient villages, monuments, quiet towns. Provence is evocative of a gentler life. *ISBN 1 85284 293 8 248pp*

**THE PYRENEAN TRAIL: GR10** *Alan Castle* From the Atlantic to the Mediterranean at a lower level than the Pyrenean High Route. 50 days but splits into holiday sections. *ISBN 1 85284 245 8 176pp*

**WALKS AND CLIMBS IN THE PYRENEES** *Kev Reynolds See entry under FRANCE/SPAIN*
**THE TOUR OF THE QUEYRAS** *Alan Castle* A 13 day walk which traverses wild but beautiful country, the sunniest part of the French Alps. Suitable for a first Alpine visit. *ISBN 1 85284 048 X 160pp*

**THE ROBERT LOUIS STEVENSON TRAIL** *Alan Castle* 140 mile trail in the footsteps of Stevenson's *Travels with a Donkey* through the Cevennes, from Le Puy to St Jean du Gard. This route is ideal for people new to walking holidays. *ISBN 1 85284 060 9 160pp*

**ROCK CLIMBS IN THE PYRENEES** *Derek Walker See entry under FRANCE/SPAIN*
**WALKING IN THE TARENTAISE AND BEAUFORTAIN ALPS** *J.W. Akitt* The delectable mountain area south of Mont Blanc includes the Vanoise National Park. 53 day walks, 5 tours between 2 and 8 day's duration, plus 40 short outings. *ISBN 1 85284 181 8 216pp*

**ROCK CLIMBS IN THE VERDON - An Introduction** *Rick Newcombe* An English-style guide, which makes for easier identification of the routes and descents. *ISBN 1 85284 015 3 72pp*

**TOUR OF THE VANOISE** *Kev Reynolds* A 10-12 day circuit of one of the finest mountain areas of France, between Mt. Blanc and the Écrins. The second most popular mountain tour after the Tour of Mont Blanc. *ISBN 1 85284 224 5 120pp*

**WALKS IN VOLCANO COUNTRY** *Alan Castle* Two LD walks in Central France, the High Auvergne and Tour of the Velay, in a unique landscape of extinct volcanoes. *ISBN 1 85284 092 7 208pp*

**THE WAY OF ST JAMES** *Two titles - see below*

## FRANCE/SPAIN

**ROCK CLIMBS IN THE PYRENEES** *Derek Walker* Includes Pic du Midi d'Ossau and the Vignemale in France, and the Ordesa Canyon and Riglos in Spain. *ISBN 1 85284 039 0 168pp PVC cover*

**WALKS AND CLIMBS IN THE PYRENEES** *Kev Reynolds* Includes the Pyrenean High Level Route. Invaluable for any backpacker or mountaineer who plans to visit this still unspoilt mountain range. (3rd Edition) *ISBN 1 85284 133 8 328pp PVC cover*

**THE WAY OF ST JAMES: Le Puy to Santiago - A Cyclist's Guide** *John Higginson* A guide for touring cyclists follows as closely as possible the original route but avoids the almost unrideable sections of the walkers' way. On surfaced lanes and roads. *ISBN 1 85284 274 1 112pp*

**THE WAY OF ST JAMES: Le Puy to Santiago - A Walker's Guide** *Alison Raju* A walker's guide to the ancient route of pilgrimage. Plus the continuation to Finisterre. *ISBN 1 85284 271 7 264pp*

## SPAIN AND PORTUGAL

**WALKING IN THE ALGARVE** *June Parker* The author of *Walking in Mallorca* turns her expert attention to the Algarve, with a selection of walks to help the visitor explore the true countryside. *ISBN 1 85284 173 7 168pp*

**ANDALUSIAN ROCK CLIMBS** *Chris Craggs* El Chorro and El Torcal are world famous. Includes Tenerife. *ISBN 1 85284 109 5 168pp*

**COSTA BLANCA ROCK** *Chris Craggs* Over 1500 routes on over 40 crags, many for the first time in English. The most comprehensive guide to the area. *ISBN 1 85284 241 5 264pp*

**MOUNTAIN WALKS ON THE COSTA BLANCA** *Bob Stansfield* An easily accessible winter walking paradise to rival Mallorca. With rugged limestone peaks and warm climate. This guide includes the 150 km Costa Blanca Mountain Way. *ISBN1 85284 165 232pp*

**ROCK CLIMBS IN MAJORCA, IBIZA AND TENERIFE** *Chris Craggs* Holiday island cragging at its best. *ISBN 1 85284 189 3 240pp*

**WALKING IN MALLORCA** *June Parker.* The 3rd edition of this great classic guide, takes account of rapidly changing conditions. Revised reprint for 1999. *ISBN 1 85284 250 4 288pp PVC cover*

**BIRDWATCHING IN MALLORCA** *Ken Stoba* A complete guide to what to see and where to see it. *ISBN 1 85284 053 6 108pp*

**THE MOUNTAINS OF CENTRAL SPAIN** *Jaqueline Oglesby* Walks and scrambles in the Sierras de Gredos and Guadarrama which rise to 2600m and remain snow capped for 5 months of the year. *ISBN 1 85284 203 2 312p*

**ROCK CLIMBS IN THE PYRENEES** *Derek Walker See entry under FRANCE/SPAIN*

**THROUGH THE SPANISH PYRENEES: GR11** *Paul Lucia* An updated new edition of the long distance trail which mirrors the French GR10 but traverses much lonelier, wilder country. With new maps and information. *ISBN 1 85284 307 1 232pp*

**WALKING IN THE SIERRA NEVADA** *Andy Walmsley* Spain's highest mountain range is a wonderland for the traveller and wilderness backpacker alike. Mountain bike routes indicated. *ISBN 1 85284 194 X 160pp*

**WALKS AND CLIMBS IN THE PICOS DE EUROPA** *Robin Walker* A definitive guide to these unique mountains. Walks and rock climbs of all grades. *ISBN 1 85284 033 1 232pp PVC cover*

## SWITZERLAND - including parts of France and Italy

**ALPINE PASS ROUTE, SWITZERLAND** *Kev Reynolds* Over 15 passes along the northern edge of the Alps, past the Eiger, Jungfrau and many other renowned peaks. A 325 km route in 15 suggested stages. *ISBN 1 85284 069 2 176pp*

**THE BERNESE ALPS, SWITZERLAND** *Kev Reynolds* Walks around Grindelwald, Lauterbrunnen and Kandersteg dominated by the great peaks of the Oberland. *ISBN 1 85284 243 1 248pp PVC cover*

**CENTRAL SWITZERLAND - A Walking Guide** *Kev Reynolds* A little known but delightful area stretching from Luzern to the St Gotthard, includes Engelberg and Klausen Pass. *ISBN 1 85284 131 1 216pp PVC cover*

**CHAMONIX TO ZERMATT** — *see entry under Walking and Trekking in the Alps*

**THE GRAND TOUR OF MONTE ROSA Vols 1 & 2** *See entry under Walking and Trekking in the Alps*

**WALKS IN THE ENGADINE, SWITZERLAND** *Kev Reynolds* The superb region to the south-east of Switzerland of the Bregaglia, Bernina Alps, and the Engadine National Park. *ISBN 1 85284 003 X 192pp PVC cover*

**THE JURA: WALKING THE HIGH ROUTE** *Kev Reynolds and* **WINTER SKI TRAVERSES** *R. Brian Evans.* The High Route is a long distance path along the highest crest of the Swiss Jura. In winter it is a paradise for cross-country skiers. Both sections in one volume. *ISBN 1 85284 010 2 192pp*

**WALKING IN TICINO, SWITZERLAND** *Kev Reynolds* Walks in the lovely Italian part of Switzerland, little known to British walkers. *ISBN 1 85284 098 6  184pp  PVC cover*

**THE VALAIS, SWITZERLAND - A Walking Guide** *Kev Reynolds* The splendid scenery of the Pennine Alps, with such peaks as the Matterhorn, Dent Blanche, and Mont Rosa providing a perfect background. *ISBN 1 85284 151 6  224pp  PVC cover*

## GERMANY, AUSTRIA AND EASTERN EUROPE

**MOUNTAIN WALKING IN AUSTRIA** *Cecil Davies* An enlarged second edition. 25 mountain groups, 98 walks from half a day to a good week. *ISBN 1 85284 239 3  126pp*

**WALKING IN THE BAVARIAN ALPS** *Grant Bourne & Sabine Korner-Bourne* 57 walks of variety in the Allgau, Ammergau, Wetterstein, Tegernsee, Chiemgau and Berchtesgarden Alps on the German-Austrian border. *ISBN 1 85284 229 6  184pp*

**WALKING IN THE BLACK FOREST** *Fleur & Colin Speakman* Above the Rhine valley, the Ortenauer Wine path (64km) and the Clock Carriers Way (10 day circular walk) are described, together with practical walking advice for the area in general. *ISBN 1 85284 050 1 120p*

**GERMANY'S ROMANTIC ROAD A Guide for Walkers and Cyclists** *Gordon McLachlan* 423km past historic walled towns and castles of southern Germany. *ISBN 1 85284 233 4 208pp*

**WALKING IN THE HARZ MOUNTAINS** *Fleur & Colin Speakman* 30 walks in Germany's most northerly mountains, some from the narrow gauge steam railway. *ISBN 1 85284 149 4  152pp*

**KING LUDWIG WAY** *Fleur and Colin Speakman* Travels the Bavarian countryside from Munich to Füssen. King Ludwig was responsible for the fabulous castle of Neuschwanstein and sponsored Wagner's operas. *ISBN 0 902363 90 5  80pp*

**KLETTERSTEIG - Scrambles in the Northern Limestone Alps** *Paul Werner Translated by Dieter Pevsner* Protected climbing paths similar to the Via Ferrata in the German/Austrian border region. *ISBN 0 902363 46 8  184pp  PVC cover*

**THE MOUNTAINS OF ROMANIA** *James Roberts* A definitive guide to the newly accessible Carpathian mountains. Potentially one of the best walking destinations in Europe, with mountain wilderness and friendly people. *ISBN 1 85284 295 4  296pp*

**WALKING THE RIVER RHINE TRAIL** *Alan Castle* A spectacular 170mile (273km) walk along Germany's most famous river from Bonn to Alsheim near Worms. Excellent public transport assists the walker. *ISBN 1 85284 276 8 176pp*

**WALKING IN THE SALZKAMMERGUT** *Fleur and Colin Speakman* Holiday rambles in Austria's Lake District. Renowned for its historic salt mines. *ISBN 1 85284 030 7  104pp*

**HUT TO HUT IN THE STUBAI ALPS** *Allan Hartley* The Stubai Rucksack Route and The Stubai Glacier Tour, each around 10 days. Easy peaks and good huts make it a good area for a first Alpine season. *ISBN 1 85284 123 0  128pp*

**THE HIGH TATRAS** *Colin Saunders & Renata Narozna* A detailed guide to the Tatras, popular area between Poland and Slovakia. *ISBN 1 85284 150 8  248pp  PVC cover*

## SCANDINAVIA

**WALKING IN NORWAY** *Constance Roos* 20 walking routes in the main mountain areas from the far south to the sub-arctic regions, all accessible by public transport. *ISBN 1 85284 230 X  200pp*

## ITALY AND SLOVENIA

**ALTA VIA - HIGH LEVEL WALKS IN THE DOLOMITES** *Martin Collins* A guide to some of the most popular mountain paths in Europe - Alta Via 1 and 2. *ISBN 0 902363 75 1  160pp PVC cover*

**THE CENTRAL APENNINES OF ITALY - Walks, Scrambles and Climbs** *Stephen Fox* The mountainous spine of Italy, with secluded walks, rock climbs and scrambles on the Gran Sasso d'Italia and some of Italy's finest sport climbing crags. *ISBN 1 85284 219 9  152pp*

**WALKING IN THE CENTRAL ITALIAN ALPS** *Gillian Price* The Vinschgau, Ortler and Adamello regions. Little known to British walkers, certain to become popular. *ISBN 1 85284 183 4 230pp PVC cover*

**WALKING IN THE DOLOMITES** *Gillian Price* A comprehensive selection of walks amongst spectacular rock scenery. By far the best English guide to the area. *ISBN 1 85284 079 X  PVC cover*

**WALKING IN ITALY'S GRAN PARADISO** *Gillian Price* Rugged mountains and desolate valleys with a huge variety of wildlife. Walks from short strolls to full-scale traverses. *ISBN 1 85284 231 8  200pp*

**LONG DISTANCE WALKS IN THE GRAN PARADISO** *J.W. Akitt* Includes Southern Valdotain. Supplements our Gran Paradiso guide by Gillian Price. Describes Alta Via 2 and the Grand Traverse of Gran Paradiso and some shorter walks. *ISBN 1 85284 247 4 168pp*

**THE GRAND TOUR OF MONTE ROSA** *C.J. Wright*
*See entry under Walking and Trekking in the Alps*

**ITALIAN ROCK - Selected Climbs in Northern Italy** *Al Churcher.* Val d'Orco and Mello, Lecco and Finale etc. A good introduction to some great crags. *ISBN 0 902363 93 X  200pp PVC cover*

**WALKS IN THE JULIAN ALPS** *Simon Brown* Slovenia contains some of Europe's most attractive mountain limestone scenery. 30 walks as an introduction to the area, from valley strolls to high mountain scrambles. *ISBN 1 85284 125 7  184pp*

**WALKING IN TUSCANY** *Gillian Price* 50 itineraries from brief strolls to multi-day treks in Tuscany, Umbria and Latium. *ISBN 1 85284 268 7  312pp*

**VIA FERRATA SCRAMBLES IN THE DOLOMITES** *Höfler/Werner Translated by Cecil Davies* The most exciting walks in the world. Wires, stemples and ladders enable the 'walker' to  enter the climber's vertical environment. *ISBN 1 85284 089 7 248pp  PVC cover*

## OTHER MEDITERRANEAN COUNTRIES

**THE ATLAS MOUNTAINS** *Karl Smith* Trekking in the mountains of north Africa. Practical and comprehensive. *ISBN 1 85284 258 X  136pp  PVC cover*

**WALKING IN CYPRUS** *Donald Brown* Without a guide getting lost in Cyprus is easy. Donald Brown shares undiscovered Cyprus with 26 easy to moderate routes for walkers. *ISBN 1 85284 195 8  144pp*

**THE MOUNTAINS OF GREECE - A Walker's Guide** *Tim Salmon* Hikes of all grades from a month-long traverse of the Pindos to day hikes on the outskirts of Athens. *ISBN 1 85284 108 7  PVC cover*

**CRETE - THE WHITE MOUNTAINS** *Loraine Wilson* Describes 49 walks graded from modest to demanding, in this spectacularly beautiful range of mountains in the west of Crete. Includes Samaria gorge, high mountains up to 2500 metres, and glorious coastal walks. *ISBN 1 85284 298 9  152pp*

**THE MOUNTAINS OF TURKEY** *Karl Smith* Over 100 treks and scrambles with detailed route descriptions of all the popular peaks. Includes Ararat. *ISBN 1 85284 161 3  184pp  PVC cover*

**TREKS AND CLIMBS IN WADI RUM, JORDAN** *Tony Howard* The world's foremost desert climbing and trekking area. Increasingly popular every year as word of its quality spreads. *ISBN 1 85284 254 7  252pp  A5 Card cover*

**JORDAN - Walks, Treks, Caves, Climbs, Canyons in Pella, Ajlun, Moab, Dana, Petra and Rum** *Di Taylor & Tony Howard* The first guidebook to the superlative routes found in Jordan's recently formed Nature Reserves. These are walks, treks, caves and climbs described in this little known landscape by the authors of our Wadi Rum guide. *ISBN 1 85284 278 4 192pp A5*

**THE ALA DAG, Climbs and Treks in Turkey's Crimson Mountains** *O.B. Tüzel* The best mountaineering area in Turkey. *ISBN 1 85284 112 5 296pp PVC cover*

## HIMALAYA

**ADVENTURE TREKS IN NEPAL** *Bill O'Connor*
*ISBN 1 85223 306 0 160pp large format*

**ANNAPURNA - A Trekker's Guide** *Kev Reynolds* Includes Annapurna Circuit, the Annapurna Sanctuary and the Pilgrim's Trail, with lots of good advice. *ISBN 1 85284 132 X 184pp*

**EVEREST - A Trekker's Guide** *Kev Reynolds* A new second edition of this guide to the most popular trekking region in the Himalaya. Lodges, tea-house, permits, health - all are dealt with in this indispensible guide. With updated information, clear mapping and superb photography, including detailed descriptions of approach routes from both Nepal and Tibet. *ISBN 1 85284 306 3 184pp*

**GARHWAL AND KUMAON - A Trekker's and Visitor's Guide** *K.P. Sharma* Almost at the centre of the Himalayan chain culminating in Nanda Devi. Garhwal consists of rugged mountains and valleys, Kumaon is more gentle. *ISBN 1 85284 264 4 200pp*

**KANGCHENJUNGA - A Trekker's Guide** *Kev Reynolds* Known as the Five Treasures of the Snows because of its five summits, Kangchenjunga is the world's third highest peak (8586m). The trek to base camp is regarded by many as the most beautiful walk in the world. Various options are described by one of the best of current guide book writers. *ISBN 1 85284 280 6 184pp*

**LANGTANG, GOSAINKUND & HELAMBU - A Trekker's Guide** *Kev Reynolds* Popular area, easily accessible from Kathmandu. *ISBN 1 85284 207 5*

## OTHER COUNTRIES

**MOUNTAIN WALKING IN AFRICA 1: KENYA** *David Else* Detailed route descriptions and practical information. *ISBN 1 85365 205 9 180pp A5 size*

**OZ ROCK - A Rock Climber's Guide to Australian Crags** *Alastair Lee* An overall view of Oz rock with details of each crag and how to get there. *ISBN 1 85284 237 7 184pp A5 size*

**TREKKING IN THE CAUCAUSUS** *Yuri Kolomiets & Aleksey Solovyev* The great mountains once hidden behind the Iron Curtain. 62 walks of which half demand basic climbing skills. Included are the walks to the highest tops in Europe, the summits of Mt Elbrus. *ISBN 1 85284 129 X 224pp PVC cover*

**ROCK CLIMBING IN HONG KONG** *Brian J. Heard* Great climbing for both locals and travellers. *ISBN 1 85284 167 2 136pp A5 size*

**TREKKING IN THE CAUCAUSUS** *Yuri Kolomiets & Aleksey Solovyev* The great mountains once hidden behind the Iron Curtain. 62 walks of which half demand basic climbing skills. Included are the walks to the highest tops in Europe, the summits of Mt Elbrus. *ISBN 1 85284 129 X 224pp PVC cover*

**THE GRAND CANYON and the American South-West** *Constance Roos* The long awaited walking and trekking guide to this spectacular region. With clear mapping, superb photographs of the breathtaking scenery and extensive information. *ISBN 1 85284 300 4*

**ADVENTURE TREKS WESTERN NORTH AMERICA**
*Chris Townsend ISBN 1 85223 317 6 160pp large format*

**CLASSIC TRAMPS IN NEW ZEALAND** *Constance Roos* The 14 best long distance walks in both islands. Each "tramp" takes between 2-7 days. *ISBN 85284 118 4 208pp PVC cover*

Origination & Printing by Next Century Ltd